W9-BKI-142

The Impact of Geographic Deregulation on the American Banking Industry

The Impact of Geographic Deregulation on the American Banking Industry

Ann B. Matasar and Joseph N. Heiney

Q

QUORUM BOOKS
Westport, Connecticut • London

Library of Congress Cataloging-in-Publication Data

Matasar, Ann B.

    The impact of geographic deregulation on the American banking industry / Ann B.
Matasar and Joseph N. Heiney.

      p. cm.

    Includes bibliographical references and index.

    ISBN 1–56720–350–7 (alk. paper)

    1. Banks and Banking—United States. 2. Banks and Banking—Deregulation—
United States. I. Heiney, Joseph N. II. Title.

HG2491.M33 2002

332.1'0973—dc21   2001049180

British Library Cataloguing in Publication Data is available.

Library of Congress Catalog Card Number: 2001049180
ISBN: 1–56720–350–7

First published in 2002

Quorum Books, 88 Post Road West, Westport, CT 06881
An imprint of Greenwood Publishing Group, Inc.
www.quorumbooks.com

Printed in the United States of America

The paper used in this book complies with the
Permanent Paper Standard issued by the National
Information Standards Organization (Z39.48–1984).

10 9 8 7 6 5 4 3 2 1

Contents

Preface

There are three potential relationships between law and society. Ordinarily, laws mirror and defend currently accepted social values and realities. Laws also can guide a society by leading it in new directions. Finally, laws may reflect a bygone era and lag behind changing social norms.

Discomfiture with the law by one or more segments of society can occur under all of these scenarios but is, most likely, problematic and divisive when the law is out of synch with generally accepted views or practices. Ultimately, therefore, the rule of law requires an alignment of law and society. Gradual realignment results in changes that are often less noticeable and traumatic while they are in progress even though they may be far-reaching in their consequences. Rapid realignment, however, increases social anxiety and can be unsettling.

This book is the study of the institutional and systemic changes in banking in the United States as the result of the passage of the Riegle-Neal Banking and Branching Efficiency Act of 1994, the first revision of a major banking law associated with the era of the Great Depression. In the intervening years between the late 1920s or the early 1930s and the approaching end of the 20th century, the environment of banking changed dramatically on a domestic and international plane while the laws associated with banking in this country remained fixed and intransigent. During the lengthy interim, no amount of regulatory flexibility or bankers' ingenuity was able to substitute fully for the modernization of the banking laws necessary to keep pace with the dynamic domestic and international revolution occurring in banking and financial services. Thus Riegle-Neal represents a rapid realignment of American banking law to catch up to the changes that had already taken place over a 70-year period.

Celebrated by some as the dawn of a new banking era in America, Riegle-Neal was fraught with uncertainty for individual banks and the banking industry and its constituents (e.g., stockholders, customers, and employees). By examining public data from 1994, when Riegle-Neal was enacted, until 1999, this book seeks answers to some of the uncertainties regarding the implications associated with the consolidation and resulting increased average size of American banks in the wake of a deregulatory tide.

Several challenges had to be met in dealing with the data. It was not always possible to delineate circumstances created solely by Riegle-Neal from those resulting from other systemic changes in the banking system. Inference, therefore, was required to segregate interstate experience from other banking transitions. The Gramm-Leach-Bliley Financial Services Modernization Act, which was passed in 1999 and eliminated major portions of the Glass-Steagall Act (Banking Act of 1933), will further exacerbate the difficulty in the future. In combination, however, it is certain that these two new laws forever altered American banking.

This study of Riegle-Neal may also appear somewhat premature or preliminary because of the short period of time since the law was enacted and fully enforceable. Nonetheless the findings herein reveal the direction that changes associated with the law are likely to take and thus serve as a baseline for future analysis.

The snowball of change in the banking community continues to roll and pick up speed even as this book is being written. What is being presented here, therefore, is a still photo of a moment in time, as well as comparison with the past. The future of banking and of financial services in the 21st century is likely to differ considerably from what it was at the end of the 20th century. Hopefully this book offers a foundation for further thought and understanding of the future now being chartered.

ACKNOWLEDGMENT

The authors would like to thank Dr. Deborah D. Pavelka, Professor of Accounting and Director of the School of Accountancy in the Walter E. Heller College of Business Administration at Roosevelt University, for her extensive professional assistance. Her cogent and timely comments were of great value. We remain appreciative and in her debt. She is an extraordinary colleague.

Chapter 1

$

Introduction

U.S. GEOGRAPHIC BANKING REGULATION: THE LEGISLATIVE ODYSSEY

The Backdrop to Regulation

As a country of immigrants from all parts of the globe, the United States has been influenced since its founding by a variety of political and economic philosophies. This difference in weltanschauung or worldview has left its imprint throughout American life, including the laws of the land dating from the inception of the Constitution to the present. In no set of legislation or regulation is this influence more marked than that that affects the fundamental structure and underlying principles of the American banking system.

The uniqueness of the American banking system is largely attributable to the original differences between the Hamiltonian Federalists and the Jeffersonian Republicans. The former favored a strong central government; believed that large, even monopolistic, businesses added to the economic strength of the country; supported protectionism of strategic and infant industries; and anticipated an international role for the country as part of a larger economy. By contrast, the latter preferred the nexus of authority close to the average citizen, believed that the inherent strength of the country was dependent on the existence of small shopkeepers and rural farmers,

and maintained a basically domestic set of reference points in their think-
ing. American economic life continues to reflect these disparate visions and
to generate passions and fears associated with them. The banking system,
so central to the life of the nation, has been a "battleground" for this ideo-
logical conflict, the outcome of which has made the industry the most
heavily regulated field in the country.

Federalism, a basic principle of the American Constitution, also resulted
from a philosophical struggle between the proponents of national suprem-
acy and the advocates of states' rights. As in the case of economic differences among the founders, this compromise influenced all components of
the political system, including banking. The dual banking system, which
divides regulatory authority between three federal regulators (the Office of
the Comptroller of the Currency [OCC], the Federal Reserve Board [Fed],
and the Federal Deposit Insurance Corporation [FDIC]) and the banking
officials of the 50 states, is attributable entirely to federalism and the average citizen's concerns regarding big business and banking power. The result has been that a large number of small, community-based, and territori-
ally separate institutions have co-existed profitably and stubbornly along-
side domestically headquartered, international behemoths—the American
banking anomaly.

Regulation in American Banking: A Brief Overview

Three types of regulation emerged from these political and economic
disagreements: pricing regulation, product regulation, and geographic
regulation.

Pricing regulation took two forms–limits on the amounts banks could
pay to obtain funds, particularly deposits, as well as on the amount they
could charge on loans. Interest on deposits, a competitive issue between
banks and thrifts, was for many years a major stumbling block in gaining
any deregulation of the banking industry. Thrifts, particularly savings and
loans, faced substantially more restrictions regarding the products they
could offer and became heavily dependent on long-term loans such as
mortgages. To offset this situation and make it possible for them to attract
funds, thrifts were permitted to pay slightly higher interest than banks on
deposits. In the negotiations regarding reform of financial services, thrifts
sought to diversify their portfolio of services. In return, banks demanded
the equalization of interest on deposits and, ultimately, the elimination of
ceilings on the amount of interest that could be paid. Passage of the Depository Institutions Deregulation and Monetary Control Act of 1980
(DIDMCA), which eliminated Regulation Q, the interest rate ceilings established by Glass-Steagall, allowed both parties to obtain their goals and
made deposit pricing part of the financial marketplace. DIDMCA also ef-

fectively ended pricing regulation on loans through the elimination of usury ceilings.

Product regulation limited the services banks could offer and the businesses they were permitted to enter. These regulations were exemplified by the Banking Act of 1933 (Glass-Steagall), which separated commercial banking from investment banking, and by the Bank Holding Company Act, which, in conjunction with amendments by the Depository Institutions Act of 1982 (Garn–St. Germain), separated banking from insurance. The rules resulted in the creation of a panorama of highly specialized, uniquely American financial institutions, which were disadvantaged in the global financial arena where they were confronted with opponents able to offer a wide range of products and services to their clientele. After years of erosion through bankers' innovations, regulators' leniency, and judges' interpretations, restrictive product regulations also have been dismantled with passage of the Gramm-Leach-Bliley Financial Services Modernization Act of 1999. The future of American banking and financial services generally is about to be rewritten for the new millennium.

Geographic regulation governed the location of banking headquarters, as well as the placement of banks' deposit-taking branches on an intrastate, interstate, and international basis. With passage of the Riegle-Neal Interstate Banking and Branching Efficiency Act of 1994, geographic deregulation at the national level was completed. Symbolic of federalism and states' rights, however, intrastate branching restrictions remained in force. This book, therefore, studies the recently acquired freedom of American banks to avail themselves of the entire national market without interstate constraints.

Branching and the Location of Banking Facilities: A Legislative Overview

Until the early 20th century, unit or one-office banks predominated in the United States for several reasons. Most state-chartered institutions, as well as private banks, eschewed branching to avoid competition. This aversion was formalized in states, which legislated branching prohibitions. Additionally, the National Bank Act of 1863–1864, which established the OCC to charter and supervise national banks, limited these banks to a single location. In so doing, it missed the opportunity to create a national branching system. At the turn of the century, therefore, only 87 banks out of 13,000 in the nation accounted for the 119 branches in existence. Until the depression era, the rise in branching continued to be moderate despite easing of state and national restrictions because of continued opposition of the American Bankers Association and the concern that branches would lead to the accumulation of financial power in a few hands.[1]

The McFadden Act (1927), which was a part of the National Bank Act, maintained intrastate or interstate branching limitations on nationally chartered banks. On an intrastate basis, it gave state legislatures the power to govern within their state's borders the branching activities of all banks, both national and state chartered. Additionally, after amendment by the Banking Act of 1935, national banks were prohibited from branching across state lines. When the Fed extended this prohibition to state-chartered banks, virtually all banks were limited to having a physical presence in only one state. Having been eliminated on an interstate basis, branching— where it existed—was under the authority of the individual states and was limited by the borders of any one state.

The states, in turn, adopted one of 3 broadly based approaches to intrastate branching: unit banking, limited branching, or statewide branching: unit banking was the most restrictive because it permitted banks to have only one home office and no branches. Limited branching, on the other hand, included a plethora of options depending on (a) varying definitions of a branch (e.g., whether an automatic teller machine or ATM was a branch); (b) the existence or extent of ceilings on the number of branches; and (c) the geographic distribution or distance between branches. Statewide banking was the most generous because it allowed banks the freedom to locate facilities throughout their state.

Despite the post–World War II prosperity, which increased the demand for banking services and created a mushrooming of new banks and branching networks, banks remained frustrated and confined within the borders of one state. They sought to break out of this restriction by developing bank holding companies (BHC), which substituted interstate banking or the ownership by an umbrella organization or holding company of two or more separately chartered banks in more than one state for interstate branching. This proved to be a short-lived and futile solution to the problem with the adoption of the Douglas Amendment to the Bank Holding Company Act of 1956. Under this provision, multibank BHCs were not permitted to operate banks in more than one state unless an individual state voluntarily permitted out-of-state BHCs to buy a bank or establish one de novo within its borders. No state allowed out-of-state BHCs to enter its territory prior to 1975. Over the course of the next 20 years, all states, other than Hawaii, permitted some degree of interstate activity by BHCs within their borders. They did so by entering into regional compacts, developing either regional or national reciprocity agreements, or simply opening their borders to out-of-state BHCs without restriction. Despite this erosion of McFadden's intent, however, the law remained on the books.

In addition to the McFadden and Douglas amendment prohibitions, branching and the location of banking facilities were affected peripherally by several banking laws, which were focused primarily on other issues.

The Bank Merger Act of 1960 required national banks to receive regulatory approval prior to participating in a merger or acquisition. Intended primarily to avoid anticompetitive activities, the law looked with favor upon mergers and acquisitions, which had an offsetting public benefit. This provision ultimately paved the way for the emergency powers accorded regulators in 1982 by Garn–St. Germain. Under this law, regulators permitted out-of-state banks to merge with or acquire large failing banks or thrifts if no viable alternative buyer was present within the home state of the failing institution. It was determined that saving the FDIC from additional bailout costs and avoiding disruptions in the banking system and the economy at large outweighed the negative effect on McFadden's interstate geographic barriers.

Title VIII of the Housing and Community Development Act of 1977, better known as the Community Reinvestment Act (CRA), attacked "redlining," a discriminatory lending practice that caused local disinvestment when banks exported deposits from a poor, old, or racially transitional area in order to provide credit in another usually richer and more stable area. Little consideration was given to an individual's or business' credit worthiness or income level or to a community's general viability if it was viewed as declining. The banks' generic analysis, therefore, became a self-fulfilling prophecy supporting their contention that redlining was not a discriminatory practice but rather a prudent investment policy intended to protect stockholders and depositors. CRA required federal supervisory agencies to encourage institutions they examined to help meet the credit needs of the communities from which they drew their deposits in a manner consistent with safe-and-sound business practice and simultaneously to discourage the exportation of funds which adversely affected a community. The geographic distribution of credit extensions, including the physical presence of banks throughout their community in order to encourage lending, became a central precept of CRA.

The importance of CRA, however, far exceeded the provisions of the law itself. Satisfactory or outstanding CRA audit ratings became the litmus test for banks seeking to avail themselves of the interstate banking and branching privileges after Riegle-Neal and the merger and acquisition possibilities in financial services opened up by the Gramm-Leach-Bliley Financial Services Modernization Act.

Riegle-Neal addressed five areas of interstate banking and branching activity: (1) interstate BHC acquisitions, (2) interstate bank mergers, (3) de novo interstate bank branching, (4) foreign bank interstate branching, and (5) interstate affiliate banking.

1. *Interstate Bank Holding Company Acquisitions.* The ability of BHCs to acquire banks across state lines was restricted to those BHCs that were adequately capitalized and managed, a proviso frequently used to control the activity of BHCs. States were not permitted to disallow this activity within their borders or to discriminate against out-of-state firms. However, they were allowed to protect young banks up to the age of 5 from out-of-state BHC acquisition.

In order to avoid excessive consolidation, the loss of competition within the banking industry of any state or within the nation as a whole, or subject the Federal Deposit Insurance Corporation (FDIC) to undue insurance risk, BHC interstate acquisitions were limited by market share. No BHC was permitted to acquire a bank if, in so doing, it would control more than 30% of the federally insured deposits in any one state or 10% of them in the nation. An exception was made to this provision for the initial acquisition made by a BHC within any state. Additionally, the market share provisions could be waived with the approval of the appropriate regulator under a variety of conditions intended to protect depositors or the banking system.

2. *Interstate Bank Mergers.* Banks headquartered in two different states are allowed to seek regulatory approval for merging across state lines. This opportunity, however, was denied initially to banks headquartered in Texas and Montana, the only two states that chose "to opt out" of this provision prior to the June 1, 1997, deadline. Texas opted out until September 1999, whereas Montana extended its exclusion until October 2001.[2] As in the case of BHC acquisitions, the 30% in state and 10% nationwide market share restrictions are generally applicable with exceptions involving the goals of regulatory agencies.

3. *De Novo Interstate Bank Branching.* Riegle-Neal allows an out-of-state bank to branch de novo into a state other than the one in which it is headquartered if the state has expressly permitted this activity and approval is obtained from the appropriate regulator. States are permitted to take no action regarding de novo interstate branching within their borders, thus prohibiting this activity within their state. De novo branches are subject to all the laws of the state in which they are located, as well as to CRA provisions regarding community lending. They are not bound, however, by the 10% or 30% concentration rules. In states that have not authorized de novo branching and also have not "opted out," interstate branching is possible only by purchasing a bank and converting it into a branch or branches.[3]

4. *Foreign Bank Interstate Branching.* With the approval of the Fed and the appropriate national or state banking regulator, a foreign bank also can participate in an interstate merger or de novo interstate branching. This privilege, however, is limited to well-capitalized foreign banks, a requirement that may necessitate the establishment of a separate subsidiary to allow for capitalization verification. Foreign banks seeking to participate in new interstate activity must comply with CRA provisions, a requirement many foreign banks have been able to avoid because they were uninsured by the FDIC.[4] Uninsured foreign bank branches are limited in taking deposits of less than $100,000 and must comply with all consumer protection legislation. [5]

Riegle-Neal has altered the landscape of American banking by eliminating the prohibitions against interstate banking and branching with only minor exceptions and restrictions and paved the way for banking mergers and acquisitions across state lines.[6]

II. THE THEORY OF ECONOMIC REGULATION

Much has been written concerning the economic theory of regulation, and many studies have provided empirical evidence regarding the effects of government regulation and deregulation. These studies have focused largely on the utility, transportation, telecommunication, and banking industries, which historically are or were the most heavily regulated industries in the U.S. economy. To provide a context for this study of geographic deregulation in the U.S. banking industry, it will be helpful to first review the literature concerning the theory of economic regulation and its empirical effects.

The Natural Monopoly Theory

A historical consideration of the economic theory of regulation must begin with natural monopoly theory. A natural monopoly is said to exist when economies of scale are so extensive that only one firm can exist in a market at a profit, so that the market is "naturally monopolistic." Since two of the earliest regulated industries, utilities and railroads, were thought to exhibit significant economies of scale, it was only a small leap to argue that the notion of natural monopoly provided a theoretical justification for utility and railroad regulations.

Regulations designed to deal appropriately with the problem of natural monopoly would set maximum prices at levels equal to marginal cost or, at least, equal to average cost in those cases in which economies of scale were so extensive that marginal cost was still below average cost at the level of output for which price equals marginal cost. In any case, the regulation appropriate to deal with a natural monopoly situation would set a maximum price. The Interstate Commerce Act of 1887, in fact, gave the Interstate Commerce Commission (ICC) the authority to set the maximum rates that could be charged by railroads. Utility regulations, on the other hand, were stated in terms of maximum rates of return rather than maximum prices. Much has been written about the extent to which rate of return regulation reduces a firm's incentive to minimize costs and operate efficiently, beginning with Averch and Johnson.[7]

As the regulation of the transportation industry extended from railroads in 1887 to motor carriers in 1935 and airlines in 1938, the nature of the regulations changed and became more difficult to explain in the context of the natural monopoly theory of regulation. The Motor Carrier Act of 1935 gave the ICC the authority to set not only maximum prices but also minimum prices. The Civil Aeronautics Act of 1938 gave the Civil Aeronautics Board similar authority to set maximum, minimum, and actual rates.

These regulations, which set rates of return and minimum prices, are difficult to explain in terms of the natural monopoly argument for regulation that would justify maximum prices. Furthermore, studies such as Stigler and Friedland[8] have shown that regulations in the utility industry have had little effect on prices. Spann and Erickson[9] as well as Sloss[10] showed that regulations in the railroad and trucking industries, respectively, in fact, have resulted in higher rather than lower prices. These findings—that regulations do not take the form appropriate to deal with natural monopoly and do not have the effect expected of regulations appropriate to deal with natural monopoly—led to the development of alternative theories of economic regulation.

The Producer Protection Theory

Regulations that set minimum rather than maximum prices and findings that regulations did not reduce rates in the utility industry and that they actually seemed to increase rates in the transportation industry seem inconsistent with the natural monopoly rationale for government regulation which would predict that regulations would be designed to protect consumers by setting maximum prices and holding prices down.

Therefore, the existence of regulations that set minimum prices and appear to hold prices higher than they would otherwise be might be thought to be designed to protect producers in the regulated market rather than consumers. Jordan[11] suggested a theory that regulations are intended to protect the producers in the regulated industry and that the differential impacts of regulations in the utility and transportation industries is due to their market structure prior to regulation.

If utilities were natural monopolies and regulations are designed to protect them, then regulations will have no appreciable affect on utility rates. If the trucking and especially the airline industries were unstable collusive oligopolies, then regulations designed to protect them would set minimum prices to police secret price cuts, and the stabilization of the collusion would result in higher prices.

This producer protection theory of regulation is consistent with the effects of regulation in the utility and transportation industries at the time. However, this theory does not make clear why the regulators would want to protect the producers rather than the consumers in the regulated industry.

The Political Support Maximization Model of Government Regulation

The most recent economic theories of government regulation proposed by Stigler[12] and formalized by Peltzman[13] have empirical implications consistent with those of the producer protection theory.

This political support maximization model of government regulation suggests that a government regulatory agency, such as the Civil Aeronautics Board (CAB), has the authority to set airfares for passengers. Because passengers prefer lower airfares whereas airlines prefer higher airfares, members of the CAB make their decisions in such a manner as to maximize their political support from the consumers and the producers.

Suppose the issue is whether to increase airfares by $10. Each consumer and each producer considers the extent to which they should express their political support to the CAB in favor of or against this fare increase. Each consumer or producer makes their decision as to whether to express their political support or opposition based on the costs and benefits that will result from their activity.

The benefit to each individual consumer from expressing opposition to the $10 fare increase is $10 times the number of times the consumer flies per year. The benefit to each individual airline from expressing its support in favor of the fare increase is $10 times the number of passengers ticketed per year. Clearly, the benefit to each airline from expressing support in favor of the fare increase is significantly greater than the benefit to passengers from expressing their opposition. Therefore, each consumer has less incentive to express opposition than each producer has to express support.

The costs of expressing credible political support or opposition include the costs of becoming well informed on the merits of the issue as well as the costs of organizing effectively for political action. Although the consumers, for example, airline passengers, are a much larger group, they are unlikely to be technically well informed on the issue of whether a fare increase is justified. More importantly, passengers have very little in common other than the fact that they occasionally fly on airplanes. The economic theory of collusion predicts that large and heterogeneous groups are not likely to organize effectively to represent their interests as a group.

Conversely, the producers, airlines in this example, are by the nature of their business well informed on the issues justifying a fare increase and are small in number and already well organized for expressing political opinions concerning fare increases.

This theory predicts that small numbers of well-organized producers will be more likely to clearly and articulately express support for regulations that favor them, and large numbers of diverse, and therefore not well-organized, consumers will be less likely to effectively express support for regulations in their favor. Hence the possibility of the outcome of the producer protection theory of regulation, that is, regulations favor the producers rather than the consumers in the regulated industry.

This theory can be expanded to explain the differential effectiveness of subgroups of consumers and producers within the regulatory purview of an agency, such as industrial and commercial users of electricity relative to residential users or trucking firms relative to railroads under ICC regulations. It is relatively clear from sources such as Hilton[14] that ICC regulations were extended to the trucking industry not to protect customers in the trucking industry, but to protect the railroads from competition from the newly developing trucking industry. The National Transportation Act of 1940 contains language that appears to be intended to protect different modes of transportation from competition by others.

Most recently, Economides, Hubbard, and Palia used this political economy model of regulation with a model of monopolistic competition among small and large banks to analyze branching restrictions and deposit insurance. They analyzed the congressional voting records on the branching provisions of the McFadden Act along with other variables for each state. They concluded, "the introduction of federal branching restrictions was designed to maintain the viability of poorly capitalized small banks and against the interests of large banks."[15]

Economic regulation clearly operates through restrictions on pricing and the restriction of entry of new firms into certain markets, either on the basis of geography or product. Regulations are usually rationalized by the concern that in certain cases unregulated markets might allow increasing concentration, resulting in higher prices and reduced services to customers. These studies seem to confirm that economic regulation in the industries examined have generally not had the effect of reducing prices and have protected more inefficient firms from competition by more efficient operators. The implication is that deregulation might reduce prices, increase services, and result in more efficient operations within an industry. Several recent studies have indicated that deregulation in the utility and transportation industries has indeed resulted in lower prices, increased service, and more efficient operations. Winston provides a good summary of the effect of recent deregulation in which he concludes that, "deregulation has been and continues to be a success, and further, that this success is the result of an adjustment process that is common to all major industries that have been completely or partially deregulated."[16]

CONSOLIDATION OF THE AMERICAN BANKING SYSTEM

Reasons for Consolidation

In the wake of Riegle-Neal the deregulation of the banking industry, particularly the elimination of its geographic restrictions, ushered in the era of U.S. banking consolidation. The path of consolidation that is likely to be expanded beyond banking in the future in light of the Gramm-Leach-Bliley Financial Services Modernization Act's repeal of product regulation exemplified by Glass-Steagall was the result of several disparate as well as interrelated phenomena.

Foremost was the desire to provide greater customer convenience through easier physical access to financial service centers. This was more than altruistic; it was imperative because of the mobility of the population both regionally and nationally. As people moved easily across state lines to take new positions or to accept transfers within their companies or as companies themselves moved for reasons of economic advantage, banks were forced to keep pace in order to retain as well as increase their customer base. Although the advent of technological improvements enhanced the ability of banks to deliver services and communicate across state lines with ease, it did not substitute fully for the lack of institutional presence and representation.

Second banks, particularly larger ones, sought to augment their safety, stability, and profits by expanding their asset size and diversifying their product line. Asset growth was required to gain opportunities for cost savings through economies of scale. Additionally, substantial asset strength was essential to meet the challenge posed by two formidable competitors: domestic financial service firms that were unencumbered by banking rules and international banks operating in less regulated and often more supportive systems. Although asset growth alone could not level the playing field for American banks, it was needed to keep them in the ball game at all.

There also is substantial consensus that minimum asset size is a factor in determining a bank's efficiency and its ability to control costs through economies of scale and ultimately to make a profit. Scale efficiencies in banking measured by the decline in average cost per unit of assets increase with a bank's size up to $75 million in assets. Between $75 million and $300 million, the scale economies become exhausted so that above $300 million in assets efficiencies are no longer related to size.[17]

Size also was a factor in gaining economies of scope, the development of greater product breadth, and subsequent, related savings. These synergies, however, did more than add to revenues. They also reduced risk by creating new sources of funds, increased banks' appeal by augmenting the number of services available to depositors, and helped banks compete with unregulated firms that offered banklike products.

Banking regulators seeking to solve some of the systemic problems of banking and thus reduce the failure rate that added to the FDIC's exposure also supported consolidations. After passage of Garn–St. Germain, healthy banks were given regulatory blessing to acquire or merge with banks experiencing declining loan quality or jeopardized by the increased cost of obtaining funds after Regulation Q interest rate ceilings were phased out by DIDMCA.

Ironically, the FDIC itself exacerbated the failure and insurance problem. The flat fees charged all banks for obtaining FDIC insurance provided no reward for prudence. Additionally, the higher ceilings on insured accounts after DIDMCA made the insurance fund even more vulnerable. Until passage of the Federal Deposit Insurance Corporation Improvement Act

(FDICIA) in 1991, bankers could accept inappropriate risks without consideration of adverse consequences, a situation that led to the demise of many institutions.

Finally, regulators also stimulated merger and acquisition activity among banks as the former became less concerned with protecting the dual banking system or antitrust legislation. Aware of the changes in the competitive landscape but unable to alter the underlying regulatory framework, regulators favored a growth in bank size and demonstrated little concern for the consequent reduction in the number of separate banking institutions.

The Extent of Banking Consolidation

It is evident from Table 1.1 that the decade of the 1990s was one in which the American banking industry experienced extensive consolidation, resulting in a steady and dramatic decline in the number of banking institutions in the nation. From 1990 to 1998, the number of banks in the United States decreased by 3,288 from 12,303 to 9,015, a decline of 26.7%.

This trend was pervasive throughout the nation. Only 5 states (Arizona, Connecticut, Maine, Massachusetts and Nevada) were able to counter the tide and retain or increase the number of banks operating within their borders. If one were to review the changes on an annual basis during the period 1990—1998, however, it would be apparent that even within these 5 states, only Nevada had a steady growth in its banking institutions, whereas the other 4 had several years of decline during the same time frame.

Mergers and Acquisitions. The reduction in the number of banks was primarily, and in some states exclusively, the result of merger and acquisition activity. Although this activity preceded the passage of Riegle-Neal, it became more extensive and widespread after passage of the law as the possibility for interstate business expanded along with the ability to reduce competitive costs. Interstate expansion afforded banks the opportunity to enlarge and diversify their customer base, create economies of scale, replace inefficient management, and reduce the risk associated with fixed costs, geographic restrictions, and asset quality.[18]

Failures. Few, if any, reductions in the number of banking institutions were attributable to failures, a result of the passage of the FDICIA of 1991. From 1960–1980, only 134 banks or an average of just 6 per year had failed. From 1981–1991, however, 1,431 banks failed, an average of 130 per year. This drastic increase in failures during the 1980s created substantial pressure on the FDIC. It also was the impetus for passage of the FDICIA which required banking regulators to take preemptive action to avoid failures by critically undercapitalized banks, defined as having a ratio of tangible equity capital to risk adjusted assets below 2% for 270 days.[19] The FDIC also avoided failures by encouraging healthy banks to merge with or acquire unhealthy institutions within their state or across state lines in order to re-

Table 1.1

Changes in the Number of Banking Institutions and Branches in the United States from 1990–1998 by State

	De Novo	Failures	Mergers & Acquisitions	Institutions 1990	Institutions 1998	Change 1990 to 1998	Branches
Alabama	10	0	68	220	156	-64	297
Alaska	1	0	3	8	7	-1	13
Arizona	27	1	30	38	43	5	62
Arkansas	22	0	62	256	194	-62	274
California	67	18	161	482	332	-150	-403
Colorado	34	2	283	446	196	-250	726
Connecticut	11	4	43	68	68	0	408
Delaware	14	0	19	47	37	-10	41
Florida	53	5	216	432	243	-189	821
Georgia	72	2	111	409	340	-69	304
Hawaii	0	2	7	21	12	-9	-5
Idaho	8	0	11	22	17	-5	71
Illinois	69	0	423	1087	740	-347	1052
Indiana	12	1	162	301	168	-133	209
Iowa	24	2	146	562	444	-118	289
Kansas	16	0	196	555	392	-163	407
Kentucky	32	0	95	332	260	-72	328
Louisiana	17	1	104	231	148	-83	261
Maine	5	0	4	21	36	15	123
Maryland	7	2	33	103	77	-26	-37
Massachusetts	5	5	67	85	215	130	576
Michigan	26	1	132	235	161	-74	-206
Minnesota	29	0	164	626	511	-115	277
Mississippi	10	0	36	123	95	-28	158
Missouri	26	0	193	544	377	-167	535
Montana	13	1	86	156	89	-67	141
Nebraska	27	0	119	392	314	-78	195
Nevada	18	0	6	19	25	6	100
New Hampshire	6	0	40	45	34	-11	170
New Jersey	28	3	79	131	77	-54	328
New Mexico	9	1	30	91	58	-33	119
New York	18	4	52	193	196	3	504
North Carolina	34	0	44	78	68	-10	168
North Dakota	5	0	43	150	113	-37	90
Ohio	21	1	81	289	217	-72	404
Oklahoma	8	1	150	419	311	-108	365
Oregon	16	0	23	50	43	-7	154
Pennsylvania	21	1	116	300	211	-89	504
Rhode Island	3	0	6	11	10	-1	25
South Carolina	23	0	23	85	76	-9	83
South Dakota	8	0	24	125	108	-17	96
Tennessee	38	0	102	253	200	-53	428
Texas	67	11	671	1184	806	-378	1672
Utah	19	0	20	55	50	-5	95
Vermont	1	0	8	27	24	-3	26
Virginia	26	1	60	178	150	-28	156
Washington	32	0	41	94	82	-12	336
West Virginia	10	0	107	180	90	-90	176
Wisconsin	19	0	199	473	343	-130	428
Wyoming	4	0	45	71	51	-20	52
United States	1071	70	4944	12303	9015	-3288	13396

Source: Statistics on Banking, 1998, pp. B-4–B-9; 1997, pp. B-4–B-9; Historical 1934–1966, pp. E-119–E-169.

duce the burden on the FDIC while continuing to protect savers. Table 1.1 reveals that from 1990 to 1998 only 70 banks, an average of slightly under 8 per year, failed throughout the nation. Given the fact that 29 of the failing institutions were either in California or Texas, the rest of the nation averaged only 5.7 failures per year including 28 states that had no bank failures at all.

De Novo. The decline in the number of banks would have been even more dramatic without an increased number of de novo or start-up institutions. Several factors, many of them related to provisions in Riegle-Neal, stimulated the establishment of new banks. The limitations on market share contained in Riegle-Neal curtailed the plans of some banks to increase their regional or national dominance, thus making it possible for new banks to be formed in a less competitive environment. Additionally, in the historic tradition of Alexander Hamilton's protection of infant industries, states were permitted to protect young banks for 5 years from acquisition by an out of state BHC, thus giving the former an opportunity to incubate, grow, and afford investors the hope of future rewards either from operating profits or capital gains from a future sale.[20]

Several factors unrelated to Riegle-Neal also motivated the growth of de novo banks. Grassroots support for new banks came from individuals and businesses disenchanted with the prospect of less personalized and less responsive service from banks headquartered outside their community whether intra state or inter state. Many bank executives worried about their future employment prospects or comfort level if their institutions were to be involved in a merger or acquisition that chose to open new institutions in their community. Finally, new banks had several economic advantages that attributed to their early profitability and stability, namely, lower overhead, the ability to obtain new communications networks and computer technology at reasonable cost, and their ability to avoid extraordinary costs because of the built-in Y2K preparedness of their new equipment.[21]

Table 1.1 shows that 1,071 de novo banks were established from 1990 to 1998. Clearly these banks did not compensate for the reduction of institutions due to mergers and acquisitions. However, further analysis suggests a relationship between de novo banking and the reduced number of institutions. The number of de novo banks is higher in states in which the number of institutions shows the greatest decrease. Simple regression of de novo banks on the number of mergers and acquisitions reveals a regression coefficient of +.1024 with a t-statistic of +6.15, indicating a positive and statistically significant relationship between de novo banks and the number of mergers and acquisitions. De novo banks, therefore, partially offset the effects of mergers and acquisitions in reducing the number of institutions and service to communities.

Although the general decline in the number of banking institutions had the potential for adversely effecting the service received by small and rural communities, small businesses, and the average customer, the growth in branching networks afforded amelioration of these problems.[22] Table 1.1 reflects the mushrooming of branches throughout the nation with the exception of California and Hawaii from 1990—1998. Although the growth rate in the 48 effected states varied considerably, the trend was clearly upward and served to offset the decline in the number of institutions within most states. Figure 1.1 provides a graphic illustration of the growth of interstate branching on a national basis immediately before and after passage of Riegle-Neal.

Branching. Branching networks grew in popularity for many reasons. First and foremost was the fact that they were a less costly form of organization than separately chartered institutions for reaching a broadly scattered clientele. This factor was particularly attractive to BHCs that could consolidate their banks in several states into a branching network that could reduce expenses through economies of scale. The number of branches in the United States increased by 13,396 from 49,848 to 63,244 from 1990–1998, respectively, or by 26.8%. The percentage change in the number of branches, therefore, fully offset the decline in the number of banking institutions.

The regression of the net change in the number of branches on the net change in the number of institutions gives a regression coefficient of—2.4, with a t-statistic of—6.2 indicating a negative and statistically significant relationship between the decrease in the number of banking institutions and the increase in the number of branches. Therefore, it appears that the decrease in the number of institutions is more than compensated for by the increase in the number of branches. This finding is enhanced by the statistical analysis of the relationship between the change in the number of branches and the number of mergers and acquisitions. The simple regression of the change in the number of branches on the number of mergers and acquisitions results in a regression coefficient of +2.22 with a t-statistic of +9.5.

Table 1.2 reveals the importance of interstate branching per state as of June 30, 1999. Most notable is the fact that in 12 states, branches of banks headquartered outside of the state accounted for 30% or more of all the bank branches within the host state.

The Affect of Consolidation on Asset Size

Asset size was a concern both for the proponents and opponents of Riegle-Neal. The former favored consolidation of the banking industry and the growth in the average size of banks because they believed that asset strength was necessary for risk reduction through diversification of the customer base. Additionally they believed that the nation's largest banks needed to expand in size in order to remain competitive in the international arena. Those who feared growth in the average size of banks believed that large banks would grow at the expense of smaller ones.

Figure 1.1
Number of Interstate Branches Operated by FDIC-Insured Commercial Banks and Savings Institutions 1994–1999

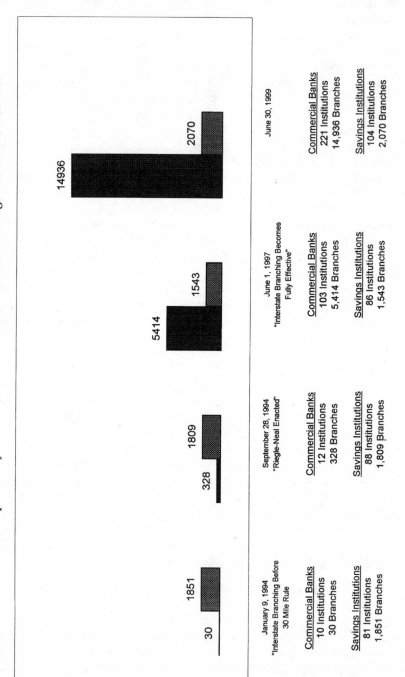

January 9, 1994
"Interstate Branching Before
30 Mile Rule

Commercial Banks
10 Institutions
30 Branches

Savings Institutions
81 Institutions
1,851 Branches

September 28, 1994
"Riegle-Neal Enacted"

Commercial Banks
12 Institutions
328 Branches

Savings Institutions
88 Institutions
1,809 Branches

June 1, 1997
"Interstate Branching Becomes
Fully Effective"

Commercial Banks
103 Institutions
5,414 Branches

Savings Institutions
86 Institutions
1,543 Branches

June 30, 1999

Commercial Banks
221 Institutions
14,936 Branches

Savings Institutions
104 Institutions
2,070 Branches

Source: www.fdic.gov

16

Table 1.2
Interstate Branches as a Percent of Total Offices
FDIC-Insured Institutions, June 20, 1999

States	
Alabama	5.5
Alaska	14.6
Arizona	44.9
Arkansas	21.4
California	3.2
Colorado	27.0
Connecticut	38.2
Delaware	6.3
Florida	56.0
Georgia	40.9
Hawaii	0.3
Idaho	79.5
Illinois	14.0
Indiana	16.4
Iowa	15.1
Kansas	17.6
Kentucky	17.4
Louisiana	10.1
Maine	14.9
Maryland	37.2
Massachusetts	14.1
Michigan	8.9
Minnesota	1.2
Mississippi	24.0
Missouri	17.0
Montana	1.8
Nebraska	7.1
Nevada	57.6
New Hampshire	16.4
New Jersey	35.8
New Mexico	16.4
New York	19.5
North Carolina	3.3
North Dakota	7.5
Ohio	3.3
Oklahoma	8.9
Oregon	69.5
Pennsylvania	11.8
Rhode Island	24.0
South Carolina	32.9
South Dakota	4.8
Tennessee	14.9
Texas	17.2
Utah	21.0
Vermont	14.2
Virginia	34.0
Washington	46.5
West Virginia	17.0
Wisconsin	0.9
Wyoming	13.9

Source: FDIC Web site.

17

Appendix 1 reflects that the asset size of American banks has grown substantially from 1990 to 1998. Banks with assets under $25 million declined by 62.16% or by 2,065, the largest declining category. They were followed by declines in banks with assets from $25–$50 million (39.24% or 1,231) and those with assets from $50–$100 million (19.42% or 539). Clearly what the regulators characterize as small banks, namely, those with assets under $100 million, were the major losers during the decade of consolidation.

The category with the greatest percentage increase during the same period was the largest banks, namely, those with over $10 billion in assets. Their number was augmented by 21 or 42.86% during the 1990s. It is likely that this growth accounts entirely for the decline of 17 banks or 14.28% among those institutions with assets from $3 to $10 billion. One can conclude that the regulators' definition of a large bank as one having $10 billion or more in assets now reflects the need for large banks to have sufficient asset size to be internationally competitive.

The greatest growth in the number of institutions during the 1990s was among the intermediate-sized banks with assets between $100 million and $3 billion. They grew by 9.6% overall or by 279 institutions.

As in the overview of consolidation, these trends also were generalized throughout most of the nation. Smaller institutions declined in number among 49 states. At the other end of the spectrum, 15 states had an increase in the number of large banks with assets of at least $10 billion whereas 8 states declined in this category. Among the 27 states experiencing no change in the category, 19 of them had never had large banks.

Consolidation of the American banking industry and the concomitant growth in the asset size of its institutions should have enhanced its profitability and stability. To what, if any, extent this was accomplished at the expense of servicing small businesses and the average individual customer is a major cause of concern. Chapter 2 pursues the answer to the first issue. Chapter 3 considers the second issue.

NOTES

1. Benjamin J. Klebaner, *American Commercial Banking: A History* (Boston: Twayne Publishers, 1990), pp. 70, 71, 102 and 133.

2. Timothy W. Koch and S. Scott MacDonald, *Bank Management* (Fort Worth, TX: Dryden Press, 2000), p. 66.

3. "Interstate Branching: Who's Opting In, Who's Opting Out, Who's Looking at the Options," *ABA Banking Journal* LXXXVII, no. 10 (October 1995): p. 12.

4. Ann B. Matasar and Deborah D. Pavelka, "Industry-Specific Corporate Responsibility with an International Dimension: The Case of Foreign Bank Compliance with CRA," *Business and Society* 36 no. 3 (September 1997): pp. 280–295.

5. Daniel L. Goelzer, Simon Zornoza and Eli D. Cohen, "New Banking Legislation: The Riegle-Neal Interstate Banking and Branching Efficiency Act of 1994" (unpublished paper from the law firm of Baker and McKenzie, October 1994), pp. 1–7.

6. Peter Rose, *Banking across State Lines: Public and Private Consequences* (Westport, CT: Quorum, 1997), pp. 43–44.

7. H. Averch and L.L. Johnson, "Behavior of the Firm under Regulatory Constraints," *American Economic Review* 53 (December 1963), pp. 1052–1069.

8. George J. Stigler and Claire Friedland, "What Can Regulators Regulate? The Case of Electricity," *Journal of Law & Economics*, V (October 1962): pp. 1–16.

9. Robert M. Spann and Edward W. Erickson, "The Economics of Railroading: The Beginning of Cartelization and Regulation," *Bell Journal of Economics and Management Science* 1, no. 2 (autumn 1970): p. 227.

10. James Sloss, "Regulation of Motor Freight Transportation: A Quantitative Evaluation of Policy," *Bell Journal of Economics and Management Science*, 1, no. 2 (autumn 1970): p. 327.

11. William A. Jordan. "Producer Protection, Prior Market Structure and the Effects of Government Regulation," *Journal of Law & Economics* XV no. 1 (April 1972): pp. 151–176.

12. George J. Stigler, "The Theory of Economic Regulation," *Bell Journal of Economics and Management Science* 2, no. 1 (spring 1971): pp. 3–21.

13. Sam Peltzman, "Toward a More General Theory of Regulation," *Journal of Law & Economics* XIX, no. 2 (August 1976): pp. 211–240.

14. George W. Hilton, "Consistency of the Interstate Commerce Act," *The Journal of Law & Economics* IX (October 1966): pp. 87–114.

15. Nicholas Economides, R. Glen Hubbard, and Darius Palia, "The Political Economy of Branching Restrictions and Deposit Insurance: A Model of Monopolistic Competition among Small and Large Banks," *Journal of Law and Economics*, XXXIX, no. 2 (October 1996): p. 700.

16. Clifford Winston, "U.S. Industry Adjustment to Economic Deregulation," *Journal of Economic Perspectives* 12, no. 3 (summer 1998): p. 103.

17. Paul S. Calem, "The Impact of Geographic Regulation on Small Banks," *Business Review* (Federal Reserve Bank of Philadelphia) (November–December 1994): pp. 26 and 27.

18. John W. Spiegel and Alan Gart, "What Lies Behind the Merger and Acquisition Frenzy," *Business Economics* XXXI, no. 2 (April 1996): p. 49.

19. Koch and MacDonald, *Bank Management*, p. 398; Peter Rose and James W. Kolari, *Financial Institutions*, 5th ed. (Chicago: Irwin, 1995), p. 245.

20. Melissa Wahl, "As Banks Merge, New Ones Emerge," *Chicago Tribune*, June 30, 1998, p. 2.

21. Ibid., pp. 1 and 2.

22. William R. Keeton, "Multi-Office Bank Lending to Small Businesses: Some New Evidence," *Economic Review* (Federal Reserve Bank of Kansas City) 80, no. 2 (Second Quarter 1995): p. 45.

Chapter 2

$

The Economic and Financial Health of America's Banks: The Effects of Consolidation on the Private Sector

The number of American banks that ushered in the new millennium was substantially diminished by the ongoing consolidation occurring in the American banking industry during the 1990s. To what extent this represented a healthy and desirable phenomenon was not immediately apparent or assured. As Peter Rose noted, "Relative to most other controversial areas in banking, the volume of research focusing upon interstate banking still remains comparatively limited. Few issues can be really marked down as 'decided,' and the current body of evidence must be considered 'thin' by conventional scientific standards."[1]

Using data collected by the FDIC for all insured banks, which encompass all domestic banks as well as any foreign banks doing retail banking in the United States, it is now possible to develop a composite picture of the financial health, particularly the profitability and risk exposure, of American banks at the end of the 20th century and to determine to what degree, if any, this condition has improved, deteriorated, or remained unchanged in the era of consolidation.

AGGREGATE CONDITION AND INCOME DATA

Net Income

Net income or profitability is the key component of any business's present fortunes and future viability. As profit-making institutions, banks are no exception to this rule.

Banks obtain their operating income from a variety of sources, including interest and fees on loans, income from the investment securities held in the bank's own portfolio, underwriting income associated with leases, fees for fiduciary activities, earnings on foreign exchange transactions, service fees, and noninterest income. Each of these sources of funds has different levels of significance for banks of varying size (e.g., small- and medium-sized banks are likely to have little, if any, income from foreign exchange transactions). Additionally the relative significance of each source of funds can alter over time because of changing circumstances, for example, service charges for demand deposits (checking accounts) have declined as an important source of income as banks have had to compete for deposits in these noninterest-bearing accounts which are less attractive because banks have been able to offer negotiable orders of withdrawal (NOW) accounts and money market deposit accounts (MMDA), both of which pay interest while providing checklike products. Nonetheless demand deposits remain attractive transaction options for those not wanting to maintain the minimum balances usually required by the interest bearing alternatives.

The operating expenses of banks resemble those of other businesses in that they include salaries, employee-related expenditures, and overhead charges. Banks, however, also have expenses associated with interest owed on deposits, interest on borrowed funds, money that must be put aside for potential losses on loans and leases, and the payment of miscellaneous noninterest expenses. Additionally, during the last years of the 1990s, noninterest charges related to mergers, acquisitions, and restructuring have been responsible for a major portion of the increased expenses and, according to the FDIC, have been "a key determinant of industry profitability."[2]

Rose notes that "one of the most widely voiced claims in support of the spread of interstate banking . . . [was] the belief that spreading out geographically into multiple markets . . . [would] reduce a banking organization's dependence upon any particular market and, thereby, help to stabilize its cash flows and earnings."[3] He goes on to state, however, "it is *not necessarily* true that the spread of interstate banking will reduce the overall risk exposure of either individual banks or of the banking system as a whole."[4] Appendix 2 provides empirical data for evaluating the impact of interstate banking on the earnings of the nation's banks. It reflects the net income or total income minus total expenses on an aftertax basis for banks in each of the 50 states from 1996, the year in which Riegle-Neal was almost fully effective, to 1999, the last full year for which data was available. On a nationwide basis, the banking system's total net income during this period rose by 36.97% or $19,353 million to a record high of $71.7 billion in 1999.[5]

The change in net income levels among the states, however, was decidedly mixed. During this 4-year period, 29 states recorded an increase in the net income of their banks, and 21 states had declines. Only 13 of the 29 states that showed an increase in their net income had a percentage increment greater than the national one. Among the states in which there were increments, the percentage of change ranged dramatically from 1.4% in Kentucky to 1,437.3% in Rhode Island. The change in income among those states reflecting declines, though substantial, was considerably less startling, ranging from –3.5% in Louisiana to –76.9% in Washington.

If one looks at absolute rather than relative change, the results also show great disparities. Among the states in which there was an increase in net income, Alaska had the smallest change, that is, $2 million. North Carolina had the largest change, $9,439 million. In terms of absolute dollar disparities among those states with declining banking net incomes, the state that was least effected was Wyoming with a decline of –$4 million. The state most adversely effected was Florida, whose banks had a decline in net income of –$933 million.

Although, as Rose has pointed out, "state-by-state is preferable to only a broad regional view of U.S. banking markets,"[6] it is interesting to note that regionally the results also were mixed with no one region appearing to be the clear beneficiary of change. Nonetheless it appears that the central portion of the nation fared rather well whereas a large portion of both coastal regions experienced a substantial number of declines in statewide banking net income.

Looking at net income figures alone, however, provides an incomplete picture of the effect of consolidation on the banks in various states. Although net income changes can reflect the improvement or declining nature of the banking business in a state, it also can be attributed to the effects of interstate consolidation and the out-of-state relocation of the head office that reports the data. Taking into account the change in the number of banks shown in Table 1.1, there is reason to believe that the declining net income among banks in Connecticut, Florida, Maine and Washington is, in part, effected by consolidation, a fact supported by the FDIC's statement on noninterest charges of banks for several quarters at the end of the 1990s. On the positive side, several states, most notably Alabama, Minnesota, New Hampshire and Rhode Island benefited from consolidation when recording a growth in net income.

Total Assets

The assets of a bank include cash (money readily available to meet the needs of customers, the reserve account at the regional Federal Reserve bank, demand and time deposits held at other depository institutions, and cash items in process); investment securities in the bank's own portfolio; loans and leases, the variety of which is determined by the size, location, and customer base of the bank; fixed assets such as the building and equipment of the bank; other real estate holdings; and a variety of tangible and intangible assets. Without exception, the single most important category is net loans and leases resulting from the deduction of a loss allowance from the actual loans and leases outstanding.

The total assets of banks as well as other businesses affect liquidity, solvency, and income potential and, therefore, serve as a benchmark against which the well-being of an institution can be measured. Appendix 2 reflects the total assets of the American banking industry on a state-by-state basis during the period 1996 to 1999. Banking assets rose nationally by $1,156,529 million or 25.26% during this period.

As in the case of net income, however, the growth of American banks was unevenly distributed throughout the nation. Thirty-one states registered asset growth for their banking industry whereas the banks in 19 states diminished in asset size. Here, too, as in the case of net income disparities, the range for asset growth was greater than the range for asset decline. The former ranged from an almost insignificant change of $2 million in Alaska to a substantial jump of $9,439 million in North Carolina, the same two states representing the polar points for increases in net income. Among the declines, the least significant was –$4 million in Wyoming and the most substantial was –$933 million in Florida. These two states also represented the extremes for net income declines.

On a relative rather than absolute basis, increases in assets ranged from 1.48% in Colorado to 1,496.5% in Rhode Island. Among the states with declining banking assets, the state experiencing the smallest decline was –.58% in Nevada. The state with the greatest decline in its banking assets was Connecticut with a –70.99%.

A correlation of net income changes to changes in assets among the states' banks reveals a positive and clearly statistically significant relationship that may be explained, in part, by interstate consolidations, as well as other factors such as the costs associated with acquiring the assets, the earnings derived from the assets, and the costs attached to attracting deposits.

Total Deposits

As depository financial institutions, banks derive the vast majority of their money or liabilities from one source, deposits. Deposits can be categorized in a several ways: (1) by type of customer or holder of the deposits; (2) the type of deposit (e.g., demand deposits, savings deposits), time deposits (e.g., certificates of deposit [CDs]); and (3) interest-bearing or non-interest bearing.[7] Although the mix of deposits effects the liquidity requirements of a bank in that demand deposits require higher liquidity than time deposits while the latter pay higher interest than the former, the total deposits of a bank reflect its ability to attract money, a basic concern in garnering loanable funds and competing with other financial institutions for the deposits and investment money available from the complete customer base.

Appendix 2 reflects the total deposits in American banks on a state-by-state basis from 1996 to 1999. On a nationwide basis, deposits during the period rose by $633,640 million or by 19.82%. On a statewide basis, the states were evenly divided between those in which the deposits grew and those in which they declined.

Among the 25 states experiencing deposit increases, the smallest actual dollar increase ($787 million) occurred in Iowa and the largest one ($483,540 million) was in North Carolina, the state that benefited most consistently and substantially in virtually all categories. The state with the smallest actual dollar decline (–$249 million) was Alaska; the largest was –$95,224 million in California. On a relative basis, the greatest increase in deposits, 920.3%, was in Rhode Island, and the smallest, 2.2% was in Iowa. Among the states in which deposits declined, the most severe drop, –70.6%, occurred in Connecticut, and the least severe was –1.1% in Nebraska.

Equity Capital

The equity capital of banks has several components, some of which are similar to other businesses (e.g., par value of issued common and preferred stock and retained earnings), whereas others are unique to a depository, financial institution, for example, capital reserve for future contingencies. Banks are highly leveraged businesses that have a relatively small proportion of total equity capital on their balance sheets to protect depositors against operating losses. As noted by Rose and Kolari, "because the equity cushion is quite small, the soundness of a bank depends principally on the competence and prudence of its management and the stability of the financial system."[8]

Appendix 2 reflects the absolute amounts of bank equity by state from 1996 to 1999. In conjunction with the ratio for the return on equity capital and the ratios for equity capital to total assets, core capital, and total capital to risk-weighted assets, a relatively clear picture of the safety of American banks during the last year of the 1990s can be derived.

Nationwide equity capital rose by $91,049 million or 23.42%. Banks in 29 states increased their equity capital as compared with 21 states in which equity capital declined. To a notable degree, as would be expected, the increase in equity capital occurred in those states where the level of assets also rose. The relationship of equity to assets is reviewed at greater length in conjunction with the capital/asset ratio.

SELECTED PERFORMANCE RATIOS

Performance ratios evaluated on a time series basis provide insight into the effects of consolidation on the efficiency, cost reduction from economies of scale, levels of assumed risk, profitability, and future, as well as current prospects for a bank's success. When viewed on a state-by-state basis for all banks as they are in Appendix 3, performance ratios also are a reflection of the health of the entire banking system.

The end of interstate geographic restrictions on America's banks gave them the opportunity to break out of restrictive or nonprofitable markets and pursue new customers in more vibrant business locales. Performance ratios, therefore, also provide initial insight into the ability of America's banks to take advantage of their new, national marketplace. Additionally these ratios help to determine the value of market diversification for banks and whether or not "geographic determination . . . [is] a two-edged sword, reducing bank earnings risk but increasing other dimensions of bank risk exposure."[9]

Net Interest Margin

Banks must be concerned with the interest rate spread because they are particularly sensitive to interest rate fluctuations that effect both sides of their balance sheet. The net interest margin considers the spread or relationship of total interest income on the asset side minus total interest expenses on the liability side compared with earnings assets. Because this ratio is directly representative of bank profitability, the higher the ratio, the better the bank's performance.

From 1996–1999, the net interest margin of the entire American banking industry declined by –4.68%. The net interest margin declined in 36 states, rose in 13 states, and remained unchanged in one state, Alaska. During this period, therefore, states experienced a decline in their net interest margin nearly 3 times more often than they experienced an increase in their net interest margin. The states whose net interest margin was most adversely affected were Arizona, Connecticut, Delaware, Ohio, and Wyoming. On a relative basis, the most fortunate states were California, New Hampshire and South Dakota.

The widespread decline in the net interest margin reflected the heavy competitive pressures banks were experiencing in attracting new deposits on the one hand and remaining a desirable source of loans on the other hand. Banks had to maintain high-interest rates on deposits in order to vie successfully for investment money that had many other opportunities for placement. Other financial institutions, especially thrifts and credit unions, also offered high rates, equivalent insurance on deposits, and a personal and community appeal that was enhanced as banks became larger and were perceived, rightly or wrongly, as less concerned with the average customer.

On the asset side, banks were unable to increase their interest charges because of the growth of the commercial paper market that was attractive to large, commercial customers. The pricing of loans also was reduced by the ability of thrifts, credit unions, and other financial institutions to make competitive loans to a broader customer base because of the regulatory changes of the 1980s.

Noninterest Income to Average Earning Assets

This ratio focuses on those balance sheet items unaffected by interest rates. On the asset side, these items include fee income and service charges, whereas on the liability side, they are salaries and expenses for building maintenance and equipment, particularly information technology. Consolidation within the banking industry sought the reduction of these expenses and, therefore, in addition to providing insight into the changing asset and liability mix of banks, this ratio is a bellwether regarding the success that banks have had in increasing their earnings as a result of the expenditure reductions associated with consolidation.

In light of the nationwide increase in banking income and the decline in the net interest margin, it is not surprising to find that the national ratio for noninterest income to average earning assets rose from 1996 to 1999. Thirty-one states registered increases in this ratio for their banks; 18 states experienced declines, and only Montana remained unchanged.

To a considerable extent, this ratio does not testify fully to the growing importance of noninterest income because it only relates to those items that are recorded on the balance sheet. Many services and fee-producing products upon which banks have become ever more reliant do not appear on the balance sheet. They, therefore, are referred to as off balance sheet items. Off balance sheet items are activities of a bank that are not included on their balance sheet.

Banks have been attracted to off balance sheet items such as loan commitments, standby letters of credit, futures contracts, and swaps because they generate fee income, are not subject to the vagaries of interest rates, and reduce the perceived risk of the bank. These items are of concern, however, because they obligate banks to assume future contingent risks that can jeopardize their safety. Fees are earned for underwriting future situations over which the bank has little, if any, control. Therefore, the perceived risk may be reduced by off balance sheet items, and the actual risk may be heightened.

Net Charge-Offs to Loans and Leases

Net charge-offs represent the money that banks had expected to receive from their loan and lease portfolio but that will not materialize. Obviously the results of this ratio are preferably lower than higher.

Net charge-offs to loans and leases rose by 5.17% nationwide during the 4-year period from 1996 to 1999. Here, too, the national figure masked underlying experiential diversity among the states. Twenty-four states had banks with greater net charge-offs on their loans and leases. Among these, some states, such as Minnesota in which the net charge off ratio rose by

1,595%, were especially hard hit. Twenty-two states had banks with lower results, and 4 states experienced no change.

The extent to which mergers and acquisitions, particularly across state lines, affected the performance of the loan and lease portfolio of the banks within a state is of particular interest in light of regulators' willingness to allow cross-border activity for the purchase of insolvent banks in order to protect the FDIC. Although net charge offs could be exclusively related to acceptance of greater risk in the loan and lease portfolios, it also, in part, could be linked to interstate marriages for regulatory convenience.

Credit–Loss Provision to Net Charge-Offs

Although net charge-offs reflect the actual, current losses that a bank has incurred for its loans and leases, the credit-loss provision reflects the estimation of future loan losses. Additionally the money put aside to fund the anticipated credit losses increase current expenses, thus representing a loss of future income.

The credit–loss provision to net charge-offs ratio, therefore, is more than a reflection of banking health in the present; it casts light on the assessment of the quality of the bank's loans and leases and its anticipated future performance. If the ratio increases, it portends for a poorer performance in the loan and lease portfolio because the credit–loss provision will have become progressively larger than the current net charge-offs.

From 1996 to 1999, this ratio rose on a national basis by a modest 1.6%. Among the individual states, 30 had increases in this ratio, and 20 declined. Texas had the least significant increase, .59%. At the other extreme was Connecticut which had a staggering increase of 12,765.18%. The range of the declines was substantially smaller, extending from the smallest reduction of –1.00% in Kentucky, to the greatest reduction, –36.63% in Arizona.

Of these states the most interesting case appears to be Connecticut, which experienced an enormous reduction in its indigenous banking population during this period. This leaves the impression that the Connecticut banks that remained were in a weakened financial condition with poor loan portfolios and were unattractive merger or acquisition partners for out-of-state banks.

Return on Assets (ROA)

Although providing general insight into how well a bank is managing or using its assets overall, ROA does not pinpoint those assets that either are underperforming or doing well. Each of the items on both sides of the balance sheet must still be evaluated separately to determine the specific problems or successes of a particular bank. Nonetheless, for purposes of evaluating the health of the banking system and banks in general, ROA is a useful ratio for gaining a composite view.

One would assume that states in which the banks had high net charge-offs and/or high credit loss provisions might also have poorer ROAs because loans, and to a lesser extent leases, are the largest categories among the assets of most banks, as well as their major sources of income.[10] This, however, did not occur either nationally or in several states. Nationally, the ROA rose from 1996 to 1999 by 10.08% despite the increase of 1.60% in the credit–loss provision to net charge-offs and an increment of 5.17% in net charge-offs to loans and leases. Throughout the states, as shown in Appendix 3, the relationship of ROA to the loan/lease portfolio ratios was unpredictable. Assets other than loans and leases were obviously having a major impact on ROA.

Thirteen states reported an increase in their net charge-offs to loans and leases as well as an increase in their ROA. Fourteen states, however, experienced declines in their net charge-offs to loans and leases, along with an increase in their ROA. Nine states had declines in both their net charge-offs to loans and leases and their ROA. Ten states had increases in their net charge offs to loans and leases but declines in their ROA. Among the 4 states that had no changes in their net charge offs to loans and leases, 2 had increases in their ROA, and 2 had declines in their ROA.

Return on Equity (ROE)

As noted by Madura, "[a] bank's ROE is affected by the same income statement items that affect ROA as well as by the bank's degree of financial leverage [as represented by the equity or leverage multiplier]."[11] This ratio is of key concern to shareholders and is a major factor in determining the value of a share of bank stock. The extent to which ROE has improved or deteriorated during the era of banking consolidation, therefore, is of crucial importance inasmuch as banks, like other for-profit organizations, are expected to enhance shareholders' wealth.

The national banking industry posted a gain of 6.16% in the composite ROE from 1996 to 1999. Half the states recorded expanded ROEs among their banks, whereas the other half had ROEs that contracted.

Percent of Unprofitable Institutions

Most disconcerting was the extremely large increase, 68%, in the number of unprofitable banking institutions during the period 1996–1999. In the final analysis, this was a most telling figure because it clearly demonstrated that the period of banking consolidation had either injured or been unable to save a substantial portion of the industry members experiencing financial difficulties. The anticipated benefits of cross-border mergers and acquisitions are brought into question by this finding.

Percent of Institutions with Earning Gains

The national decline of −10.82% in the number of banking institutions with earnings gains augments the findings related to the growth in unprofitable institutions. Nonetheless there is no definitive pattern between these two factors among the individual states.

Profitability or asset utilization ratios collectively reflect a mixed message for the end of the 1990s and provide a basis for uncertainty for looking toward the future. Although giving little credence to those projecting doom and gloom for the banking industry because of geographic expansion, the generally poor profitability performance of the nation's banks as a group must be viewed as discouraging.

SELECTED CONDITION RATIOS

When reviewed in conjunction with one another, the condition ratios included in Appendix 4 create an image of the general economic and financial health of the American banking system in the last years of the 20th century. Each of the ratios contributes a tile to the mosaic that comes into focus as the information is viewed collectively. Taken together, these ratios provide an insight into the risks associated with the banking system and the impact that consolidation and geographic expansion had on America's banks.

Net Loans and Leases to Assets

Loans and leases represent the single largest asset category for all banks. To what extent banks' dependence on lending and leasing has grown or diminished in the last several years, therefore, is a significant question because it reveals the degree of asset diversification risk contained in banks' balance sheets. If banks retained or increased their dependence on lending, it would be appropriate for them to seek a reduction in their portfolio risk by diversifying this asset category. One means for accomplishing this would be to expand across state lines in search of new customers.

Appendix 4 shows that from 1996 through 1999 the national ratio of net loans and leases to assets remained relatively constant at approximately 60%. The apparent stability of this ratio for the entire nation masks the substantial range of changes at the state level. Although 7 states had changes in this ratio of less than 1%, 22 states reported an increase, and 22 reported a decrease. On a relative basis, the greatest increase occurred in Minnesota (14.14%), and the most substantial decline was in Wyoming (−27.33%). On an absolute basis in 1999, the state with the highest ratio was South Dakota (75.55%), and the one with the smallest ratio was Massachusetts (41.20%). The dependency on one category of assets, therefore, differed considerably among the states despite the appearance of little overall nationwide change.

Loss Allowance to Loans and Leases

The provision for losses reflects banks' and regulators' perception of risk in relation to a bank's loan and lease portfolio. A higher ratio is associated with a perception of greater risk. In light of the primary position occupied by loans and leases in a bank's asset mix, it is of vital concern to know if the risk of loss associated with this asset category was viewed as having grown or diminished during the period of consolidation.

Appendix 4 attests to an overall improvement in the quality of the loan and lease portfolio of the nation's banks. During the period 1996–1999, the nationwide loss allowance ratio was reduced from 1.84% to 1.68% or by –11.58%. With the exception of 9 states, namely, Georgia, Indiana, Nevada, New Hampshire, North Carolina, North Dakota, Rhode Island, South Dakota, and Wyoming, all other states experienced declines in their banks' loss allowance ratio. In the case of the loss allowance ratio, therefore, the national quality of loan portfolios was reflected in the vast majority of the states, signifying a generalized decline in the risks associated with loan portfolios during the last years of the 20th century.

Nonperforming Assets to Assets

Assets are the lifeblood of any business in that they are intended to produce the revenues needed to meet and exceed the obligations associated with liabilities in order to produce a profit. Nonperforming assets not only are unable to assist banks in the manner anticipated but also represent a drain on profits because they are an expenditure of funds for which no return or an inadequate return is being derived. The percentage of nonperforming assets, therefore, is a very important measure of a bank's present and future viability, as well as a reflection of the wisdom of the management.

Nonperforming banking assets nationwide diminished by 16% during the period from 1996 through 1999. Among those states in which the loss allowance had risen, 4 states, namely, Georgia, Nevada, New Hampshire, and Wyoming, saw their banks' nonperforming assets decline. Overall 31 states reported that their banks lowered their nonperforming assets during these years, a sign of improvement in their asset mix, and undoubtedly, in their loan portfolios.

Core Deposits to Total Liabilities

Core deposits are passive deposits that a bank receives without solicitation from its most loyal customers. They are extremely important as a source of continuing liquidity on the liability side of the balance sheet because they are largely inelastic in relation to interest rate fluctuations. According to Rose, "interstate firms were more heavily dependent upon so-called core deposits . . . and displayed higher non-interest operating expenses and lower earnings margins than comparably sized non-interstate banking companies, suggesting that interstate-bound banks seek lower cost and more stable deposits, economies of scale, and improved margins when they cross state lines."[12]

From 1996 to 1999, core deposits in banks throughout the nation declined by −10.31% from 54.6% to 51.24%, thus increasing the risk of reduced liquidity from liabilities. The proportion of core deposits in banks in different states showed an enormous disparity ranging in 1996 from a high of 86.37% in Vermont to a low of 19.87% in Delaware. By 1999, the range of the disparity had been reduced slightly with Vermont continuing to have the highest amount of core deposits, 82.27%, and the lowest percentage was 23.24% in New York.

Equity Capital to Total Assets

This capital ratio is one method by which a bank's capital adequacy and the risk associated with it are assessed. Although capital can be considered a drain on a bank's profitability, ordinarily a higher ratio is interpreted as representing lower risk. This occurs because, inversely, the capital ratio becomes the leverage multiple used in calculating the ROE. By lowering the leverage multiple, therefore, a higher capital ratio lowers the level of risk associated with the ROE.

Throughout the nation from 1996 to 1999, equity capital to total assets remained relatively constant, changing by a modest 2.07% from 8.2% to 8.37%. Among the states the greatest increase in this ratio occurred in Idaho, 42.70%. The most substantial decline in the capital ratio was −14% in Illinois. Most importantly, with the exception of Massachusetts (6.7%) and New York (7.14%), all states in 1999 had equity capital ratios that equaled or exceeded 7.4%, reflecting a relatively stable and secure situation throughout the nation. The highest capital ratio in 1999 was 14.45% in Georgia.

Total Capital to Risk-Weighted Assets

Not all items in a bank's asset mix are viewed in the same light by regulators. Assets are divided among those that are viewed as "risk free," namely cash and U.S. government securities and all the other assets that are seen as containing elements of risks and are called "risk-weighted assets." When assessing the degree of risk associated with the risk-weighted assets in a bank's portfolio, regulators also determine the amount of capital required to compensate for it.

This ratio, therefore, reflects the accumulated risk of the asset portfolio, including the proportion of "risk free" to risk-weighted assets, as well as the degree of risk contained in the latter and the amount of compensatory capital that must be put aside by the bank. Ordinarily as the risk of the portfolio increases, so does this ratio.

During the period 1996 to 1999, the total capital to risk-weighted asset ratio for the nation declined by -2.59%. Among the states, 19 reported higher ratios and, therefore, higher perceived risk in their portfolios, whereas 31 states reported reductions in their ratios. Idaho's ratio rose by the highest percentage, 29.21%, during these years, whereas the smallest ratio growth was .28% in North Carolina. In the states in which this ratio declined, the greatest reduction was -17.97% in Rhode Island. The lowest reduction was -.38% in Vermont.

Gross 1–4 Family Mortgages to Gross Assets

In light of the concern that consolidation within the banking industry would create larger banks that were less sensitive to the needs of the average customer, this ratio has been included to assess to what extent, if any, banks have altered their willingness to provide mortgage loans in the last several years.

During the final years of the 1990s the awarding of mortgages for 1–4 family dwellings remained relatively stable at just above 14% throughout the nation despite consolidation within the banking industry. This apparently benign national result, however, concealed substantial changes in several states.

From 1996 to 1999, the number of mortgage loans for 1–4 family dwellings increased in 23 states but declined in 27. Among the former the state experiencing the most substantial change was North Dakota at 56.28%. The state with the smallest positive percentage change in its lending pattern was Kentucky at 1.47%. Wyoming's -59.77% was the greatest percentage decrease in lending, whereas South Carolina's lending decline of -1.69% was the smallest percentage decline.

Although the range of increases and declines appears similar, the overall pattern was for the reductions in lending to be greater than the increases. Among the 23 states in which banks increased lending, the average of this increase was 15.33%. In the 27 states in which banks reduced their lending, the average of this reduction was -19.19% with 10 of these states reporting declines of approximately -20% or more. This result supports the fears of the opponents of banking consolidation concerning the anticipated unwillingness of larger banks to offer loans to smaller borrowers.

CONCLUSION

An assessment of the changing financial and economic health of America's banks from 1996 to 1999 provides mixed messages. Macroanalysis or an overview at the national level contains several optimistic signs of vitality and strength. Aggregate condition and income data reflect growth of net income, deposits, and equity. Respectively these results create a picture of increasing profitability, adequate liquidity and lower risk. The microview, however, at the state level is substantially less certain. Although many states reported advancement in one or more of the areas related to aggregate condition and growth, other states suffered sharp declines.

The national and state-by-state evaluations of the performance ratios reflected inconsistency and provided no clear pattern at either level or between them. If one looked at net charge-offs, the percentage of unprofitable institutions, and the percentage of banks with earnings gains, the national picture looked bleak. Focusing on the ROA, however, provided an entirely different outcome. As one moved to a more detailed assessment at the state level, what had appeared clear at the national level began to lose its clarity. Only one trend held true at both the state and national levels, namely, a greater reliance on noninterest income.

As in the case of aggregate condition and income data, the condition ratios created an optimistic and steady pattern of growth at the national level. The performance among the states as viewed from the vantage point of the condition ratios also appeared healthier. Loss allowances, nonperforming assets, and risk-weighted capital were particularly strong among the individual states and throughout the nation. Only the core deposits gave any cause for concern.

Although not a factor related, per se, to the strength of the banks, caution also should be taken regarding the number of states in which the level of mortgage lending declined despite the increase in this type of lending nationwide. Critics of interstate banking and branching, as noted earlier, were concerned that this type of pattern might arise, and it is important to keep track of this ratio in order to protect banking customers in states in which out-of-state banks are gaining dominance.

One further note must be added to the overview of the health of America's banks now and possibly even more so in the future. It is no longer possible to look solely at published data to determine the well-being of a bank or of the banking system as a whole because of the growing importance of off balance sheet activities. These fee-generating activities have increased in popularity because they are not subject to the vagaries of interest fluctuations and, therefore, are more fully controlled by management decisions and ingenuity, as well as the competitive marketplace. Among the items included on an off balance sheet basis are loan commitments, standby letters of credit, future contracts, and swaps. Inasmuch as these activities obligate banks by creating future, contingent risks, they pose a concern for the safety of the banking system. To what extent banking consolidation and the newest changes in the banking laws that have broken down the barriers between previously segregated financial institutions, in turn, have adversely or favorably altered the risks of the banking system cannot be determined at this time. Nonetheless they pose many questions that must be addressed in the future.

NOTES

1. Peter Rose, *Banking across State Lines: Public and Private Consequences* (Westport, CT: Quorum, 1997) p. 83.

2. *FDIC Quarterly Banking Profile*. Last Quarter of 1999. Obtained from the FDIC web site.

3. Rose, *Banking across State Lines*, pp. 84 and 85.

4. Ibid., p. 86.

5. *FDIC Quarterly Banking Profile*, Last Quarter of 1999. Obtained from the FDIC's web site.

6. Rose, *Banking across State Lines*, p. 94.

7. Peter Rose and James W. Kolari, *Financial Institutions*, 5th ed. (Chicago: Irwin, 1995), p. 169.

8. Ibid., p. 170.

9. Rose, *Banking across State Lines*, p. 86.

10. Emmanuel N. Roussakis, *Commercial Banking in an Era of Deregulation*, 3rd ed. (Westport, CT: Praeger, 1997), pp. 14–16.

11. Jeff Madura, *Financial Markets and Institutions*, 4th ed. (Cincinnati, OH: South-Western College Publishing, 1998), p. 533.

12. Rose, *Banking across State Lines*, p. 98.

Chapter 3

$

The Public Effects of Interstate Banking Expansion: The Impact on Bank Customers

In anticipation of geographic deregulation, Peter Rose stated that the public effects of this change could include any of the following mutually exclusive and contradictory results: "Increased or decreased quality of banking services supplied to the public," as well as "[l]arger or smaller quantity of banking services made available to the public."[1] He was not alone in expressing uncertainty regarding the fate of the U.S. public in the aftermath of Riegle-Neal's fundamental alteration of the banking system through the introduction of full-scale interstate branching and interstate banking.

Supporters of change projected and applauded a system in which there would be fewer, bigger, and stronger domestic banks able to compete more effectively at home and abroad. Detractors of interstate banking and branching concurred that consolidation would occur, but they maintained that an increase in the average size of American banks "would reduce the services provided by the banking industry to individuals, small businesses, farmers and small communities or increase the cost of these services to these customers."[2] This chapter seeks to determine whether this pessimism was justified.

Prior to reflecting on the banking industry itself, it is interesting to note that opponents of change expressed similar concerns regarding deregulation in the railroad, trucking, and airline industries in the late 1970s and early 1980s. In those situations, the concerns proved to be unfounded.

"Consumers have turned out to be the primary beneficiaries of deregulation. The evidence to date suggests that since deregulation, each industry has significantly improved its service quality and reduced its average prices from 30 to 75 percent."[3]

Initial analysis of data for 1997 and 1998 presented by the board of governors of the Federal Reserve Board (Fed) in its June 1999 *Annual Report to the Congress on Retail Fees and Services of Depository Institutions* confirms that deregulation of the banking industry has had an impact on customers similar to that in the other industries that were deregulated in prior years. The Fed's information base for this report comes from surveys of a randomly selected sample of 700 commercial banks in 29 to 33 states as opposed to a complete set of information from the entire banking population as found in the FDIC's 1997 *Statistics on Banking*. The Fed's sample adequately represents different regions of the country and institutions of different sizes; reflects a broad, cross section of the entire domestic banking community; and provides a sufficient base for analysis of Riegle-Neal's impact on banking customers.

SERVICE AVAILABILITY

An Overview

Four different services offered by a wide range of banks have been used to evaluate the level of service offered by banks in the years immediately after Riegle-Neal became fully effective. These services are automatic teller machines (ATMs), noninterest bearing checking accounts (demand deposits), interest bearing transaction accounts (negotiable orders of withdrawal or NOW accounts), and Savings Accounts. In summary, the Fed noted that 1 in 4 changes in the availability of these banking services between 1997 and 1998 were statistically significant and that of these, half were in the direction of more availability.[4]

Automatic Teller Machines (ATMs). ATMs or cash stations are a relatively new and increasingly important service offered by banks to the public at large. This broad accessibility to noncustomers as well as customers differentiates ATMs from many other banking services that are offered exclusively or primarily to a bank's own customers.

ATMs provide access to cash and serve as depositories for individuals during times when banks are closed. Additionally travelers or persons unable to get to their regular banking facility are served by ATM networks which link several different banks across the nation and worldwide. As "round the clock" tellers in a vast and growing number and variety of locations, ATMs have added flexibility, as well as accessibility for individuals with an immediate need for cash. In today's world, those persons without access to an ATM are inconvenienced and at a distinct disadvantage in obtaining cash for emergencies, unexpected opportunities, or pocket money.

In the 29 states included in this portion of the Fed's survey, 86.5% of the banks reported having ATMs in 1998. This represented an increase of 7.1% from the 79.4% of banks having ATMs in 1997. Only 7 surveyed states (Indiana, Kentucky, Massachusetts, Pennsylvania, Tennessee, Texas, and Virginia) reported declines in the percentage of banks making ATMs available. Two states (Florida and Washington) reported no change because 100% of their banks offered ATMs in both years. The states having the greatest percentage change in banks providing ATMs over the 2-year period were Kansas (+56.3%) and Massachusetts (–31.0%).[5] A statistical analysis of the relationship between the availability of ATMs and the change in the number of banking institutions across the states surveyed indicates, however, that there is a negative, but not statistically significant, relationship between the reduction in the number of banks and the increase in ATM availability.

Demand Deposits. Demand deposits or noninterest bearing checking accounts were offered by virtually all banks, 98.7% and 98.5%, respectively, in 1997 and 1998, in the 33 states included by the Fed in this section of the survey. Twenty states reported no change in this service between 1997 and 1998 because 100% of their banks offered demand deposits in both years. Of the other states reporting, only 6 (Alabama, Arkansas, California, Illinois, Massachusetts, and Ohio) indicated a decrease in the number of banks offering demand deposits.[6]

The distinction between the states became greater when demand deposits were separated by classifications, namely, single-balance, single-fee accounts; fee only accounts; and free accounts. Single-balance, single-fee accounts, which involve no fee if the account holder maintains a minimum balance but add a fee if the required balance is not maintained, decreased by –3.7% among all demand deposits from 39.3% in 1997 to 35.6% in 1998. If one interprets the maintenance of a minimum balance as a deterrent to the accessibility of a service, one would interpret this change as an increase in availability of noninterest bearing checking accounts between the two years.

On the other hand, fee-only accounts "in which the customer incurs a monthly fee regardless of the account balance" with or without the addition of a per check charge increased in availability by 3.0% from 33.3% in 1997 to 36.3% in 1998. Flat-fee accounts can be interpreted as being less accessible because they are regressive and therefore, represent an unwelcome change for customers.

Finally, free accounts, which as one would expect charge no fees under any circumstances, became substantially more available during the two-year period from 1997 to 1998. The surveyed states reported a sharp increase of +14.3% in availability, from 3.0% in 1997 to 17.3% in 1998.[7] On balance, therefore, it appears reasonable to conclude that the availability of demand deposit services taken as a whole expanded after the passage of Riegle-Neal and that this increase was largely beneficial to customers.

Negotiable Orders of Withdrawal (NOW) Accounts. Between 1997 and 1998, the percentage of the 33 surveyed states in which banks offered interest-bearing transaction accounts known as NOW accounts declined by 3.3% from 97.6% to 94.3%. If one compares the change in the availability of demand deposits, with that of NOW accounts on a per state basis, one finds that of the 16 states reporting reductions in the availability of NOW accounts, 11 of them also reported that 100% of their banks offered demand deposits. Of the remaining 5 states, 2 reported reductions also in the availability of demand deposits, and 3 reported increases in the availability of demand deposits. Apparently the reduction in NOW accounts was made possible frequently by the continued or increased availability of demand deposits, a phenomenon that occurred in 14 of the 16 states in which fewer banks supplied NOW accounts. One might surmise, therefore, that the elimination of NOW accounts was a cost-cutting move on the part of banks.[8] The reduction in service should not have inconvenienced most customers because of the availability of demand deposits. Nevertheless, the fact is that disparity in interest payments between the two forms of transaction accounts would have had a negative impact on persons unable to continue using NOW accounts.

Savings Accounts. The 30 states surveyed regarding savings accounts reported an increase of +.7% in the availability of this service from 98.6% in 1997 to 99.3% in 1998. This increase occurred in 3 of the 4 categories of savings accounts, namely, simple passbook account (+.6%), no-fee passbook account (+1.7%), and simple statement account (4.1%). The no-fee statement account was the only category of savings accounts that declined by –1.0%. Only 3 states (California, Massachusetts, and Texas) reported decreases in the number of institutions offering savings accounts.[9]

At this point, the impact of Riegle-Neal on the general availability of banking services would be largely favorable. Despite consolidation within the banking system, banks maintained or increased the variety of services available to the public. In fact, it may be argued that the economies derived from consolidation that, in turn, was stimulated by Riegle-Neal may have made it economical for banks to offer a wider array of services to their customers.

Size of Institution

As both the proponents and opponents of interstate banking anticipated, the average size of American banks has grown substantially in the last several years, a pattern that both preceded and was accelerated by Riegle-Neal. The influence of bank size on the availability of banking services, therefore, is a crucial issue in determining whether the movement toward a more consolidated banking system with fewer, but larger banks, will benefit or adversely affect the average customer.

ATMs. The increased number of banks sponsoring ATMs in the 29 sampled states is attributable primarily to an increased willingness of small banks to supply this service. From 1997 to 1998, the percentage of small institutions sponsoring ATMs rose by +10.1% from 71.3% to 81.4%. During the same time period, medium-sized banks offering this service increased in percentage by +1.4% from 96.0% to 97.4%. Simultaneously the percentage of large banks reduced their ATM networks by –1.8% from 97.3% to 95.5%.[10] The latter development may reflect an elimination of duplicate machines, an economic benefit of consolidation, rather than a true reduction in service.

The Fed survey does not reveal the actual number of ATM machines that were in operation nor does it show if the decline in ATMs offered by large banks was offset by the increases in small- and medium-sized banks providing this service. Given the high percentage of large- and medium-sized institutions already offering ATMs, it is clear that the future growth of this service will rely upon the further expansion of current ATM networks and the number of smaller banks willing to offer ATM facilities. In light of the increase in the average size of banks, the latter does not appear to be an optimistic reality. Conversely, however, de novo banks, which have proven to be able competitors, may enhance the ATM offerings among smaller banks.

Demand Deposits. The impact of institutional size on the availability of demand deposits is decidedly mixed. Among the 33 surveyed states, the percentage of small banks making this service available decreased by –.3% from 98.9% to 98.6% from 1997 to 1998, respectively. Despite this negative finding, it is interesting to note that the smaller institutions reduced single-balance, single-fee accounts while expanding fee-only accounts and free accounts, the latter by a substantial +15.1%.

On a percentage basis, the medium-sized banks providing demand deposits in the surveyed states also decreased by –.1% from 98.6% in 1997 to 98.5% in 1998. Medium-sized institutions targeted fee-only accounts, as well as single-balance, single-fee accounts for reduction. The former decreased by –1.1% from 48.1% to 47.0%, whereas the latter declined by –1.5% from 49.7% to 48.2%. As in the case of small institutions, medium-sized banks offering free accounts increased substantially from 2.9% to 15.7% or by 12.8%.

Although most large banks offered single-balance, single-fee accounts, the percentage of banks with these accounts declined by –2.3% from 54.9% to 52.6%. Large banks, like the small ones, increased the availability of fee-only accounts and free accounts. The percentage of large banks that offered fee-only accounts rose by +3.3% from 46.6% to 49.9%. Free accounts' availability at large banks expanded by +12.8% from 1.1% to 13.9%.[11] One can only surmise that the willingness of banks of all sizes to offer free accounts is attributable to a healthy, competitive environment that benefited customers.

NOW Accounts. With the exception of the large institutions, NOW accounts lost popularity among the banks in the surveyed states from 1997 to 1998. The number of large banks offering NOW accounts increased by 6.1% from 86.1 % to 92.2%. The types of NOW accounts emphasized for expansion during this period by larger banks were single-fee or no-fee accounts rather than single-fee, single-check-charge accounts.

Among medium-sized institutions the percentage offering NOW accounts declined by .9% from 96.1% to 95.2%. These institutions were most likely to eliminate single-fee accounts. Of great interest, however, is the fact that in neither year did any medium-sized institution in any of the 33 surveyed states report having any no fee NOW accounts.

The percentage of small institutions offering NOW accounts decreased by 4.9% from 98.9% to 94.0% in 1997 and 1998, respectively. Small banks targeted all types of NOW accounts for reductions, –6.8% for single-fee accounts, –1.4% for single-fee, single-check-charge accounts, and–.1% for no fee accounts. The last reduction is particularly significant because it represented an elimination of this type of account at the small institutions.[12]

In summary, it appears that large banks were the most generous in making NOW accounts of all types, including no-fee NOW accounts, available to their customers. This finding substantiates the arguments of the proponents of interstate banking who believed that larger institutions could afford a greater variety of services and/or better pricing. Given the trend toward larger banks, customers will be the beneficiaries regarding NOW accounts.

Savings Accounts. The percent of institutions of all sizes reporting savings accounts among their services increased from 1997 to 1998. Large banks reported the largest percentage change, +2.3%, as compared with +.7% for both medium-sized and small banks, respectively.

Among larger banks and smaller ones, the growth in this service covered all types of accounts except no-fee passbook accounts. Medium-sized banks also increased the availability of all types of savings accounts except one, but in their case the exception was the simple passbook account.[13]

Savings accounts like the other service areas did not appear to be adversely affected by the consolidation of the American banking system or the increase in the average size of American banks. If anything, the reverse may have been true.

In summary, the increased asset size of American banks appears to have had a positive impact on the domestic public.

Single State Versus Multistate Institutions

Unlike the other portions of the Fed's survey, the data regarding single-state versus multistate institutions are only provided for 1998, thus making trend analysis impossible. Nonetheless a comparison between banks residing in one state as opposed to those that have taken advantage of cross border expansion is a vital part of determining the significance of Riegle-Neal for banking customers.

ATMs. Multistate banks (96.5%) were substantially better represented than single-state banks (84.8%) in providing ATMs. This difference of 11.7%, which was significant at the 95% confidence level,[14] may be attributable to the fact that multistate banks tend to be larger than many single state banks. Nonetheless it supports the position that the expansion of interstate banking will benefit the consumer by making it possible for banks to offer a greater number of services.

Demand Deposits. The Fed's data indicates that 99.1% of multi-state institutions offered non-interest checking accounts as opposed to 98.4% of single-state institutions, a difference of .7% that is not statistically significant. The types of demand deposits offered by the two types of institutions, however, varied considerably. Multistate banks exceeded the percentage of single-state banks offering every type of demand deposit. Single-balance, single-fee accounts were offered by 54.7% of multistate banks compared with 32.5% of the single-state banks. Fee only accounts were offered by 47.8% of the multistate banks and by 34.5% of the single-state banks. In the case of free accounts, 20.8% of the multistate banks offered them, whereas only 16.7% of the single-state banks offered them.[15] In summary, it is apparent that more multistate banks offer a wider variety of demand deposits than do single-state banks, a fact that also supports the potential public benefits of Riegle-Neal.

NOW Accounts. As in the case of demand deposits the initial difference between the percentage of multistate institutions (95.8%) in comparison to a similar percentage among single-state institutions (94.0%) offering NOW accounts is a statistically insignificant 1.8%. Closer scrutiny, however, leads to a different conclusion. Multistate banks (64.1%) were more likely than single-state banks (48.6%) to offer single-fee accounts. Single-fee, single-check-charge accounts were offered more frequently by single-state banks (16.4%) than multistate banks (12.0%). Only a few multistate banks (.6%) offered no-fee accounts. No single-state banks offered these accounts.[16] Thus the range of choices among varying types of NOW accounts was not as clearly demarcated between multistate banks and single-state banks as was the situation with demand deposits.

Savings Accounts. Savings accounts are offered by the vast majority of multistate institutions (99.7%) and single-state institutions (99.3%). This difference, too, is not statistically significant. Simple passbook accounts were available at 32.0% of single-state banks and 36.8% of multistate banks. When one considers the other types of savings accounts, however, major discrepancies between multistate and single-state banks become apparent. The former shows a marked preference (72.8%) for simple statement accounts as opposed to 7.1% for no-fee passbook accounts or 9.8% for no-fee statement accounts. Single-state banks, on the other hand, appear equally divided among no-fee passbook accounts (31.6%) and simple statement accounts (38.4%). The percentage of single-state banks offering no-fee statement accounts is 15.9%, a significantly higher figure than the 9.8% of multistate banks.[17] Single-state banks, therefore, appear more generous in offering no-fee savings accounts than do multistate banks, a fact that advances the arguments of the detractors of interstate banking expansion.

FEES

The availability of a service cannot be evaluated apart from the fee(s) being charged for that service because the latter can negate or reduce the usefulness of the former if the service is too expensive to be affordable for many people. In its summation of the fee data, the Fed stated that nearly one-half of the banking fees examined changed significantly and that all of these changes were increases.[18] This finding brings into question, therefore, the benefits of interstate banking expansion.

ATMs. There are several different types of fees associated with the use of ATMs. These include annual fees, card fees, fees for customers of the bank using the bank's own ATM facility, fees for customers of other banks using the ATM facility of a bank other than their own, and, finally, a surcharge or flat fee imposed on each transaction conducted by a noncustomer of the ATM.

Between 1997 and 1998, large banks charging fees for use of their ATM increased in number in regard to annual fees, balance inquiries by their own customers, and surcharges on noncustomers. In all other categories, the percentage of large banks imposing fees declined.

Medium-sized banks also reacted differently for various charges. The number of these banks imposing charges pertaining to their own customers decreased in every category. In every category in which charges were imposed on noncustomer usage of ATMs, medium-sized banks increased their fees. The number of small banks imposing fees on their own customers rose regarding some transactions and decreased for others. Those banks like the medium-sized ones, however, were increasingly likely to impose new or higher charges and fees on noncustomers using their ATMs.[19]

In summary it appears that larger banks more so than medium-sized or small banks were more willing to give less expensive access to their ATMs to noncustomers, a fact that favors interstate expansion and reflects a broader outlook on the need for interbank cooperation in the networking of ATMs. The relatively positive treatment of non-customers by large banks also contradicts the expectation of critics of interstate expansion who believed that larger banks would increase their ATM fees for noncustomers to entice those people to leave their small banks to avoid the fees.[20] Banks of all sizes favored their customers as opposed to the public-at-large, a factor that will take on considerably greater significance with the continued expansion of states into new markets.

For those who would criticize the disparity in treatment for customers versus noncustomers, one need only look at the differential between in- and out-of-state tuition at state universities to find a counterargument. Although state institutions use in-state tax revenue to argue in favor of lower in-state tuition, banks also can claim that favoring customers through lower charges is justified and equitable in light of their larger customer relationship, which included other fees and business activities.

Special Fees. Special fees are service charges imposed on unique transactions in which the customer requires assistance of or special handling by the bank. Among the transactions included in this category are stop-payment orders, check with insufficient funds known as not sufficient funds (NSF) checks, overdrafts, and deposit items returned.

Stop-payment orders carried charges at 100% of large institutions, 98.9% of medium-sized institutions, and 99.9% of small institutions. This apparent similarity among banks of varying size was dispelled, however, by the discrepancies in the average fees: $20.06 in the large institutions, $17.27 in the medium-sized institutions, and only $12.80 in the small institutions. Although the average fee increased in each size category between 1997 and 1998, the extent of the increase was statistically significant only for medium-sized institutions.

Service fees for NSF checks were imposed by 100% of the banks in all size categories. The average fee was $22.10 among large institutions, $19.78 among medium-sized institutions, and $15.48 for small institutions. Although the average fee increased in all size categories between 1997 and 1998, none of the increases were statistically significant.

Overdraft charges are charges for checks written against insufficient funds but honored by the institution. Such charges were imposed by 99.4% of the large institutions, 99.1% of the medium-sized institutions, and 97.5% of the small institutions. The percent of institutions charging for overdrafts in the medium-sized category decreased but not significantly between 1997 and 1998. The average fee was $21.19 for large institutions, $19.61 for medium sized institutions, and $15.03 for small institutions. The average fee increased for each size category between 1997 and 1998, but the increase was only statistically significant in the medium-sized category.

The percent of institutions charging for deposit items returned was 91.8% for large institutions, 75.3% for medium-sized institutions, and 54.3% for small institutions. In each size category, this charge increased between 1997 and 1998. The average fee for deposit items returned was $5.89 for large institutions, which was a decrease of $.62 from 1997. The average fee for medium-sized institutions was $6.78, which was a statistically significant increase of $1.24 from 1997. For small institutions the average fee was $4.66, which was a decrease of –$.08 from the previous year.

Data on special fees charged by single-state and multistate institutions indicate significant differences. A greater percent of multistate institutions charged for stop-payment orders. The average fee charged in multistate institutions was $18.82 as opposed to $13.61 in single state institutions. The $5.21 difference was statistically significant.

All banks charged for NSF checks. However, the average fee for multistate banks were $20.87. The average fee for single-state banks was $16.32. The difference of $4.55 was statistically significant.

Regarding overdraft charges, 98.4% of multistate banks as opposed to 97.9% of single-state banks imposed such charges. The average fee among multistate banks was $20.34 compared with single state banks charges of $15.92. This difference of $4.42 was statistically significant.

For deposit items returned, 76.8 % of multistate institutions charged a fee in comparison to 59.3% of the single-state institutions that charged a fee. The average fee in multi-state institutions was $5.33 compared with $5.52 in single-state institutions. This was a rarity, a situation in which single-state banks charged more than multistate ones.[21]

The higher fees charged by larger and medium-sized institutions as well as by multi-state versus single-state banks for most special services do not bode well for customers as the banking system continues to consolidate. This also tends to add credence to some of the fears of interstate banking opponents and to explain, in part, why some people continue to do business with small or de novo banks even though they offer fewer services.

Rather than providing a definitive answer to the question of whether the average customer would benefit from the interstate banking expansion, the data on service availability and fees published by the Fed sent a mixed message. It does appear, however, that larger institutions have more services with better terms for customers and noncustomers alike but are more apt to charge higher fees, a factor that has a regressive effect on poor communities, many of which are located in rural or minority areas.

LOANS

Opponents of interstate banking and interstate branching also feared that large, impersonal banks headquartered outside of a community, particularly in another state, would reduce the amount of lending and/or increase the costs associated with borrowing. Despite the Community Reinvestment Act (CRA), which requires banks seeking to merge with or acquire another bank to prove that they have serviced and will continue to service small businesses, minorities, and women within the communities in which they are and will be doing business, detractors also believed that large, out-of-state banks would be less favorable lenders to these often under serviced groups.

Using data provided by the Federal Deposit Insurance Corporation (FDIC) in its publication *Statistics on Banking* for 1996 and 1999, it is possible to address the issue of lending preference only. The state by state comparison included here reflects the relative changes occurring in asset size, in total lending and in four categories within loan portfolios, namely real estate backed loans, agricultural loans, commercial loans and individual loans during the first 4 years of Riegle-Neal's enforcement. This information provides an initial review of the impact of banking consolidation and the increased asset size of banks on lending patterns and the composition of loan portfolios.

During the 4-year period under consideration, the asset size of banks rose in 31 states while declining in 19. Focusing on those states in which asset size rose, one finds that total lending also rose in 26 of these states but declined in the other 5. In only one state, Alabama, however, was the relative increase in total lending greater that the relative increase in asset size. Total lending did not increase in proportion to change in assets growth, and, therefore, the latter was attributable to increments in asset categories other than loans.

In the states in which banks declined in asset size, the percentage reduction in lending was similar to or less than the relative decrease in asset size. Thus lending retained its importance among banks experiencing a reduction in size and did not gain in importance among banks experiencing growth. In total, therefore, lending increased absolutely but not proportionately.

The lending patterns among states in which banks were experiencing growth and those in which the banks faced asset reductions, however, is substantially alike if one looks at the specific types of loans that were being made. Most dramatic is the fact that loans to individuals declined in 43 states and rose in only 7. The asset growth of banks within a state appeared to have no linkage to lending to individuals. One is led to believe that the movement toward larger banks has hurt lending to individuals and that interstate activity has contributed to, if not been exacerbated by, this problem. Unlike the historical examples of deregulation in the trucking and airline industries, the early results of banking deregulation do not clearly benefit individual consumers.

Among the four types of loans studied, real estate loans had the greatest relative growth during the period 1996–1999. Real estate lending played a more prominent role in 37 states and fell off in 13. States with and without asset growth in their internal banking community were represented in both groups. A similar pattern was seen for commercial lending which rose in 32 states and declined in 18.

Like individual lending, loans for agriculture declined more often than they increased. Agricultural loans were made less frequently in 26 states and more frequently in 21 states with 3 states showing no change. What is of interest here is the inverse relationship between the increase in agricultural lending and the change in bank size. In the 21 states in which agricultural lending increased, average bank size decreased in a majority of them. Among the 26 in which agricultural lending declined, most states experienced growth in the size of their banks. This provides some substantiation of the criticisms that larger banks will pay less attention to rural areas.

CONCLUSION

Riegle-Neal's early impact on bank customers is inconsistent and inconclusive regarding the availability of services. ATMs have become more available because they are being offered by an increasing number of smaller and medium-sized banks. Larger, multistate banks, however, retain a lead in offering ATMs. Although banks of all sizes and with a presence in one or in several states favor customers over noncustomers in the cost of using their ATMs, noncustomers received better treatment from larger, multistate institutions.

All banks appeared to expand the availability of demand deposits, but larger, multistate institutions offered a more diverse array of accounts than did smaller banks. The same held true for the number and diversity of NOW accounts despite a trend among some states for this type of account to show a decline. Although available at virtually all banks, savings accounts, however, had more advantageous terms at smaller banks. The benefits of doing business with a small bank also extended to special fees. Most banks charged fees in similar situations, but the size of the fees tended to be lower at smaller banks.

The most unsettling finding for individual bank customers relates to banks' loan portfolios. Throughout a substantial portion of the nation in states whose banking industry was either constricting or expanding, individual lending declined. Agricultural borrowing also appeared to wane but less dramatically and on a less widespread basis. However, commercial borrowers and, in particular, real estate borrowers appeared much more likely to obtain loans after passage of Riegle-Neal.

Before concluding that the discrepancy in lending patterns by loan category was totally attributable to Riegle-Neal, it is necessary to recall that during the period under consideration individual incomes and employment levels rose substantially and may have reduced the demand for loans rather than the supply of them. Simultaneously, real estate and commercial expansion and loan demand may have increased for the same reasons. Additionally, individual borrowing for consumer usage may have been transformed into real estate borrowing for mortgages.

NOTES

1. Peter Rose, *Banking across State Lines: Public and Private Consequences* (Westport, CT: Quorum Books, 1997), p. 84.
2. Ann B. Matasar and Joseph N. Heiney, "Big Banks/Small Customers: The Impact of Riegle-Neal on the Banking Relationship," *1999 Proceedings* of the International Association for Business and Society (IABS) Tenth Annual Conference, Paris, France, June 24–27, 1999, p. 362.

3. Clifford Winston, "U.S. Industry Adjustment to Economic Deregulation," *Journal of Economic Perspectives* 12, no. 3 (Summer 1998): p. 100.

4. *Annual Report to the Congress on Retail Fees and Services of Depository Institutions*, Board of Governors of the Federal Reserve System, June 1999, p. 1.

5. Ibid., pp. 7, 8, and 111–139.

6. Ibid., pp. 3 and 48–64.

7. Ibid., pp. 3 and 4.

8. Ibid., pp. 4, 5, and 64–80.

9. Ibid., pp. 5, 6, and 81–95.

10. Ibid., pp. 18–20.

11. Ibid., pp. 12 and 13.

12. Ibid., pp. 13 and 14.

13. Ibid., pp. 15 and 16.

14. Ibid., p. 10.

15. Ibid., p. 8.

16. Ibid., p. 9.

17. Ibid.

18. Ibid., p. 1.

19. Ibid., pp. 18–20.

20. Testimony of John E. Taylor, president and CEO, National Community Reinvestment Coalition. U.S. Congress, House, Committee on Banking and Financial Services, *Hearing on Bank Mergers*, 105th Congress, 2nd session, April 29, 1998, p. 121.

21. Ibid., pp. 16 and 17.

Chapter 4

The Public Effects of Interstate Banking Expansion: The Impact on Employees

Consolidation within the banking industry and the concomitant growth in the average size of American banks in the 1990s, particularly in the years subsequent to the passage of Riegle-Neal, raised natural concerns about the impact this deregulation would have on employment in the banking industry. The accepted wisdom was that merger and acquisition "mania" would create fewer and larger banks capable of functioning more efficiently and economically with reductions in personnel. Expansion in the number of de novo banks and branches, which was the offshoot of consolidation, was not expected to temper this trend.

Simultaneously, technological advances in the banking industry, such as the increased use and availability of ATMs, also were expected to exacerbate the anticipated decrease in employment opportunities in the industry. In describing the potential benefits and costs of interstate banking, Rose wrote that "[a]s the number of banks continues to fall, many bankers foresee a continuing shrinkage in the number of bank employees, especially with continuing advances in information and service delivery technology, which tend to expand the role of capital equipment, making those employees who do remain more productive."[1] He went on to note that "[m]any authorities have predicted large scale lay offs as interstate bank expansion proceeds and as automation replaces many teller and back-office positions."[2] This chapter studies the accuracy of these forecasts.

DEREGULATION AND EMPLOYMENT:
THE HISTORICAL EXPERIENCE

In a study entitled "Deregulation and the Labor Market," James Peoples examined the effects of deregulation in the railroad, trucking, airlines, and telecommunications industries to see whether "stepped-up competition in an industry can easily place greater downward pressure on labor earnings."[3] He found that the results differed by industry.

Regarding the trucking industry, he discovered that "[a]fter a pre-deregulation period of relatively low employment growth, from 977,000 in 1973 to 1,111,000 in 1978, the number of workers employed in trucking dramatically increased to 1,907,000 in 1996," with "workers in this industry experiencing their real earnings falling from $491 in 1978 to $353 in 1996."[4] In the railroad industry, on the other hand, employment fell by more than 50% after deregulation, but earnings fell only slightly. Conversely, the airlines industry experienced significant employment gains, though real labor earnings declined but by much less than in the trucking industry. Finally, in the telecommunications industry there was modest growth in employment and real earnings.

Peoples concluded that "industry labor earnings premiums fell sharply in trucking, somewhat in airlines, slightly in telecommunications, and barely in railroads. It is perhaps no coincidence that the size of the workforce dramatically increased in trucking and airlines, held roughly steady in telecommunications, and fell dramatically in railroads—a pattern roughly the opposite of the changes in earnings."[5]

Peoples's study demonstrated that despite generally accepted assumptions regarding deregulation's adverse effects on the levels of employment and compensation in an industry, the factual results could vary substantially and that no one pattern was guaranteed.

LEVEL OF EMPLOYMENT

The banking community's deregulatory experience in the aftermath of Riegle-Neal was that the changes in the level of employment paralleled that of the trucking, airlines, and telecommunications industries in that it did not decline nationally. Table 4.1, which presents data on the number of full-time equivalent employees in the banking industry on a state-by-state basis from 1996 to 1999, illustrates this finding.

Although the number of banking institutions decreased nationwide during this period by almost 10%, the number of full-time equivalent employees increased by almost 15%. This inverse relationship clearly demonstrates that consolidation in the banking industry immediately after passage of Riegle-Neal did not adversely effect employment in the industry nationwide.

Table 4.1
Number of Full-Time Equivalent Employees by State

Employees States	Years	1999	1998	1997	1996	Change 1996-1999	% Change 1996-1999
Alabama		59227	49343	38267	27664	31563	114.09
Alaska		2378	2165	2165	2483	-105	-4.23
Arizona		13209	13636	13850	16692	-3483	-20.87
Arkansas		11012	10295	12242	13182	-2170	-16.46
California		97198	147507	153170	142352	-45154	-31.72
Colorado		14100	14322	14738	17167	-3067	-17.87
Connecticut		1196	1885	1768	3227	-2031	-62.94
Delaware		59268	53746	53460	42165	17103	40.56
Florida		27358	27837	46641	58327	-30969	-53.10
Georgia		31087	30127	26884	43637	-12550	-28.76
Hawaii		7605	8265	8624	8445	-840	-9.95
Idaho		1131	931	762	2663	-1532	-57.53
Illinois		75090	74284	72960	70987	4103	5.78
Indiana		23140	24716	24084	26058	-2918	-11.20
Iowa		15031	15651	15864	16427	-1396	-8.50
Kansas		13426	13238	12820	12632	794	6.29
Kentucky		15891	16520	17946	19187	-3296	-17.18
Louisiana		18350	19302	18825	21540	-3190	-14.81
Maine		1705	1724	1720	3037	-1332	-43.86
Maryland		16141	16239	13936	15184	957	6.30
Massachusetts		54628	53637	45505	52957	1671	3.16
Michigan		42175	42141	42907	41816	359	0.86
Minnesota		39149	41382	41300	24715	14434	58.40
Mississippi		12628	11666	16215	13906	-1278	-9.19
Missouri		29794	29145	25524	34429	-4635	-13.46
Montana		4166	4110	3887	3933	233	5.92
Nebraska		13627	13176	12578	13017	610	4.69
Nevada		7333	7176	6134	7508	-175	-2.33
New Hampshire		2165	2365	2051	1952	213	10.91
New Jersey		24285	21391	19668	22006	2279	10.36
New Mexico		5672	5772	5127	7346	-1674	-22.79
New York		209668	212944	196636	200091	9577	4.79
Nor Carolina		247435	189639	109782	58821	188614	320.66
Nor Dakota		4621	4700	3784	3803	818	21.51
Ohio		107721	100717	80788	61994	45727	73.76
Oklahoma		16515	15812	16139	17018	-503	-2.96
Oregon		4281	3802	3635	11423	-7142	-62.52
Pennsylvania		64141	69986	94226	91611	-27470	-29.99
Rhode Island		34443	23921	18420	3265	31178	954.92
South Carolina		7411	7051	6866	9653	-2242	-23.23
South Dakota		11291	10504	10062	9904	1387	14.00
Tennessee		38236	41749	30923	31468	6768	21.51
Texas		65679	67289	93254	89437	-23758	-26.56
Utah		13410	11986	11868	11244	2166	19.26
Vermont		2828	3130	3116	2607	221	8.48
Virginia		37922	32546	31644	32758	5164	15.76
Washington		55483	5432	5288	16867	38616	228.94
West Virginia		8893	9407	9013	9472	-579	-6.11
Wisconsin		19951	25369	23985	23794	-3843	-16.15
Wyoming		2318	2298	2303	2247	71	3.16
Total 50 states		1691412	1611976	1523354	1474118	217294	14.74

Source: FDIC State Banking Performance Summary.

A more detailed analysis at the state level, however, supports the common assumption by linking the number of bank employees directly to the growth or decline either in the number of institutions located in a given state or the banking assets held within that state. Thus, the variation in the number of employees working in banks in different states not only mirrors the changes in the number of institutions in the states, but it also follows the path of interstate acquisitions in which some states' banks grew at the expense of those in other states. For acquisitive states, in particular, the initial results were especially beneficial because employment growth often equaled or exceeded the growth in banking industry in the state. As an example, North Carolina, which had a 27% increase in the number of banks headquartered in the state, had an even higher increase of over 321% in the number of full-time equivalent employees.

A similar employment situation could be found in states in which the assets of the banking community expanded even when the number of banking institutions declined. An example of this occurred in Rhode Island which had a 955% increment in banking employees, as well as an increase in assets of 1,496.51% despite the loss of one bank.

Those states in which there were substantial percentage reductions in the number of banks headquartered within their borders as well as the assets of their indigenous banks also had declining employment in banking. Stark examples include Connecticut, which lost 4 banks, almost 71% of its banking assets, and 63% of its banking employees and Florida, which lost 17 banks, 46% of its banking assets, and 53% of its banking employees. A similar pattern was consistent in all states in which banking contracted.

The employment data presented here provide no surprises or new insights. However, it should be noted that the results are not necessarily as grim at the state level as they appear at first glance because the employee count by state relates employees to the home office of their institution rather than to their actual place of personal residence or work location. Therefore, many of the banking jobs remained in the same state even when the statistical reports transferred them elsewhere. In this regard the statistical record is somewhat confusing and misleading. Nonetheless the alteration of employment levels in banking by state testifies to the importance of interstate activity after Riegle-Neal and the relocation of power within the American banking community.

SALARIES AND COMPENSATION

Although Table 4.1 clearly demonstrates that the period of consolidation following Riegle-Neal did not adversely effect employment levels in the banking industry nationwide, it does not adequately address the related issue of employee welfare or the impact of deregulation on salaries and compensation. Table 4.2 presents data on salaries and compensation for employees in the banking industry by state from 1996 to 1999. Here, too, is

Table 4.2
Salaries and Employee Benefits by State

States	Years	1999	1998	1997	1996	Change 1996-1999	% Change 1996-1999
Alabama		2419	1930	1366	943	1476	156.52
Alaska		111	102	97	108	3	2.78
Arizona		543	568	523	635	-92	-14.49
Arkansas		384	351	392	416	-32	-7.69
California		5360	8370	7961	7361	-2001	-27.18
Colorado		611	577	550	628	-17	-2.71
Connecticut		69	94	83	126	-57	-45.24
Delaware		2986	2615	2356	1798	1188	66.07
Florida		1256	1187	1978	2191	-935	-42.67
Georgia		1229	1113	1073	1669	-440	-26.36
Hawaii		398	405	393	379	19	5.01
Idaho		41	33	25	100	-59	-59.00
Illinois		3841	3604	3405	3191	650	20.37
Indiana		979	1008	854	256	723	282.42
Iowa		631	578	603	614	17	2.77
Kansas		513	496	454	433	80	18.48
Kentucky		602	613	618	669	-67	-10.01
Louisiana		717	726	709	742	-25	-3.37
Maine		67	68	65	116	-49	-42.24
Maryland		730	716	590	626	104	16.61
Massachusetts		3623	3183	2700	2889	734	25.41
Michigan		2093	1876	1816	1658	435	26.24
Minnesota		1957	1933	1920	1085	872	80.37
Mississippi		476	420	569	470	6	1.28
Missouri		1183	1135	832	1173	10	0.85
Montana		154	149	137	132	22	16.67
Nebraska		547	503	457	458	89	19.43
Nevada		337	265	231	270	67	24.81
New Hampshire		88	93	78	77	11	14.29
New Jersey		1015	941	838	843	172	20.40
New Mexico		219	204	169	238	-19	-7.98
New York		17830	16422	15002	14770	3060	20.72
North Carolina		12794	8436	5006	2631	10163	386.28
North Dakota		182	167	139	135	47	34.81
Ohio		4786	4341	3199	2281	2505	109.82
Oklahoma		609	558	538	563	46	8.17
Oregon		139	121	110	423	-284	-67.14
Pennsylvania		3050	3046	3877	3720	-670	-18.01
Rhode Island		1901	1083	881	109	1792	1644.04
South Carolina		281	254	242	335	-54	-16.12
South Dakota		427	400	368	353	74	20.96
Tennessee		1734	1878	1269	1238	496	40.06
Texas		2829	2770	3642	3252	-423	-13.01
Utah		563	505	439	405	158	39.01
Vermont		120	121	107	99	21	21.21
Virginia		1119	992	1119	1307	-188	-14.38
Washington		246	228	212	751	-505	-67.24
West Virginia		279	290	258	280	-1	-0.36
Wisconsin		778	1024	930	909	-131	-14.41
Wyoming		85	83	72	75	10	13.33
Total 50 states		84931	78575	71252	65930	19001	28.82

Source: Statistics on Banking, 199, FDIC Web site, 1998, pp. D-2–D-205; 1997, pp.D-2–D-205;
Historical 1934–1996, pp. E-368–E-418.

seen an inverse relationship in the number of banking institutions and the impact on banking employees at the national level, in this case their salaries and compensation. Although the number of banks decreased by 10% and banking employment rose by almost 15%, the level of salary and compensation in the banking industry nationwide increased by almost 30%. It appears that banking deregulation, unlike the deregulation in trucking, railroad, airlines, and communications industries, benefited employees in two ways—it increased rather than decreased the employment opportunities and simultaneously enhanced salaries and compensation.

As expected, the pattern of compensation variation across the states substantially mirrors the variation in employment levels. In several states, however, the increment in salary and compensation not only equaled that of employment, but it also exceeded it. For instance, in North Carolina, where the number of full-time equivalent employees rose by 321%, salary and compensation grew by 386%. In Rhode Island, salary and compensation grew by 1,644%, thus far surpassing the enormous increment of 955% in employment. Only in states such as Connecticut, Florida, Idaho, Maine, and Texas, in which employment levels, gross salaries, and compensation all declined, were the benefits of deregulation in banking brought into question.

Nationally, however, the macroview of employment, salaries and compensation in the banking industry after Riegle-Neal paints a relatively pleasant picture. Employment increased by about 15%, a figure that doubles when one looks at salaries and compensation. The view is even rosier in regard to salaries and compensation when viewed against the larger economic setting that factors in inflation. During the period 1996 to 1999 when inflation averaged 2.4% and never exceeded 2.9%, salaries and compensation in the banking community rose by almost 29% or approximately 7.25% annually for 4 years. It can be argued that the health of the banking system as a result of Riegle-Neal's deregulation actually allowed the industry to expand the ranks and pocketbooks of its personnel in real as well as nominal terms.

COMPENSATION PER EMPLOYEE

The aggregate analysis of the data on salaries and compensation both nationally and by states masks possible differential effects on individual employees. In some states where employment, salaries, and compensation all increased, it is possible that on average, individual employees did not benefit because salaries and compensation increased less rapidly than employment. Similarly, it is possible that in some states in which overall employment, salaries and compensation all decreased that employment decreased more rapidly than salaries and compensation so that level of compensation per employee, in fact, increased.

Information on the levels and changes in employment and compensation per employee across the 50 states from 1996 to 1999 is presented in Table 4.3. During this period of time when yearly inflation averaged 2.4% and salaries and compensation in the banking industry increased on average by over 7% annually, the banking employees in 34 states received percentage wage increments greater than the inflation rate.

Employees working for banks headquartered in states that expanded their banking industry after deregulation benefited the most. For instance, employees of banks in North Carolina received an increase of 15.6% in salary and compensation over the four year period or 3.9% annually. Similarly in Rhode Island, compensation per employee increased by just over 65% for the four years or an average of 16.25%. Comparable results also were found in Alabama (4.95% per year), Delaware (4.54% per year), and Minnesota (3.47% per year), other states with the large increases in employment and compensation after Riegle-Neal.

However, the most starling result is that in all but one of the states that experienced decreases in both employment and overall compensation in their banking industry, the level of compensation per banking employee increased. For example Connecticut, which had a decrease of almost 63% in employment and over 45% in salaries and compensation, had an almost 48% increase in compensation per employee during the four years, an average of 12% per year or a fivefold multiple of the inflation rate. Even in Florida, where overall salaries and compensation decreased by almost 43%, compensation per employee increased by over 22% or 5.5% per year, twice the inflation rate. A similar pattern of results was found in such other major states as Texas.

A deviation from this pattern was found in Maine and Idaho. In Maine salaries and compensation decreased by just over 42% and compensation per employee increased by only 3% for the 4 years, falling short of the inflation rate per year. However, in Idaho, where overall salaries and compensation decreased by 59%, did compensation per employee also decrease—in this case by almost 3.5%. Finally only 3 states, Oregon, Virginia and Washington, had increased aggregate salary and compensation levels but declining levels of compensation per employee in the banking industry. These declines per employee salary were 12%, 26%, and 90% respectively for these 3 states.

CONCLUSION

Despite the few states where banking employees appeared to suffer individually in their salary and compensation gains in the post–Riegle-Neal years, most banking employees were favorably effected by changes that ensued from deregulation. More jobs at salary and compensation levels exceeding inflation were the norm, and individual employees were able to see this benefit personally in their own accounts.

Table 4.3
Salaries and Benefits per Employee by State

Compensation States	1999 comp	1999 employees	1999 c/e	1996 comp	1996 employee	1996 c/e	Change c/e	% Change c/e
Alabama	2419	59227	0.040843	943	27664	0.034088	0.006755	19.82
Alaska	111	2378	0.046678	108	2483	0.043496	0.003182	7.32
Arizona	543	13209	0.041108	635	16692	0.038042	0.003066	8.06
Arkansas	384	11012	0.034871	416	13182	0.031558	0.003313	10.50
California	5360	97198	0.055145	7361	142352	0.05171	0.003435	6.64
Colorado	611	14100	0.043333	628	17167	0.036582	0.006752	18.46
Connecticut	69	1196	0.057692	126	3227	0.039046	0.018647	47.76
Delaware	2986	59268	0.050381	1798	42165	0.042642	0.007739	18.15
Florida	1256	27358	0.04591	2191	58327	0.037564	0.008346	22.22
Georgia	1229	31087	0.039534	1669	43637	0.038247	0.001287	3.36
Hawaii	398	7605	0.052334	379	8445	0.044879	0.007455	16.61
Idaho	41	1131	0.036251	100	2663	0.037552	-0.0013	-3.46
Illinois	3841	75090	0.051152	3191	70987	0.044952	0.0062	13.79
Indiana	979	23140	0.042308	256	26058	0.009824	0.032483	330.65
Iowa	631	15031	0.04198	614	16427	0.037377	0.004602	12.31
Kansas	513	13426	0.038209	433	12632	0.034278	0.003931	11.47
Kentucky	602	15891	0.037883	669	19187	0.034867	0.003016	8.65
Louisiana	717	18350	0.039074	742	21540	0.034448	0.004626	13.43
Maine	67	1705	0.039296	116	3037	0.038196	0.001101	2.88
Maryland	730	16141	0.045226	626	15184	0.041228	0.003999	9.70
Massachusetts	3623	54628	0.066321	2889	52957	0.054554	0.011768	21.57
Michigan	2093	42175	0.049627	1658	41816	0.03965	0.009977	25.16
Minnesota	1957	39149	0.049989	1085	24715	0.0439	0.006088	13.87
Mississippi	476	12628	0.037694	470	13906	0.033798	0.003896	11.53
Missouri	1183	29794	0.039706	1173	34429	0.03407	0.005636	16.54
Montana	154	4166	0.036966	132	3933	0.033562	0.003404	10.14
Nebraska	547	13627	0.040141	458	13017	0.035185	0.004956	14.09
Nevada	337	7333	0.045957	270	7508	0.035962	0.009995	27.79
New Hampshire	88	2165	0.040647	77	1952	0.039447	0.0012	3.04
New Jersey	1015	24285	0.041795	843	22006	0.038308	0.003488	9.10
New Mexico	219	5672	0.038611	238	7346	0.032399	0.006212	19.17
New York	17830	209668	0.085039	14770	200091	0.073816	0.011223	15.20
North Carolina	12794	247435	0.051707	2631	58821	0.044729	0.006978	15.60
North Dakota	182	4621	0.039385	135	3803	0.035498	0.003887	10.95
Ohio	4786	107721	0.04443	2281	61994	0.036794	0.007636	20.75
Oklahoma	609	16515	0.036876	563	17018	0.033083	0.003793	11.47
Oregon	139	4281	0.032469	423	11423	0.037031	-0.00456	-12.32
Pennsylvania	3050	64141	0.047551	3720	91611	0.040606	0.006945	17.10
Rhode Island	1901	34443	0.055193	109	3265	0.033384	0.021808	65.32
South Carolina	281	7411	0.037917	335	9653	0.034704	0.003212	9.26
South Dakota	427	11291	0.037818	353	9904	0.035642	0.002176	6.10
Tennessee	1734	38236	0.04535	1238	31468	0.039342	0.006008	15.27
Texas	2829	65679	0.043073	3252	89437	0.036361	0.006712	18.46
Utah	563	13410	0.041984	405	11244	0.036019	0.005964	16.56
Vermont	120	2828	0.042433	99	2607	0.037975	0.004458	11.74
Virginia	1119	37922	0.029508	1307	32758	0.039899	-0.01039	-26.04
Washington	246	55483	0.004434	751	16867	0.044525	-0.04009	-90.04
West Virginia	279	8893	0.031373	280	9472	0.029561	0.001812	6.13
Wisconsin	778	19951	0.038996	909	23794	0.038203	0.000793	2.07
Wyoming	85	2318	0.03667	75	2247	0.033378	0.003292	9.86
Total 50 states	84931	1691412	0.050213	65930	1474118	0.044725	0.005488	12.27

Source: FDIC State Banking Performance Summary, Statistics on Banking, 1999, FDIC Web site, 1998, pp. D-2–D-205; 1997, pp. D-2–D-205; Historical 1934–1996, pp. E-368–E418.

NOTES

1. Peter Rose, *Banking across State Lines: Public and Private Consequences* (Westport, CT: Quorum Books, 1997), p. 74.

2. Ibid., pp. 74 and 75.

3. James Peoples, "Deregulation and the Labor Market," *Journal of Economic Perspectives* 12 no. 3 (summer 1998): p. 111.

4. Ibid., p. 112.

5. Ibid., p. 128.

Chapter 5

$

A Microanalysis: Case Studies

The impact of geographic deregulation on the American banking industry that was presented in Chapter 2 provided a macroperspective of the entire American banking industry in the post–Riegle-Neal era. With the exception of differentiation according to state and/or asset size, the analysis was completely global and encompassed all American banks. No attempt was made to look in depth at any one bank or local geographic area. Chapter 5 seeks to fill this void by providing detailed information about 4 banking organizations headquartered in the Chicago metropolitan area.

Case studies have been added for several reasons. In addition to providing a microanalysis, detailed case studies also help to resolve apparent inconsistencies in the costs and benefits associated with banking mergers and acquisitions in the post–Riegle-Neal era. Some consolidations create efficiencies, lower costs and produce greater profits while creating little or no adverse impact on their customers or the banking system. In other instances, however, some banks appear to approach monopolistic dominance which adversely affects competition and, ultimately, increases prices and/or reduces services for customers. Case studies in the banking industry are particularly helpful in addressing these issues of contradiction because the rapid changes taking place in the industry "make even the recent past a poor guide to the future."[1]

The Chicago metropolitan area was selected for several reasons. By virtue of its location and size, it represents the heartland of the country. Despite the growth of banking in other midwestern cities, it remains the major banking center between both coasts. Chicago also has been a central arena of merger and acquisition activity involving several banks of various sizes. Additionally several of these mergers and acquisitions have occurred across state lines or involved banking organizations from other parts of the world. Despite this activity, however, there still remain several banks of various sizes that have withstood the competitive pressures to get aboard the Riegle-Neal bandwagon and have been able to retain their independence. By focusing on Chicago, it, therefore, is possible to study the impact of Riegle-Neal on various types of banks directly in competition with one another within one banking market.

Chicago also is home to banks that have followed different strategic paths in approaching the new banking era. Some have sought efficiencies in a traditional manner by increasing their size and reach in hope of gaining economies of scale. Others, however, have chosen the path of relationship banking which focuses on economies of scope in which "[a] bank's mixture of products and services and its locational strategy are primarily set in reference to the client base that the bank is targeting rather than according to the technological costs or synergies associated with particular sets of products and services."[2] The relative success of each of these merger and acquisition strategies, therefore, also can be studied within the Chicago market.

The final, and in some ways the most interesting, reason for selecting Chicago is its location in Illinois. Through a look at Chicago, one also obtains an insight into the importance of the dual banking system on the ability of a bank to survive and thrive in an ever increasingly competitive domestic and international environment. Several years ago the Department of Tourism of the State of Illinois developed a radio commercial that said: "Just outside Chicago is the State of Illinois." Although the commercial was quickly withdrawn from the airwaves, it succinctly testified to the political division and tensions within the state which affected all statewide policies and regulations, including those related to intrastate and interstate branch banking.

Illinois is not a homogenous state. Like a large number of states, Illinois is a state with one dominant city in an otherwise agricultural environment. Influenced by suburban and downstate legislators, intrastate branching regulations in Illinois were intended to keep Chicago's banks, particularly the largest ones located in the city's Loop business district, from encroaching upon areas outside of the city. Little consideration was given to the impact of restrictive regulations upon the ability of these Loop banks to compete successfully as the banking environment changed. Chicago, therefore, is a prime example of the impact of competition in the banking industry in a big city where branching has been restricted.[3]

Like a host of midwestern states, Illinois was a strong advocate of unit banking because of the "combination of tradition, vested interests and special customer demands."[4] Because of the McFadden Act, the unit banking restrictions effected federally and state chartered institutions with home offices in the state. Unit banking protected rural banks by discouraging new banks from entering the market because it was difficult to recover high start-up costs. This, in turn, protected less efficient small banks that could charge higher fees and loan rates and pay less on deposits without fear of competition.[5]

Illinois begrudgingly relinquished unit banking when "[i]mproved transportation and communications, the growth of businesses, and a more mobile and convenience-conscious population"[6] made it imperative. Limited branching was instituted in several stages and in several ways. Initially branching was confined geographically. The first change permitted was one branch within 1000 feet as the crow flies from the home office. This was intended to keep Loop banks in their place. The next change increased the territorial distance to 2,000 feet as the crow flies, thus making expansion possible to downtown areas outside of the Loop. Another phase geographically defined branching by permitting the establishment of 5 branches in any 2–collar counties. Given the fact that Cook County, in which Chicago is located, has 6 adjacent counties, this branching regulation protected downstate, if not suburban, communities from encroachment by Loop banks.

Exacerbating the geographic branching restrictions were other regulations associated with the definition of a branch. State courts in Illinois initially considered an automatic teller machine (ATM) as equivalent to a branch, thus making it difficult to develop even suburban branching. Although Illinois remains a limited intrastate branching state in order to continue its protection of downstate communities from Chicago's influence, branching in collar communities is virtually unrestricted.

Despite its narrow view of intrastate branching, Illinois was among those states that participated in national reciprocity for the expansion of bank holding companies across state lines prior to passage of Riegle-Neal. Although apparently inconsistent with the state's restrictive internal banking rules, this liberal approach to interstate banking paralleled it in that it was assumed that it only would effect large Chicago-based banking organizations. It certainly did. Among the largest banks headquartered in Chicago, only The Northern Trust Company retains its original hometown control. All others have merged with or been acquired by banking organizations from other states or countries. Restrictive intrastate branching rules in combination with mutual reciprocity for interstate banking made banks of all sizes, particularly well known Chicago institutions, vulnerable to takeover and account for the fact that several of the most well known of them disappeared or have been taken over.

Each of the institutions selected, therefore, represents not only one of the asset categories used in the analysis but also a different dimension of the Chicago experience. By getting "up close and personal" with these banks, it may be possible to determine if the macroeffects of geographic deregulation are, in fact, accurate at the level of an individual bank and to what extent, if any, geographic deregulation has had a differential affect on banks competing within the same regional market. The 4 banking organizations that have been selected for the case studies are The Glenview State Bank (an independent, suburban, community bank), The Northern Trust Corporation (the only major, independent Loop banking organization still in existence), Harris Bankcorp (Chicago's fourth largest banking organization and a wholly owned subsidiary of the Bank of Montreal), and Bank One (an Ohio banking organization now headquartered in Chicago after its merger with First Chicago NBD Corporation).

THE GLENVIEW STATE BANK

According to information available on its web site[7], the Glenview State Bank was organized on January 1, 1920, by a group of local citizens and opened its doors for business on May 17, 1921. From its inception to the present, the bank has been a family owned and operated institution. Initially members of two families, the Rugens and the Lutters, ran it out of the Rugen's General Store. Since its inception the bank has sought to service local businesses and residents of the suburban community of Glenview where it is located. The bank quickly thrived, outgrowing the general store "facility" and building its headquarters in Glenview where it still remains.

In 1963, Paul C. Jones, an Indiana retail financier, and his son John E. Jones purchased the Glenview State Bank for $14 million. The Jones family continues to own and manage the bank which has become one of the largest independently owned and operated community banks in Illinois.

Despite its claim to independent status, Glenview State Bank is a wholly owned subsidiary of Cummins-American Corporation, a bank holding company that also is owned and operated by the Jones family. The term independent, therefore, denotes the common family ownership of the holding company and of the bank and signifies that the Glenview State Bank has neither been bought by, nor merged with any other banking institution either within the state or across state lines.

As its name implies, the Glenview State Bank is a state-chartered institution. As of June 30, 2000, it had assets totaling $637,507,000. This represented a 24.4% increment from its asset size of $512,398 at the end of 1994.[8]

Although it is headquartered in Glenview, an affluent, bedroom suburb 20 miles northwest of Chicago where it has 3 full-service offices, the Glenview State Bank has expanded its geographic presence by building one full-service facility in each of 3 similar, adjacent suburban communities, namely Arlington Heights, Northbrook, and Northfield. The expansion was made possible when Illinois eased its intrastate branching restrictions and made limited branching possible. The bank has no offices in other states or foreign countries.

Glenview State Bank prides itself on several things: commitment to its customers, excellent employee relations, and being a good corporate citizen within the communities it serves. The first of these claims can be documented through specific actions taken by the bank. For example, its customer service orientation is reflected immediately by having 8 ATMs that are located in the same suburbs as its full-service facilities plus one in Long Grove, a rapid growing suburb. In addition to convenient locations, these ATMs also offer drive-up and 24-hour access. There is no surcharge for withdrawals by the bank's own customers or by other persons who belong to the bank's AGREE network. Additionally the bank's customers are not charged a service fee for use of any ATM within the bank's AGREE network.

The bank's customer orientation also can be seen in the other services it offers. Since 1996 it has pursued direct banking through a state-of-the-art telephone system as well as Internet banking. All this was made possible by the bank's extensive investment in technology so that banking could become more convenient for customers and more efficient for employees. Its web site notes that it is "[e]xpanding hometown banking to the Internet" and that it will "provide banking services to clients the way that they want them and at their convenience [via] Personal banking, direct banking, 24-hour banking and one-stop-banking." The bank's ability to invest in technology has been enhanced through the help of a sister subsidiary within Cummins- American Corporation, namely, Cummins-Allison, which makes a variety of coin and currency sorters, scanners, dispensers, check signers, imprinters, endorsers, and shredders.

The Glenview State Bank has a very well-defined public image that is actively projected and protected in its advertising which features John Jones as its spokesman. This image underscores the bank's claim regarding good corporate citizenship. The message contained in its advertising emphasizes that the bank is large enough to provide all the services needed by individuals and businesses in the community while remaining small enough and locally based to serve its customers in a friendly and caring manner. The bank stresses that it is not a big, impersonal behemoth that views its customers as numbers rather than neighbors, and it promises to remain independent and locally focused.

Comparisons between 1994 and 2000, however, bring into question the bank's contention that it has excellent employee relations. From December 31, 1994, to June 30, 2000, the number of employees of the Glenview State Bank declined by 2 persons from 190 to 188 despite the expansion of the bank into several facilities and suburbs. To a substantial degree, this can probably be attributed to the bank's investment in technology. Nonetheless during this period the bank's salary and employee benefits were reduced from \$8,046,000 to \$5,181,000 or by a negative 35.6%. On a per employee basis, therefore, the bank reduced its expenditure from \$42,347 to \$27,559. The savings of \$14,789 per employee thus represented a reduction of 35% on an individual as well as aggregate basis. Unless employee relations are totally unaffected by salary and benefits, it is appropriate to assume that employee relations may not be as strong a suit as the bank claims and that employees, if not customers, have borne the brunt of competition.

Nonetheless because of its history and its commitment to remaining an independent, community bank, the Glenview State Bank has remained competitive even as larger banks have entered its market either from Chicago or from out of state.

SUMMARY: PERFORMANCE AND CONDITION RATIOS

In summary, an analysis of the Glenview State Bank's performance and condition ratios provides an opportunity to reflect on the success of the bank in the aftermath of Riegle-Neal's geographic deregulation and the increased competition that it created for the bank within the suburban communities it serves. Additionally it helps to assess the influence of the 4 guiding principles that govern the bank's business conduct: (1) integrity and fairness in dealing with employees and customers; (2) commitment to employees, clients and community; (3) a conservative orientation that focuses on safety and soundness, and (4) independence.

Time Series Analysis

In this section, the performance and condition ratios of the Glenview State Bank are compared on December 31, 1994, the beginning of the Reigle-Neal era and on June 30, 2000, the most recent date for which information is available. It is immediately apparent that the Glenview State Bank has thrived. The yield on earnings assets has risen from 6.39% to 7.04% or by 10% despite the fact that its cost of funding these earning assets has risen by even more. During the same time period, the cost of funding earning assets rose from 2.54% to 3.01%, an increase of 18.5%. Net interest margin widened from 3.85% to 4.03%—an increase of 4.7%—whereas noninterest income during the same period remained stable at 1.01%. Most telling is the fact that return on assets has improved from 0.80% to 1.08%—an additional 35%—whereas the return on equity has grown from 10.53% to 11.73%—an increase of only 11.4%. The disparity between the two figures, namely, the increase in the return on assets, 35%, and the increase in the return on equity, 11.4%, highlights the leverage effects of Glenview State Bank's decision to finance its assets by using debt.

Much of this improvement can be attributed to the bank's conservative orientation. For instance, its net charge-offs to loans declined from 0.12% to

0.04% or by 67%, and the credit loss provision to net charge-offs was reduced from 297.53% to 147.06% or by an impressive 50.6%. Additionally, its assets per employee rose from $2.70 million to $3.39 million, denoting not only an increased asset size but also an ability to minimize its labor force, a fact that is attributable in large part to the bank's substantial expenditure on technology.

The strengthening of its condition ratios during the 5 1/2 years under consideration here paralleled Glenview State Bank's improved performance ratios. Although its loss allowance to loans rose from 1.15% to 1.28% or by 11%, its noncurrent loans to loans dropped from an extremely low 0.05% to 0.00%.

The set of condition ratios that is most reflective of the bank's conservative orientation, however, is its capital ratios. Equity capital to assets rose during the period under consideration from 7.66% to 9.50% or by 24%. Simultaneously the core capital ratio rose from 7.91% to 9.64% or by 21.9%; the tier-1 risk-based capital ratio rose from 12.61% to 14.41% or by 14.3%; and the total risk-based capital ratio increased from 13.75% to 15.63% or by 13.7%.

Cross-sectional Analysis

Although the time series analysis supported a conclusion that the Glenview State Bank has prospered under Riegle-Neal and has benefited from its conservative stance, it is necessary to compare the bank's performance with that of its peer group to determine to what extent, if any, its performance could have been improved. In this section, therefore, the performance and condition of the Glenview State Bank is evaluated on December 21, 1994, and June 30, 2000, in relation to its FDIC Standard Peer Group, namely, banks with assets between $500 million and $1 billion.

The apparent growth in economic and financial strength experienced by the Glenview State Bank in terms of the time series analysis did not translate into as positive a picture with a cross-sectional analysis. The industry standard peer group consistently appeared to be more successful in deploying its resources to obtain superior returns, but this may simply be a reflection of Glenview's continuing conservative nature.

Yield on earning assets for the standard peer group was higher than that for the Glenview State Bank at the end of 1994, as well as in mid-2000. In 1994 the standard peer group posted a yield on earning assets of 7.68% whereas the bank's was 6.39%. This discrepancy of 1.29% expanded to 1.4% in June 2000 when the standard peer group had an 8.44% yield and that of the Glenview State Bank was 7.04%. It should be noted that though the discrepancy grew during the 5-year time period, Glenview's position was improving. The standard peer group improved by 9.89%, and Glenview improved by 10.17%. Although this may not appear to be an enormous difference, it is important to note that even with Glenview's conservative position in decision making, it is making headway in narrowing the gap.

This occurred despite the fact that the cost of funding earning assets was greater for the standard peer group in both 1994 and 2000. In the former, the standard peer group had a cost ratio of 2.85% and the bank's was 2.54%. More significantly the standard peer group's ratio rose by 1.06% to 3.91% and the bank's cost ratio rose over the same period by a substantially less .47% to 3.01%. Thus the bank's cost of funding earnings assets increased at a much slower rate than did that of the standard peer group, but, nonetheless, the bank's yield on earnings assets did not reflect this fact. Instead the bank's yield fell even further behind that of the standard peer group.

Of particular significance is the fact that all of the Glenview State Bank's income ratios were below those of the standard peer group in 1994 and 2000. The bank's net interest margin in 1994 was 3.85%, and in mid-2000 it was 4.03%. The comparable figures for the standard peer group were 4.84% and 4.53%, respectively. On a relative basis, therefore, the Glenview State Bank, despite remaining less profitable than its standard peer group, did increase its net interest margins by .18% during a time when banks of similar size nationwide were facing a reduction in their overall net interest margins of .31%.

Glenview State Bank had a noninterest income to earning assets ratio of 1.01% in both 1994 and 2000. Those ratios for the standard peer group were 1.5% and 1.47%, respectively. Thus, here, too, the bank's performance appears initially to be less favorable than that of the standard peer group in each of the 2 years under consideration but shows some strength when the performance between the two years is evaluated. The bank was able to maintain this income ratio whereas that of the standard peer group shows a slight decline.

Even this modest bloom comes off the rose, however, when one considers the ratio for noninterest expense to earnings assets. As in the case of the funding of earning assets, the Glenview State Bank posted these less favorable earnings numbers even though its noninterest expense to earnings assets were lower than that of the standard peer group in both 1994 and 2000. The bank's noninterest expense ratio was 3.39% in 1994 and an even lower 3.25% in 2000. The standard peer group's respective ratios were 4.07% and 3.55%. It is important to look at the two ratios, noninterest income to earnings assets ratio and noninterest expense ratio, together rather than in isolation. During the time period under study for the peer group, the noninterest income to earnings assets ratio decreased by 2%, whereas the noninterest expense ratio decreased by 12.8%. Glenview State Bank's ratios for the same time period showed no increase or decrease in the noninterest income to earnings assets ratio whereas the noninterest expense ratio showed a 4.1% decrease. Thus a pattern emerges in which the Glenview State Bank exhibits an ability to control its expenses to a greater extent than its competitors of similar size nationwide, and through its policies does not exhibit the volatility in either earnings or expenses that is shown by the peer group's ratios. Thus a pattern emerges in which the Glenview State Bank, despite an ability to control its expenses to a greater extent than its competitors of similar size nationwide, was still unable to show equivalent profitability.

This profitability gap was most obvious when reviewing return on assets and return on equity both at the end of 1994 and mid-2000. Glenview State Bank's return on assets was .8% in 1994 and 1.08% in 2000, an increase of 35%. Simultaneous results for the standard peer group were 1.15% and 1.27%, exhibiting an increase of 10.4%. Similar results are found when reviewing the return on equity. The bank's return on equity ratios for 1994 and 2000 were 10.53% and 11.73%, respectively, showing an increase of only 1.9%. In both 1994 and 2000, the return on equity fell short of the peer group's ratios of 13.69% and 14.44%, but the peer group's increase during the 5-year period is an increase of 5.5%. Glenview State Bank's increase in its return on assets over the 5-year period is approximately 3.5 times that of the peer group while the increase in return on equity is approximately one-third that of the peer group. This clearly shows that Glenview State Bank's policies that affect leverage are different than those adopted by their peers while Glenview's policies may be a reflection of the fact that they have been a family bank and do not have the same pressures or opportunities.

When one looks at the loan portfolio ratios, however, the Glenview State Bank compares most favorably with the standard peer group. The bank's net charge-offs to loans was .12% in 1994 and an even smaller .04% in mid-2000, a decrease of 67%. The same ratios for the standard peer group were substantially higher, namely, .46% in 1994 and .31% in 2000, a decrease of 33%.

The same pattern can be seen in relation to the credit–loss provisions to net charge-offs. The Glenview State Bank posted credit–loss ratios of 297.53% in 1994 and 147.06% in 2000. The standard peer group figure was substantially lower, 107.97% in 1994 but higher, 173.64%, in 2000. Thus, during the period under consideration the bank was able to erase much of its credit loss provision whereas the standard peer group showed a significant increase.

The Glenview State Bank had a higher efficiency ratio in both years than did the standard peer group. In 1994, the bank's was 69.72%, and in 2000, it was 64.39%, a decrease of 5.33%. Nonetheless, the comparable figures for the standard peer group were better. They were 63.21% and 57.85%, respectively, a decline of 5.36%.

The favorable loan performance of the bank was mirrored in the condition ratios associated with the loan portfolio. Although the Glenview State Bank had a slight increase in its loss allowance from 1.15% to 1.28% between 1994 and 2000, these figures remained below those of the standard peer group despite the fact that their ratio declined from 1.85% to 1.45% during this period.

Additionally the bank had relatively low noncurrent assets of .03% and noncurrent loans of .05% in 1994 and nothing in either of these categories in 2000. The standard peer group figures, on the other hand, had noncurrent assets of .95% in 1994 and .53% in 2000. Its non-current loans were 1.13% in the former year and .69% in the latter. This exhibits again the conservatism present not only in Glenview's policies, but also in the bank's peer group.

It is likely that the superior loan performance and condition of the Glenview State Bank did not translate into comparably excellent returns because of the bank's increasingly safety oriented and conservative policies, particularly those related to its capital position. In both years and in all respects, the bank exceeded the capital positions of the standard peer group. The bank's equity capital to asset ratio was 7.66% in 1994 and rose to 9.5% by mid-2000. Comparable figures for the standard peer group were 8.33% and 8.7%, respectively.

The same relationship could be seen in the core capital (leverage) ratio. The Glenview State Bank's was 7.91% in December 1994 but increased to 9.64% by the end of the first half of 2000. This was higher than either the earlier 8.33% or later 8.67% for the standard peer group. Tier 1 risk-based capital and total risk-based capital also tended to be higher for the Glenview State Bank in both years. In 1994, the bank posted 12.61% and 13.75% for these two ratios whereas the standard peer group's ratios were 12.52% and 13.83%, respectively. By June 2000, however, the bank's Tier 1 risk-based capital ratio and its total risk-based capital ratio had risen to 14.41% and 15.63% respectively, whereas these ratios for the standard peer group were only 11.82% and 13.10%, respectively.

While making substantial progress and despite healthy growth during the years after Riegle-Neal, the Glenview State Bank did not participate in the opportunities created by interstate geographic deregulation. It limited itself to modest intrastate expansion within a confined suburban area and, ultimately, began to fall behind some of its peers in its returns. Conservative policies, particularly those associated with its lending policy and capital adequacy, provided them with a trouble-free loan portfolio but ultimately cost them money by reducing their overall performance and condition. Thus one could conclude, therefore, that nonparticipation in the opportunities afforded by Riegle-Neal and the somewhat defensive strategies assumed by the Glenview State Bank during the post–Reigel-Neal era adversely effected the bank's profitability and added credence to the arguments regarding the negative impact of interstate banking on small- or medium-sized independent banks. In light of the superior profitability shown by the standard peer group, however, one must question this conclusion and possibly lay the bank's less than optimal results at the feet of its own management.

THE NORTHERN TRUST CORPORATION

On a superficial level, The Northern Trust Company and the Glenview State Bank have many similarities. They were both founded and for most, if not all, of their history, managed by one family, are state chartered, and pride themselves on excellent customer and employee relations, independence, and a conservative philosophy. Initial appearances, however, are deceiving.

The Northern Trust Company opened its doors for business on August 12, 1889, in the historic Rookery Building in the heart of Chicago's commercial district, "The Loop." Byron Laflin Smith, the founder and president of the bank, worked out of a second floor room with a 6 person staff consisting of a secretary/cashier, an assistant secretary, assistant cashier/teller, 2 bookkeepers and a general man. The influence of the Smith family continues though in a lesser capacity to this day. Edward Byron Smith, the grandson of the founder, retired as chairman of the board in 1979 and became honorary chairman of the board in 1981, a position he still retains.

From its modest beginnings, The Northern Trust Company has grown into a multibank holding company, The Northern Trust Corporation, with banking assets exceeding $37 billion, trust assets over $1.5 trillion, and assets under management of $300 billion. The Northern Trust Corporation has a network of 76 subsidiaries or offices where it offers its personal financial services. These facilities are located in 14 states, namely Arizona, California, Colorado, Connecticut, Florida, Georgia, Michigan, Missouri, Nevada, New York, Ohio, Texas, Washington, and Wisconsin, in addition to Illinois where the markets have demographic trends that compliment the bank's core corporate strategies. Since 1969 when it "became the first Illinois State-chartered bank to establish a branch outside of the United States with the opening of the London Branch,"[9] The Northern Trust Corporation has expanded selected services to clients in 35 countries with settlements in 80 countries. Its international branch offices or subsidiaries are located in the Cayman Islands, Dublin, Hong Kong, London, Montreal, New York, Singapore, and Toronto.

Given the initial similarities between the Glenview State Bank and The Northern Trust Company, the dissimilarities that now exist in their current structure, size, and stature are dramatic and reflect on the importance of strategic planning and vision. The Northern Trust Corporation has followed "a highly focused business strategy to deliver trust, investment, and banking services to individuals, corporations and institutions in select markets."[10] Its concentration on personal financial services and corporate and institutional services, in turn, has provided it with the ability to become less dependent on net interest income than most banks. In fact, The Northern Trust Corporation obtains over two-thirds of its corporate revenue from "fees, the majority of which are from fiduciary, asset custody and investment management services." Commercial banking, including checking accounts, collateral loans, and, more recently, treasury management operations, always has been intended as a complimentary and compatible auxiliary to the personal and corporate trust services that are the heart of the bank's business. The Northern Trust Corporation, unlike the Glenview State Bank, saw itself as more than a bank and, therefore, was able to diversify in terms of its products even during the years when Illinois branch banking laws were among the most rigid and restrictive in the nation.

Even in the expansion of its facilities to accommodate its growth, The Northern Trust Corporation distinguished itself from the Glenview State Bank. The Northern Trust's headquarters moved several times to leased facilities until 1904 when it chose a permanent site on LaSalle Street, the financial hub of the city, midway between the Chicago Board of Trade and the Midwest Stock Exchange. Consistent with the bank's emphasis on quality, the superior construction of its facility was deemed sag-proof by city engineers who cut a benchmark into the building's cornerstone to establish the Number Once City Datum Mark, the point from which "the heights of all future structures in Chicago would be measured."[11] The bank's physical growth continued with the expansion of the main facility in 1965 and the development of separate facilities to house its burgeoning computer and operations requirements.

However, the greatest distinction between the Glenview State Bank and The Northern Trust Company and, ultimately, the one that allowed the latter institution to thrive and emerge into one of the 20 largest money managers in the United States was the latter's belief that "conservatism need not rule out innovation and progress." Creative conservatism was the hallmark that allowed The Northern Trust Company to prosper even during the depression and to increase its volume of business by accepting customers fleeing from failing institutions.

The bank's reputation for stability and excellence spread beyond Chicago and Illinois, particularly during the Second World War when its procedures for ration banking were adopted as the national standard by the Office of Price Administration. Through the use of correspondent banking relationships and the acceptance of corporate and individual accounts from outside of the state, The Northern Trust Company overcame geographic restrictions despite being limited to one facility with no intrastate branches. The bank's ability to capitalize on new product opportunities to reach a nationwide and ultimately worldwide market from a restricted location was most clearly evidenced by The Northern Trust Company's entrance into independent master trust and custody services for corporate employee benefit funds' assets after the passage of the Employee and Retirement Income Security Act (ERISA) in 1974 mandated this type of oversight.

Like the Glenview State Bank, The Northern Trust Corporation also considers itself an excellent employer that concerns itself with the welfare of its employees. Here, too, The Northern Trust Corporation has shown itself to be more visionary than the Glenview State Bank and therefore has received greater recognition for its achievements. An example of this is the fact that The Northern Trust Company established the first corporate child care center in the Loop for employees and that its model has become a standard for several other companies. On 9 occasions, The Northern Trust Corporation has been selected as one of *Working Mother* magazine's "100 Best Companies for Working Mothers." Additionally Catalyst selected it in 1999 as one of the 3 best firms for providing outstanding initiatives for the advancement of women in their firm. *Fortune* magazine also has included the bank among its 100 best companies for which to work.

Through innovation, The Northern Trust Company, now The Northern Trust Corporation, has taken advantage of new opportunities and reduced the handicap imposed by geographic, regulatory restrictions. Its uncompromising commitment to excellence, its clear and unwavering strategic business focus which integrated all aspects of its operations, and, finally, its excellent employee relations has enabled The Northern Trust Company and The Northern Trust Corporation to grow from its single family roots to one of the most prestigious and successful banking organizations in the United States.

SUMMARY: PERFORMANCE AND CONDITION RATIOS

In summary, an analysis of The Northern Trust Corporation's performance and condition ratios provides an opportunity to reflect on the success of a highly focused, customer-based strategy that allowed a major bank to remain independent and competitive in the post–Riegle-Neal period. The Northern Trust Corporation has been highly selective in its personal and corporate clientele and has pursued policies that relate primarily and sometimes exclusively to these groups. It has chosen its products to serve the changing needs of its clientele; has taken advantage of opportunities for geographic expansion to serve further its current clientele and to add to its focused customer base; and has separated itself to a substantial degree from the vagaries of interest rate alterations.

Time Series Analysis

In order to assess the effect of the deregulations enacted by Reigle-Neal on The Northern Trust Corporation, this section examines the holding company's performance and condition ratios between December 31, 1994, and June 30, 2000, before and after the passage of the act. During this period, The Northern Trust Corporation thrived. Its yield on earning assets increased from 5.47% to 6.42%, an increase of 17%. This occurred despite the fact that during this same interim, its cost for funding earning assets increased by a substantially greater 37% from 3.28% to 4.49%.

Consistent with its corporate strategy that emphasized fee-based income rather than interest income from lending, the net interest margin, which was 2.18% in 1994, decreased to 1.93% in 2000, or by 13%. The positive effect of this strategy was reflected in the change in the corporation's ratio of noninterest income to earning assets and in its noninterest expense to earning assets. The former increased from 3.81% to 4.48%, or by just slightly less than 18%. Simultaneously the latter declined by 5% from 4.2% to 3.99%.

The bottom line results reflected the wisdom of The Northern Trust Corporation's strategic focus. Its return on assets during the 5 1/2 year period under consideration rose from 1.03% to 1.36% or by 32%, whereas its return on equity increased from 17.76% to 20.67% or by a sizable 16%. The growth in the value of its corporate shares reflected investors' appreciation, both intangible and tangible.

The highly conservative lending policies of the corporation along with its extraordinarily selective customer base were reflected in the charge-offs attached to its loan portfolio. Corporate net charge-offs to loans decreased from .08% in 1994 to .07% in 2000 or by 14%. Simultaneously its credit loss provision to net charge-offs ratio rose from 89.54% to 248.39% or by 177%, a change largely accounted for by the decline in net charge-offs.

The geographic growth of The Northern Trust Corporation from de novo operations and acquisitions in selected markets locally, nationally, and internationally was reflected in an increase in its number of employees from 6,249 to 8,391, an increase of 34.3%. This growth pattern also was reflected in the even more substantial increase in corporate asset size from $18,396,507,000 to $37,246,038,000 or just over 100%. These increments account for the alteration in the ratio of assets to employees from 2.94% to 4.44% or by 51%. Through its sharply focused customer relationship strategy, The Northern Trust Corporation took full advantage of the opportunities afforded to it by Riegle-Neal and was able to remain independent, grow, and prosper at the end of the millennium.

As in the case of its performance ratios, The Northern Trust Corporation's condition ratios show a consistent and positive pattern between the end of 1994 and the middle of 2000. Its ratio of loss allowance to loans decreased from 1.66% to 0.90%, a decline of slightly less than 46%. The corporation's conservative and selective lending policies also explained the decline from 0.52% to 0.45% or by almost 14% in its ratio of noncurrent loans to loans.

Among its condition ratios, all the Northern Trust Corporation's capital ratios demonstrated a conservative pattern leading to improved performance and greater stability. The equity capital to assets ratio increased by 3.5% from 5.86% in 1994 to 6.07% in 2000. The core capital leverage ratio increased by 10% from 5.79% to 6.35%. At the same time the tier 1 risk-based capital ratio increased slightly from 8.39% to 8.63% or by 3%, and the total risk-based capital ratio increased slightly more from 10.92% to 11.38% or by 4%.

Cross-Sectional Analysis

Although the time series analysis supported a conclusion that The Northern Trust Corporation has prospered under Riegle-Neal by retaining a clear, conservative, and selective focus, it is necessary to compare its performance with its peer group to determine to what extent, if any, its performance could have been improved. In the case of The Northern Trust Corporation, a standard peer group analysis also allows for a comparison of results between a bank holding company totally committed to a customer relationship strategy and seeking gains from economies of scope and its peers that were largely committed to obtaining benefits through economies of scale. The peer group used for this purpose is the Federal Deposit Insurance Corporation's (FDIC) largest Standard Peer Group, the multibank holding companies with assets exceeding $10 billion. As one might anticipate, the performance and condition ratios of The Northern Trust Corporation and its contemporaneous organizations frequently displayed different results.

Although The Northern Trust Corporation's yield on earning assets was substantially lower than that of its standard peer group in both 1994 and 2000, the growth in yield on earning assets from 5.47% to 6.42% or by 17% for The Northern Trust Corporation exceeded the performance of its standard peer group which had only a 4% yield growth from 7.71% to 8.05% during the period under consideration. The standard peer group as well as the corporation also experienced increases in the cost of funding earning assets. Here, too, the standard peer group appeared to fare better in that its costs rose from 3.74% to 4.28% or by 14%, whereas a similar analysis of the corporation showed an increase of 37% from 3.28% to 4.49%.

Both The Northern Trust Corporation and its peer group experienced declines in their net interest margins between the end of 1994 and mid-2000. The former revealed a decline of 13% from 2.18% to 1.93%, whereas the latter declined by 6% from 3.97% to 3.77%. What is most interesting here, however, is the noticeably greater dependence on interest income within the peer group than for the corporation. This difference takes on added strategic significance when the ratio of noninterest income to earning assets is considered. The corporation's ratio of noninterest income to earning assets rose by 18% from 3.81% to 4.48%. Even though growing at an even higher 27%, the peer group's ratio remained smaller than the corporation's both in 1994 when it was 2.67% and again in 2000 when it was 3.39%. The Northern Trust Corporation's noninterest expense to earning assets also reflected better absolute and comparative results than did the same ratio for the peer group. The corporation's ratio declined from 1994 to

2000 by 5% from 4.2% to 3.99%, whereas that of the peer group remained virtually flat between the 2 years at 4.39% and 4.4%, respectively.

In light of the different business strategies used by The Northern Trust Corporation and its standard peer group, a comparison of their efficiency ratios provides some insight into their relative success. At the end of 1994, The Northern Trust Corporation's efficiency ratio was 69.77%. By mid-2000 it had improved to 61.67% or by 13%. During the same period, comparable figures for the standard peer group were 64.72% and 59.02%, a decline of less than 10%. The Northern Trust Corporation's efficiency ratio, therefore, has improved more dramatically during the Riegle-Neal era than has that of its standard peer group although the latter continues to show slightly better performance in this regard.

The success of The Northern Trust Company's strategic decisions, however, is most clearly reflected when comparing return on assets (ROA) and ROE. The Northern Trust Corporation outperformed the reference group in both 1994 and 2000, as well as by the degree of growth between these 2 years. The ROA for the corporation grew by 32% from 1.03% to 1.36%, whereas the comparable figures for the peer group were a growth of less than 5% from 1.06% to 1.11%. The ROE for The Northern Trust Corporation simultaneously grew by 16% from 17.76% to 20.67%, whereas the peer group's results declined by 7% from 15.02% to 13.86%. One can see why rumors remained rife and continuous that The Northern Trust Corporation would be the target of a merger or acquisition.

Consideration of loan portfolio ratios reveals that The Northern Trust Corporation's conservative approach also was beneficial in this regard. The corporation's ratio of net charge-offs to loans which was a low .08% in 1994 declined by 14% to .07% in 2000. During the same period, its peers experienced an increase of 12% in net charge-offs from 0.57% to 0.64%. However, the corporation's ratio of credit loss provision to net charge-offs that rose by 177% from 89.54% to 248.39% was significantly greater relatively and absolutely than that of the peer group that saw an increase of 51% from 82.01% to 123.75%.

The comparative strength of The Northern Trust Corporation's loan performance also was reflected in its condition ratios. Its loss allowance to loans declined by approximately 46% from 1.66% to 0.90% though its peer group experienced a 32% decline from 2.56% to 1.73%. Non-current loans for the corporation declined by 16% from 0.53% to 0.45% though those of the peer group declined by a much more substantial 42% but remained absolutely higher in both 1994 when the non-current loans were 1.52% and again in 2000 when they were 1.07%.

The Northern Trust Corporation's capital ratios tended to be lower than those of its standard peer group, a reflection of the bank's stability and an additional reason for its enhanced profitability. The corporation's ratio of equity capital to assets that was 5.86% at the end of 1994 rose by 36% to

6.07% by mid-2000. The comparable figures for the standard peer group were 7.01% in 1994 and 8.06% in 2000, an increase of 15%. Similarly the corporation's core capital leverage ratio rose by almost 10% from 5.79% to 6.35%, whereas that of the standard peer group rose by 7% from 6.64% to 7.13%. The only capital ratio in which The Northern Trust Corporation posted higher numbers than its industry competitors was in its tier 1 risk-based capital ratio. The corporation's ratio rose by 3% from 8.39% to 8.63%, and the standard peer group's ratio declined by 2% from 8.56% to 8.34%. At the same time, however, the corporation's total risk-based capital ratio was 10.92% in 1994 and 11.38% in 2000 as compared with 11.91% and 11.49%, respectively, for the standard peer group.

By retaining its customer focus and a clear vision of its current position and future goals, The Northern Trust Corporation was able to attain economies of scope and to capitalize on its strong niche positions after passage of Riegle-Neal. In so doing, it also enhanced its financial strength, seized selectively upon appropriate new growth opportunities, and remained independent despite the merger and acquisition mania of the day.

HARRIS BANKCORP

For most of the first hundred years of its history, the Harris Trust and Savings Bank mirrored The Northern Trust Company in a multitude of ways, the least of which was its location immediately across the street. With 5 employees and 2 customers, Norman Wait Harris founded his family's bank in 1882 originally as an investment bank known as N.W. Harris & Co, which specialized in underwriting and selling public utility bonds. In 1907, the Harris Trust and Savings Bank was formed with a state charter in order to provide bond customers the ability to retain on deposits their uninvested cash balances.[12] The imposition of Glass-Steagall's Chinese Wall provisions separating investment and commercial banking, however, caused the Harris Bank to relinquish its investment bond activities in 1933.

Like its neighbor, The Northern Trust Company, the Harris Trust and Savings Bank survived the depression because of its conservative policies, most notably its decision to convert its bonds into cash just prior to the stock market crash. These 2 institutions which provided trust and banking services to an elite personal and corporate clientele, were so similar that they constantly vied for the position of the largest-state chartered bank in Illinois, as well as the third largest bank in Chicago. Reflecting the influence of a national charter and of the comptroller of the currency as the primary regulator, the position of the two largest banks in Chicago virtually was reserved for 2 nationally chartered institutions, Continental Illinois Bank and Trust Company, which was acquired by Bank of America, and The First National Bank of Chicago, which ultimately became part of Bank One.

By merging with Chicago National Bank in 1960, however, the Harris Trust and Savings Bank distinguished itself from its primary competitor and began to travel a new strategic road into retail banking. This merger ultimately led to the formation of a parent bank holding company known as Harris Bankcorp in 1972. Ten years later there occurred a departure from the Harris Trust and Savings Bank's original focus when it took another new path with the acquisition of a community bank. The final chapter in the strategic odyssey of the Harris Trust and Savings Bank from its initial roots occurred in 1984 when the Bank of Montreal acquired Harris Bankcorp. As Canada's first bank, the Bank of Montreal was founded in 1817 and had had an office in Chicago since 1861. At the time, this merger was the second largest banking merger in U.S. banking history.

The strategic plans of Harris Bankcorp changed substantially; one might even say they experienced a metamorphosis, after it became a wholly owned subsidiary of the Bank of Montreal. Harris Bankcorp was no longer viewed as a platform for expansion beyond Chicago and Illinois or exclusively as a provider of services to a select personal and corporate clientele. The Bank of Montreal did not need Harris Bankcorp to accomplish these objectives. Instead Harris Bankcorp provided the Bank of Montreal with the possibility of developing a greater local and regional presence from a Chicago hub by taking advantage of Illinois's Multibank Holding Company Act. The prestige of the Harris Bankcorp name and the financial strength of the Bank of Montreal made it possible for the holding company to reach out to a new clientele in the Chicago suburbs within and adjacent to Cook County. This strategic growth of Harris Bankcorp was augmented and institutionalized during the Riegle-Neal era by Vision 2002, a relationship-based strategy intended to increase Harris Bankcorp's market share in the Chicago metropolitan area through the development cross-selling synergies in a regionwide network.[13]

A first step toward accomplishing the goals of Vision 2002 occurred in October 1994 when Harris Bankcorp and Suburban Bancorp combined under the Harris name to become the third largest community-banking network in Chicago. This apparently new business pattern also revitalized an earlier community based commitment dating back to 1915 when the Harris Trust and Savings Bank created the Chicago Community Trust. By pooling individual charitable contributions and distributing award grants to good causes based upon the recommendations of a committee of experts, the Chicago Community Trust became one of the largest and most prestigious philanthropic organizations in the city and a model for similar institutions elsewhere.

The new community banking initiative of Harris Bankcorp, however, also added some new features dictated by new community realities, as well as the needs of the holding company itself. It promised to "be as local as an independent community bank"[14] and to focus on the metropolitan Chicago market, including its Hispanic population (through the addition of more Spanish-speaking mortgage lenders), small businesses (through the initiation of a new "prime rate" for them), and low- to moderate-income communities (through the expansion of a local branching network). These promises, in turn, also aided the holding company in complying with the requirements of the Community Reinvestment Act (CRA), a regulation with which Harris Bankcorp had had compliance difficulties that had impeded previous expansion plans.

Harris Bankcorp's market concentration was strengthened further in June 1996 when it acquired Household Bank and added 54 more branches to its local banking network. Today Harris Bankcorp, a wholly owned subsidiary of the Bank of Montreal, has approximately 140 community banks in the Chicago area and prides itself on being "one of the largest community bank networks in Illinois."[15]

The goals of Vision 2002 to develop a community-based branch network throughout the Chicago metropolitan area by 2002, therefore, were attained 5 years ahead of schedule. The potential value of this development was dependent on cross-selling synergies in a twofold manner: It was expected to enhance current customer relationships by offering its clientele more products and services, and a wider range of services and locations were intended to attract to new customers to whom the bank had not appealed previously. By concentrating on cross-selling, the synergistic strategy also had the added benefit of reducing disruptions caused by cost reductions related to the consolidation of operations or the reduction of management or other personnel because each of the banking organizations subsumed under the Harris Bankcorp umbrella retained its independence, separate identity, and customer base. Each part of the holding company brought something unique to the corporate table and thus the whole was expected to produce more business than the sum of the parts could have produced if they had remained unaffiliated.

The holding company gained these synergies in several ways: It received low cost deposits from suburban customers; it retained the marketing and loan origination expertise of the Harris Bank; it obtained additional fee income through the expansion of Harris Bankcorp's asset management services to a new group of suburban customers; and it combined Harris Bankcorp's expertise in residential mortgage origination and resale with mortgage origination opportunities in suburban Chicago communities. The success of the plan can be seen in the fact that after completing the acquisition of Household Bank, Harris Bankcorp served 800,000 households or one-fifth of all households in Chicagoland. This far surpassed the holding company's local market share of one-fourteenth of all households in the area in 1994.[16]

Despite its local emphasis, the Harris Bankcorp did move beyond the borders of Illinois to 2 Sunbelt states, Arizona and Florida. It has 6 locations in the former and 5 in the latter. This modest expansion further highlights the diversion from its earlier strategy of competing with The Northern

Trust Corporation for select customers. The Northern Trust Corporation by comparison has only 18 metropolitan Chicago offices but has expanded to 11 locations in Arizona and 25 in Florida plus facilities in 12 other states and overseas— a very different path indeed.

The Harris Bankcorp also has sought to capitalize with the business community both in and beyond Chicago, because of its position as a member of the Bank of Montreal Group of Companies. Particularly in the post–North American Free Trade Agreement (NAFTA) era, the Harris Bankcorp has stressed its self-proclaimed competitive edge in aiding businesses on a cross-border basis between Canada and the United States. Although Harris Bankcorp opened a London branch in 1970, its overseas presence is largely dependent upon the Bank of Montreal's 5 foreign offices and operations in 21 countries throughout the world.

As set forth in its 1994 *Annual Report*, the 10-year goal of the Harris Bankcorp was to use local growth in its community-banking network in conjunction with its position as one of North America's largest banks to triple its size by 2004. By mid-2000 the Harris Bankcorp achieved a portion of its goals through its ever larger community banking network, by being one of the top 3 private banks in Chicago, as well as one of the city's top 3 providers of personal trust and assets management services, which ranks it among the top 30 trust banks in the nation. The Harris Bankcorp's initial roots in the bond industry also were reflected by its position as the number one underwriter of municipal bond issues in the Midwest and one of the top 5 U.S. dealer banks serving as managing underwriter of general obligation tax-exempt municipal bonds. Today Harris Bankcorp has a firm footing in the Chicago region and demonstrates the success of a customer-relationship strategy of mergers and acquisitions applied at the local level.

SUMMARY: PERFORMANCE AND CONDITION RATIOS

An analysis of the Harris Bankcorp's performance and condition ratios provides insight into the success of the Vision 2002 strategy that eschewed interstate expansion in favor of greater local market share. It also helps to determine the extent to which a focus on enhancement and expansion of customer relationships rather than on cost cutting measures is a beneficial basis for takeovers.

Time Series Analysis

Between December 31, 1994, and June 30, 2000, the Harris Bankcorp performed very well. Its yield on earning assets increased by almost 10% from 6.71% to 7.36% despite a substantial increase of 56% from 3.18% to 4.96% in the cost of funding these earning assets. Harris Bankcorp's net interest margin during this period decreased from 3.53% to 2.40% or by 32%, and its ratio of noninterest income to earning assets decreased by 12% from 2.88% to

2.53%. Most telling was an increase of 70.5% in its return on assets from .61% to 1.04% and a phenomenal increase of 77% in its return on equity from 9.45% to 16.69% during the 5 1/2 year period.

Although Harris Bankcorp's net charge-offs to loans decreased from .67% to .17% or by 75%, its credit loss provision to net charge-offs increased from 91.43% to 126.89% or by 39%. Assets per employee increased from 2.86% to 4.56% or by 59%. This occurred despite an increase in the corporation's labor force by 11% from 4,179 to 4, 654 because of an even greater proportional increase in assets from $11,944,330,000 to $21,237,482,000 or by 78% between December 31, 1994, and June 30, 2000.

Just as impressive were the reduction of the corporation's loss allowance to loans from 1.42% to 1.07%, a decline of 33%, and its simultaneous reduction from 1.37% to 0.36% or by 74% of its ratio of noncurrent loans to loans.

The strength and security of the Harris Bankcorp also increased as it grew. Its ratio of equity capital to assets increased from 6.11% in 1994 to 6.22% in 2000 or by 2%. The core capital leverage ratio increased from 6.62% to 7.10% or by 7%. Despite an increase in the tier 1 risk-based capital ratio from 7.83% to 8.44% or by 8%, the total risk-based capital ratio decreased from 11.22% to 10.34% or by 8.5%. By mid-2000 the Harris Bankcorp clearly demonstrated the positive impact of the Vision 2002 strategy on its financial statements.

Cross Sectional Analysis

A comparison of Harris Bankcorp's performance for the period between the end of 1994 and mid-2000 with its standard peer group of banks and bank holding companies with assets of over $10 billion produces mixed results. Harris Bankcorp's yield on earning assets rose by almost 10% from 6.71% to 7.36%. Nonetheless, in both years despite the standard peer group's lower growth of 4% in this ratio Harris Bankcorp fell short of the standard peer group's performance of 7.71% and 8.05%, respectively. The corporation's cost of funding earning assets differed considerably from that of the standard peer group. In 1994, Harris Bankcorp's ratio was 3.18%, whereas that of the standard peer group was 3.74%. By 2000, however, this relationship has altered considerably. Harris Bankcorp's ratio had risen by 36% to 4.96% whereas the standard peer group's ratio had grown more modestly by 14% to 4.28%.

The Harris Bankcorp's net interest margin fell by 32% from 3.53% to 2.40% and thus was consistently lower than that of the standard peer group which posted a 5% decline from 3.97% to 3.77%. Similarly, Harris Bankcorp's level of non-interest income to earning assets was 2.88% in 1994 and 2.53% in 2000, a decline of 12%. Although this compared favorably with the standard peer group's ratio of 2.67% in 1994, it was well below the standard peer group's 27% increase to 3.39% in 2000.

Harris Bankcorp's ROA rose by 70.5% from .61% to 1.04%. Nonetheless, it continued to fall short of the standard peer group's level of 1.06% and 1.11%, respectively, despite the more modest growth of 5%, which this latter set of numbers represented. Harris Bankcorp's ROE, however, was more impressive than that of the standard peer group. The former's ratio rose by 77% from 9.45% to 16.69%, whereas that of the latter declined by 7% from 15.02% to 13.86%.

The Harris Bankcorp's level of net charge-offs to loans declined from .67% to .17% or by 75%, whereas that of its standard peer group rose by 12% from .57% to .64%. The corporation's credit loss provision to net charge-offs, which rose by 39% from 91.43% to 126.89%, displayed a pattern similar to that of the standard peer group which saw its ratio change by 51% from 82.01% to 123.75%. Final testament to the Harris Bankcorp's improved performance could be seen in its efficiency ratio which declined by 26% from 80.07% to 59.37%, thus bringing it into line with the standard peer group which had a decline of less than 10% from 64.72% to 59.02%.

The equity capital to asset ratio of Harris Bankcorp rose by 2% from 6.11% to 6.22%. This remained relatively and absolutely below that of the standard peer group which rose by 15% from 7.01% to 8.06% during the period under consideration. Greater similarity between the corporation and comparable institutions was apparent in the core capital leverage ratio. Harris Bankcorp's results increased by 7% from 6.62% to 7.10%, and the same ratio for the standard peer group also increased by 7% from 6.64% to 7.13%. Harris Bankcorp's tier 1 risk-based capital ratio rose by 8% from 7.83% to 8.44%. During the same period, its competitors' ratio declined by 2% from 8.56% to 8.34%. Finally, Harris Bankcorp's total risk-based capital ratio declined by 8.5% from 11.22% to 10.34%, whereas its standard peer group showed a decline of 4% from 11.91% to 11.49%.

Although The Northern Trust Corporation and Harris Bankcorp have taken different paths in pursuit of greater synergy, economies of scope, and expanded customer relationships, each of them has shown the benefits to be derived from this strategy. Harris Bankcorp, however, lost its independence and narrowed its focus when it became part of the larger Bank of Montreal organization. Although it continues to have good performance, it no longer vies with its longtime rival The Northern Trust Corporation as it did in its earlier years because only one of them has remained independent and envisioned its growth beyond the narrow confines of the Chicago metropolitan region.

BANK ONE CORPORATION

The history of Bank One Corporation mirrors in microcosm the changes that have occurred in American banking as a result of deregulatory trends, including those related to geography. Even more so it is a reflection of the impact of this deregulation on the Midwest and in particular, the transformation of the City of Chicago as a regional, national and international banking center.[17]

The Bank One corporate story could be told from the perspective of Columbus, Ohio, where Sessions and Company, the earliest Ohio forerunner of Bank One Corporation, was founded in 1868. One would then follow a path that included the City National Bank and Trust Company founded in 1929, the formation of First Banc Group of Ohio, Inc. in 1968, the adoption of the Banc One Corporation name in 1979 and an 11-year interstate acquisition spree from 1987–1998, culminating with the merger in October 1998 of Banc One Corporation and First Chicago NBD Corporation to create Bank One Corporation.

The story also could be told from the vantage point of Detroit, the original home of the National Bank of Detroit. As part of the postdepression redevelopment, the bank was founded in the motor capital in 1933 with equal capitalization from General Motors Corporation and the Reconstruction Finance Corporation, both of which divested their interests during the 1940s. Through a series of acquisitions, National Bank of Detroit (NBD) grew into the largest banking organization in Michigan and Indiana before merging with the First National Bank of Chicago in 1995 to form First Chicago NBD Corporation.

The transformation story leading up to the current Bank One Corporation, however, is not complete without analysis of the historical changes associated with the First National Bank of Chicago, the oldest, largest, and, at one time, most prestigious of the 3 institutions that came together ultimately as Bank One Corporation. In a sense, this history of what was once Chicago's largest hometown bank can be summarized in the phrase "the bigger they are, the harder they fall."

Capitalizing on a February 1863 law that permitted the formation of national banks, The First National Bank of Chicago, operating under Charter #8 from the comptroller of the currency, opened its doors on July 1, 1863, the day on which the Battle of Gettysburg commenced. From the era of the Civil War when Chicago was the central hub of rail traffic in America until its merger with NBD Corporation, the First National Bank of Chicago rightfully claimed to be Chicago's bank.

The merger and acquisition tradition of the First National Bank of Chicago predates the current deregulatory era. Because of the limits imposed by Illinois's intrastate and McFadden's interstate branching restrictions, the initial expansion of the bank occurred exclusively within Chicago commencing at the turn of the century with its merger with Union National Bank. In 1902, the First National Bank absorbed Metropolitan National Bank. This was followed in 1903 by the establishment of an independent corporation, The First Trust and Savings Bank.

Like The Northern Trust Company, the First National Bank of Chicago withstood the pressures of the Great Depression and expanded its activities during this period by taking over the Foreman State Bank in 1931. The First National Bank's fortunes and size rose steadily so that by the end of the Second World War, it had $2 billion in assets and annual earnings of approximately $5.7 million. The bank's stature was acknowledged by the appointment of its president, Edward Eagle Brown as the only American banker on the U.S. delegation to the United Nations Monetary and Finance Conference at Bretton Woods, New Hampshire, which led to the creation of the World Bank and International Monetary Fund.

During the 1950s, 1960s and 1970s, the First National Bank achieved growth through industry-specialized lending and by taking advantage of the easing of Illinois' unit banking rules through the addition of several offices in the greater Chicago metropolitan area. In the 1980s, however, the First National Bank reverted to acquisition to obtain growth, especially in its retail banking activities. In 1982, it purchased the credit card business of Banker's Trust and followed this with a 1987 purchase of the credit card business of Beneficial National Bank (now FCC National Bank). Consistent with this thrust into personal banking and the small and middle markets of commercial lending, the First National Bank acquired several banking institutions or parts thereof. Most notable were its acquisition of Chicago's fifth largest bank, the American National Bank and Trust Company in 1984; the First United Financial Services, a 5-bank, suburban holding company in 1987; Gary-Wheaton Corporation, a 4-bank suburban holding company in 1988; the retail accounts of the Continental Illinois National Bank and Trust Company in 1988; and the shareholder services operation of J.P. Morgan and Company in 1989. This acquisition pattern continued into the 1990s when opportunities arose to purchase savings and loans after the passage of the Financial Institutions Reform, Recovery and Enforcement Act (FIRREA). Entering the 1990s, therefore, the First National Bank of Chicago like Harris Bankcorp was truly making its presence felt in all portions of the Chicago market through its ever-growing network of branches.

In 1995, NBD and First Chicago dominated their local markets. Nonetheless, their ability to compete nationally and internationally with the banking behemoths was still hampered by their relatively small asset size. Therefore, on July 12 of that year, they announced their "merger of equals" which was to be effected by early 1996 and was to create the sixth largest bank holding company in the nation, the market share leader in three Midwestern states (Illinois, Indiana, and Michigan), as well as the fourth largest issuer of bank credit cards in the nation. The new holding company was expected to be more competitive because of an estimated $200 million in annual cost savings and the capital to invest in technology. This was a merger predicated upon the assumption that asset size and economies of scale were the all important factors for future success.

However, mergers of equals frequently are something other than equal as Chrysler has come to realize in its merger with Daimler. In fact, as the smaller partner NBD dominated the new entity known as First Chicago NBD Corporation even though the stock swap used to finance the arrangement gave previous First Chicago Corporation shareholders 50.1% of the new holding company. Although the headquarters of the combined organization moved to the Chicago offices of the First National Bank, individuals who had previously worked in Detroit assumed the leadership quickly. They proved that NBD did not deserve to be dubbed "Nice, Big, Dull" by its detractors.[18]

The independence of First Chicago NBD Corporation was short-lived. In 1998, history repeated itself when another "merger of equals" created Bank One Corporation and the leaders of the out-of-town institution from Columbus, Ohio, moved their offices to Chicago. This merger, too, focused on the anticipated benefits to be gained from increased asset size and concomitant economies of scale rather than synergies, development of customer relationships, or savings from economies of scope.

SUMMARY: PERFORMANCE AND CONDITION RATIOS

Time Series Analysis

Because of the multiple consolidations that led to the creation of Bank One Corporation, consideration of the effect of Reigle-Neal's geographic deregulation on Bank One Corporation requires more than a simple comparison of data from 1994 and 2000. It also must take into account the enormous changes that occurred with each of the major mergers, namely, the initial merger of NBD Corporation and First Chicago Corporation and then the subsequent merger between Banc One Corporation and First Chicago NBD Corporation.

The Intervening Mergers. As a prelude to understanding the year 2000 performance of Bank One Corporation, this section compares data from 1994 prior to the merger of NBD Corporation and First Chicago Corporation with data from 1997 subsequent to that merger. It then goes on to evaluate data from the year 2000 when the merger of all segments of Bank One Corporation had been completed.

In 1994, before First Chicago Corporation and NBD Bancorp merged, they were roughly equal in size, both in terms of assets and number of employees. First Chicago Corporation had assets of $55,436,752,000, whereas those of NBD Bancorp totaled $48,593,098,000. Regarding their pre-merger number of employees, First Chicago Corporation had 15,514 employees while NBD Bancorp had 15,343 employees. It is interesting to note that after the merger of these 2 bank holding companies in 1997, the new First Chicago NBD Corporation employed 31,898 persons or 1,041 more than had been employed separately by the two organizations participating in the merger. The anticipated economies of scale, therefore, were not achieved initially, at least, through a reduction in the labor force of the new holding company.

The early signs from the newly merged First Chicago NBD Corporation were encouraging. Whereas the 1994 premerger yield on earning assets was 6.63% for First Chicago Corporation and 7.12% for NBD Bancorp, their combined, postmerger yield on earning assets in 1997 was 8.06%. This last figure represented an increase of 16% from an average of 6.92% for the yield on earnings assets of the two corporations prior to their merger.

In 1994, prior to the merger, the cost of funding earning assets was 3.34% for First Chicago Corporation and 3.23% for NBD Bancorp. By 1997, the cost of funding earning assets for the combined corporation, First Chicago NBD Corporation, had increased to 3.93% or by 19% from their prior average of 3.29%.

Before the merger in 1994, First Chicago Corporation had a net interest margin of 3.28%, and NBD Bancorp had a net interest margin of 3.98%. After the merger, in 1997, the new First Chicago NBD Corporation had a healthier net interest margin of 4.14%. The result for noninterest income, however, was substantially different because of the considerably lower reliance of NBD Bancorp on fee business. In 1994, First Chicago Corporation's ratio of noninterest income to earning assets was 3.77%, whereas that of NBD Bancorp's was only 1.36%. After their merger, therefore, the combined First NBD Corporation ratio of noninterest income to earning assets was 2.72%, marginally higher than the average of the 2 separate ratios.

The benefits of the merger in regard to ROA and ROE was mixed. It had a positive effect on ROA. In 1994, First Chicago Corporation had an ROA of 1.21%. In that year NBD Bancorp, Inc.'s ROA was 1.22%. In 1997, after the merger, however, the ROA for the combined corporation had risen to 1.32%. In terms of ROE, the merger resulted in a less positive outcome. In 1994, the ROE for First Chicago Corporation and NBD Bancorp, Inc. were 15.61% and 16.80%, respectively. In 1997, following the merger, the ROE for the combined organization was 15.11%, less than either of the participants had experienced separately.

The merger clearly resulted in a significant increase in net charge-offs to loans. The figures for net charge-offs to loans for First Chicago Corporation and NBD Bancorp were .62% and .15%, respectively, in 1994. After the merger in 1997, the net charge-offs to loans for the combined corporation was 1.09%. On the other hand, the credit–loss provision to net charge-offs decreased following the merger. In 1994, the credit–loss provision to net charge-offs was 112.03% for First Chicago Corporation and 137.03% for NBD Bancorp. Following the merger in 1997, the figure for credit–loss provision to net charge-offs decreased to 100.05%.

The 1997 figures comparing First Chicago NBD Corporation and Banc One provide the final intermediary step for evaluating the year 2000 performance results of the final merger that created Bank One Corporation. First

Chicago NBD Corporation was the smaller of the 2 participants in the final merger. It had 31,898 employees as compared with Banc One that had 36,301. By 2000, their combined number of employees had risen from its original total of 68,199 to 70,863 employees, an increase of 2,664 employees or almost 4%. As in the case of the earlier merger of First Chicago Corporation and NBD Bancorp, the creation of Bank One Corporation did not capture economies of scale despite an increase in asset size.

First Chicago NBD's assets in 1997 were $110,111,034 and Banc One Corporation's assets were $118,918,713. In 2000, the total assets of the combined Bank One Corporation were $292,284,645. This was an increase of $6,325,490 or 2.76% over the $229,029,747, the combined 1997 total of the parties in the merger.

The yield on earning assets of First Chicago NBD in 1997 was 8.06%. Simultaneously Banc One Corporation had a yield on earning assets of 9.1%. After the merger of the 2 holding companies in 2000, their combined yield on earning assets approached the lower of the 2 prior figures; it was 8.07%.

The cost of funding earning assets, however, increased after the merger. In 1997, the cost of funding earning assets was 3.93% for First Chicago NBD Corporation and 3.90% for Banc One Corporation. In 2000, the cost of funding earning assets for Bank One Corporation was 4.54%, an increase of 16%.

Of even greater concern was the fact that the net interest margin decreased after the merger. The 1997 net interest margin of First Chicago NBD Corporation was 4.14% and that of Banc One Corporation was 5.20%. The combined net interest margin of Bank One Corporation in 2000, however, was only 3.35%, substantially less than it had been for either of its constituent parts. The ratio of noninterest income to earning assets was 2.72% for First Chicago NBD and 2.17% for Banc One Corporation in 1997. In 2000, after the merger, the ratio of noninterest income to earning assets for the combined Bank One Corporation was 2.39%, or slightly less than the 2.45% average of their 1997 figures.

Here even more so than in the case of the earlier merger, the return ratios clearly reflect the negative effects of the new combination. The ROA for First Chicago NBD Corporation in 1997 was 1.32%; the same ratio for Banc One Corporation was 1.29%. In 2000, after the merger, the ROA for Bank One Corporation was a dreadful –.07%. Similarly, the ROE of First Chicago NBD Corporation in 1997 was 15.11%, whereas that of Banc One Corporation was 14.63%. Their combined return on equity in 2000, however, also was extremely disappointing. It had declined to –.96%. Clearly increased asset size was adversely affecting performance and bringing few, if any, economies of scale.

Net charge-offs to loans for First Chicago NBD in 1997 was 1.09%. For Banc One Corporation, the 1997 figure for net charge-offs to loans was 1.33%. The combined net charge-offs to loans in 2000 for Bank One Corporation were down to .60%. The credit loss provision to net charge-offs was

100.05% for First Chicago NBD in 1997 and 108.00% for Banc One Corporation. After the merger, the 2000 figure for credit loss provision to net charge-offs for Bank One Corporation, however, had more than doubled to 238.84% or more than double the 1997 figures of either of the merger partners.

The Riegle-Neal Era: 1994–2000. For purposes of statistical symmetry and in order to complete the transitional analysis, this section looks at Bank One Corporation from 1994 and 2000. In light of the holding company's history, however, a note of caution must be given. The 1994 figures are for Banc One Corporation based in Columbus, Ohio whereas those for 2000 are for Bank One Corporation, headquartered in Chicago.

Between 1994 and 2000, Bank One Corporation's yield on earning assets remained relatively constant. It was 8.02% in 1994 and 8.07% in 2000, a modest difference 0.6%. At the same time the cost of funding earning assets rose from 2.82% to 4.54%, an increase of almost 61%. During the same period, the holding company's net interest margin decreased from 5.20% in 1994 to 3.53% in 2000 or by over 32%. The ratio of noninterest income to earning assets, however, increased by only 10% from 2.17% to 2.39% over these years.

Bank One's return ratios suffered significantly between 1994 and 2000, moving from positive to negative figures. The ROA ratio decreased from 1.14% to –.07%, a decrease of over 106%. ROE decreased from 14.26% to –.96%, a decrease of almost 107%. Clearly, the merger activity associated with the creation of Bank One Corporation did not result in a performance in the year 2000 even equivalent to that of any of the original participants in 1997. In terms of return ratios, the whole was not equal to the sum of the parts.

Between 1994 and 2000, Bank One's ratio of net charge-offs to loans increased by over 13% from .53% to .60%. At the same time, the holding company's ratio of credit–loss provision to net charge-offs increased significantly from 76.82% to 238.84% or by almost 211%.

Cross-Sectional Analysis

This section compares the performance of Bank One to its peer group of all commercial banks with assets of over $10 billion with data from June 2000.

Bank One's yield on earning assets of 8.07% was very close to the reference group's average of 8.05%. This occurred while Bank One's cost of funding earning assets was 4.54% compared with the reference group's 4.28%.

Bank One's net interest margin of 3.53% fell short of the reference group's average of 3.77%. At the same time the holding company's noninterest income to earning assets ratio was 2.39% compared with 3.39% for the reference group. Bank One's ratio of noninterest expense to earning assets was 2.39% relative to the reference group's average of 4.40%.

Bank One's return ratios fell short of the reference group's performance in both the areas of ROA and ROE. Bank One's return on assets in 2000 was –.07% compared with the reference group's average of 1.11%. ROE of –.96% fell short of the reference group average of 13.86%.

The ratio of net charge-offs to loans of .06% for Bank One was below the reference group average of .64%. The bank's credit–loss provision to net charge-offs of 238.84% was substantially above the reference group average of 123.75%. Bank One had a higher efficiency ratio of 76.17% relative to the reference group's 59.02%.

Bank One's equity capital to assets ratio was 7.39% compared with the reference group's 8.06%. At the same time, the core capital leverage ratio was 6.94% relative to 7.13% for the reference group. The tier 1 risk-based capital ratio of 7.68% fell short of the reference group's 8.34%, whereas the total risk-based capital ratio of 11.57% slightly exceeded the reference group's 11.48%.

The year 2000 cross-sectional figures add final proof of the failure to-date of the Bank One Corporation to attain economies of scale despite its increase in asset size. Although this casts doubt on the ability of management to cope with this enlarged entity, it also brings into question the wisdom of a merger in which the benefits are fully expected to result from a growth in asset size and economies of scale rather than from synergies, expanded and enhanced customer relationships, and economies of scope.

NOTES

1. Charles W. Calomiris and Jason Karceski, *Is the Bank Merger Wave of the 1990s Efficient? Lessons from Nine Case Studies* (Washington, DC: AEI Press, 1998), p. 2.

2. Ibid., p. 17.

3. Ibid., p. 11.

4. Emmanuel Roussakis, *Commercial Banking in an Era of Deregulation*, 3rd ed. (Westport, CT: Praeger, 1997), p. 43.

5. Calomiris and Karceski, *Is the Bank Merger Wave of the 1990s Efficient?* p. 4.

6. Ibid., pp. 43 and 44.

7. All information regarding the history and background of the Glenview State Bank was derived from the bank's web site.

8. All statistical information for the Glenview State Bank and its standard peer group for December 31, 1994, and June 30, 2000, were obtained from the FDIC web site.

9. This quotation and all the information regarding the history, policies, and philosophy of The Northern Trust Company were derived from information on the bank's web site under the section devoted to investor relations.

10. www.ntrs.com

11. Ibid.

12. Information regarding the history of The Harris Trust and Savings Bank was derived from information on the bank's web site, the bank's annual reports

from 1994 through 1999, and a packet of historical in-house, unpublished articles made available to the authors by the Corporate Communications Department of the Harris Trust and Savings Bank.

13. Calomiris and Karceski, *Is the Bank Merger Wave of the 1990s Efficient?* p. 39.

14. Harris Bank, *1994 Annual Report.*

15. Information from the bank's web site.

16. Calomiris and Karceski, *Is the Bank Merger Wave of the 1990s Efficient?* pp. 84–86.

17. The Corporate and Media Relations Office of Bank One Corporation made the historical information regarding Bank One Corporation available.

18. Richard A. Melcher, "Is 'Nice, Big, Dull' Good Enough?" *Business Week,* May 12, 1997, p. 84.

Chapter 6

Summary

The Riegle-Neal Banking and Branching Efficiency Act of 1994 began the deregulatory revolution that took place in the American banking system at the end of the 20th century. By overturning 2 fixed and seemingly intransigent laws, the McFadden Act of 1927 and the Douglas Amendment to the Bank Holding Company Act of 1956, Riegle-Neal effectively ended banking segregation along state lines and paved the way for a truly nationwide banking system.

In the wake of its momentous, and, some would argue, overdue changes, Riegle-Neal not only altered the American banking landscape, but it also established a greater symmetry between the legal system and a banking system which had changed over the course of 70 years in order to meet financial, economic, and business requirements. In a sense one can say that Riegle-Neal helped to reestablish the rule of law and the respect for law within the banking world. Creative legal interpretations; circumvention of the spirit of the law, if not its wording; and reliance on regulatory largesse rather than legislative intent were no longer needed for banks and bank holding companies to overcome legislative obsolescence which had prevented their expansion across state lines and their ability to capitalize on the full financial strength of the American market.

The changes and challenges of rapid realignment between the law and society that was at the heart of Riegle-Neal, however, raised unsettling questions that created uncertainty regarding the banking industry in the United States. This book has sought to resolve some of these issues. Although it is too early to gain an absolutely clear and definitive picture in the aftermath of the change in interstate banking and branching, some features and trends have become apparent.

Riegle-Neal stimulated the ongoing movement toward consolidation within the banking community by opening new avenues for mergers and acquisitions across state lines. In so doing, it helped to reduce the number of bank failures and accelerated the expansion of branching networks on a national scale. Like a forest fire that initially obliterates the landscape but ultimately makes it possible for young saplings to grow without being starved for sunlight by larger trees, Riegle-Neal also encouraged the growth of de novo banks which provided new blood and competition within the banking community.

Banking consolidation after Riegle-Neal further increased the asset size of American banks, thereby adding to the economic efficiencies of scale and scope within the industry. Additionally it eliminated the disadvantages associated with a fragmented domestic base which had made it difficult for domestic banks to achieve sufficient asset size to compete successfully in the international arena. The full effect of this has yet to be appreciated given the fact that at the end of 1999, the Federal Reserve Bank (Fed) still reported that only 8 of the nation's 10 largest bank holding companies had, at least, 6 overseas branches, a relatively modest presence that is likely to grow.

A survey of the aggregate condition and income data within the banking industry in the years subsequent to the passage of Riegle-Neal testified to a generally positive impact of the legislation. Nationally, increases were seen in net income culminating in an all time high in 1999, of total assets, total deposits, and equity capital. On a state-by-state basis, however, the results were more mixed and uneven in all categories, leaving no question that the ramifications of legal change had different implications for the banking industry in different states.

The equanimity created by the aggregate figures, however, was tempered when reviewing several performance ratios. Nationally there was improvement in non-interest income to average earning assets, a reflection of the increased importance of fees. Additionally (ROA) and (ROE) increased, too. Declines in performance, however, were seen in the reduction of net interest margins, as well as increases in net charge-offs and credit–loss provisions. Most troublesome was the rise in the number of unprofitable institutions and the reduction of the number of banks posting earnings gains. It is obvious that Riegle-Neal's geographic deregulation alone could not protect the banking industry from competitive pressures imposed by the rest of the financial community. Gramm-Leach-Bliley's product deregulation also was required to level the playing field, the results of which have yet to be seen.

Despite some pessimism created by the performance ratios, the condition ratios were somewhat more encouraging. They revealed a reduction in loss allowances and in nonperforming assets, stability in equity capital, a decline in total capital to risk weighted assets, and a slight decline in the dependence on loans and leases within the asset portfolio. The only area reviewed that created some concern was a reduction in core deposits.

Throughout the analysis of the financial statements, the most obvious result of Riegle-Neal was the disparity of the law's impact on the banking industries at the state level. The growth of the national banking industry attributable to the demise of interstate constraints has become a zero sum game with some states winning at the expense of others.

The post–Riegle-Neal effect on banking customers also appeared to vary depending on the type of service under consideration. Large- and medium-sized banks offered automatic teller machines (ATMs) more often than small ones but the latter showed noticeable growth in providing this service. Multistate banks were better represented in ATM networks than were single-state banks. All banks, regardless of size, made ATM access less expensive for customers than noncustomers but overall, larger institutions had lower fees.

Noninterest bearing checking accounts or demand deposits were available nationwide at banks of all sizes. When disaggregated by balance requirements and fees applied to the accounts, however, the accessibility of these accounts varied by bank size. Large banks were more generous in the terms offered than were small- or medium-sized banks. The same was true in the comparison of multistate banks to single-state banks. Extension of free accounts without balances or fees rose among all types of banks, the singularly best news for customers.

Interest bearing transaction accounts or NOW accounts were generally less available at small- and medium- sized banks while gaining some support at larger ones. The distinction between multistate and single-state banks regarding this type of account was nominal.

Virtually all banks offered savings accounts and registered increased offerings in all subcategories with the exception of no-fee statement accounts. No-fee accounts, which were most favorable to customers, were more frequently found in single-state rather than multi-state banks.

Lending rose nationally along with asset size but did not keep up on a proportional basis. A desegregation of loan portfolios showed a substantial nationwide trend to decrease lending to individuals and to increase real estate lending. The latter somewhat nullified the former if the increase in 1–4 unit mortgages is factored into the picture.

Consolidation in the banking industry appeared to have had few negative ramifications for employees. Prognostications of a decrease in employment and compensation levels did not materialize by the end of the century. In fact, the post–Riegle-Neal years from 1996–1999 posted increases in the number of employees and compensation throughout virtually the entire nation, including most states in which there was a reduction in the number of banks.

When the analysis of changes during the post–Riegle-Neal era was brought to the local level through the use of case studies of 4 banks headquartered in the Chicago metropolitan area, several additional findings became apparent. Most noticeable were the continuation of competitive disadvantages facing banks of all sizes located in a state such as Illinois in which intrastate branching had been restrictive; the need to take advantage of the expansion opportunities afforded by Riegle-Neal in order for a bank to claim a leadership position; the importance of developing a market niche for a bank's products; the importance of sound and focused strategy in enabling a bank or bank holding company to capture the benefits of expansion such as a larger customer base without simultaneously incurring downside costs associated with servicing a more sizable and geographically diverse clientele; the ascending importance of customer relationships in creating synergies and efficiencies of scope that add to postexpansion profitability; the difficulty in achieving postexpansion economies of scale despite increased asset size; and finally the underlying importance of fee-based income as a steady source of revenue and a safeguard against the vagaries of interest rate fluctuations.

Glenview State Bank has eschewed the post–Riegle-Neal possibilities for expansion across state lines. It has chosen instead to take modest advantage of the more liberalized intrastate branching regulations now in force in Illinois in order to develop a well-focused business in the Chicago suburbs. To a considerable extent, therefore, the changing world of banking regulation has passed by the Glenview State Bank. Nonetheless the bank continues to perform well and has remained independent. It has been content to remain a relatively small, local bank which maintains a consistent focus on service to its customer base and still earns its bread-and-butter income from traditional lending and deposit taking activities. The Glenview State Bank proves that a well-run, local bank can continue to exist despite the merger and acquisition mania in the American banking system even in the post–Riegle-Neal era.

Like many banks affected by the merger and acquisition movement of the 1990's, Harris Bankcorp lost its independence to a foreign bank in part because of the restrictive interstate banking rules which preceded Riegle-Neal. In purchasing Harris Bankcorp, the Bank of Montreal saw the opportunity to obtain a twofold market foothold in the Chicago area by capitalizing on Harris Trust and Savings Bank's expertise in servicing an elite clientele and by expanding into the suburban communities surrounding Chicago to offer these services to a new set of customers. Under the auspices of the Bank of Montreal, Harris Bankcorp relinquished its national aspirations in favor of a new set of local ones. Through its Vision 2002 plan,

Harris Bankcorp expanded within the Chicago metropolitan area by seeking acquisitions that brought it synergies and the ability to enhance its customer relationships. Harris Bankcorp's presence in the Chicago suburbs supplements and enhances its Chicago base as opposed to the Glenview State Bank that has only a suburban presence. In the post–Riegle-Neal period, Harris Bankcorp proves that geographic growth within one state remains a viable and attractive option, particularly if the branching opportunities within the state had been historically restrictive prior to passage of the law. Vision 2002 also shows the potential advantages to be accrued by a foreign bank seeking to increase its international presence in Chicago and to increase its visibility in the United States.

The Northern Trust Corporation provides the clearest example of the importance of a focused strategy and the centrality of the customer relationship in assisting a bank holding company in taking advantage of Riegle-Neal's interstate banking deregulation in order to expand its asset size and its profitability. To a substantial extent, one can say that The Northern Trust Corporation provides a textbook analysis of how to overcome the restrictions of the past, both interstate and intrastate, in the new banking era. Establishing several synergistic niches, expanding geographically in order to play to these strengths, concentrating on customer service and fee business, and avoiding the temptation to pursue growth in asset size for its own sake have kept The Northern Trust Corporation independent and profitable. In the post–Riegle-Neal era, selective opportunism may be a formula for success.

Finally, Bank One Corporation reveals the inadequacy of a merger and acquisition strategy based solely upon growth in asset size. Profitability remained elusive because of inadequate consideration of cost reductions from economies of scale or through obtaining economies of scope associated with development of customer relationships. Enticed by the new interstate opportunities associated with Riegle-Neal and fearful of falling behind in a world of increasingly larger banks and financial giants, the mergers that created Bank One Corporation provided few synergies. Bank One Corporation proved that big is not necessarily beautiful and that Riegle-Neal's liberalization of interstate regulations is fraught with dangers as well as advantages. In the case of Bank One Corporation, the whole was not even as strong as the sum of the parts.

Proponents and opponents of interstate banking and branching can each find fuel in the results of this study to fan their partisan fires. A dispassionate view, however, reveals that the benefits attributable to the growth in bank size and in the presence of multistate banks because of Riegle-Neal has been largely beneficial to the banking community, its customers, and the nation. The extent to which this was or was not apparent at the level of an individual bank or bank holding company was, in large part, dependent upon their strategic planning and their ability to create economies of scope, as well as economies of scale through expansion of their customer relationships.

Although it is necessary to remain alert and vigilant for potential dangers, there is no need for undue alarm. Deregulation of the banking industry like the deregulations that occurred at an earlier time in other industries, appears to be well on its way to strengthening the economic well-being of the country. Although the trend line is not perfectly straight, it is definitely upward sloping.

Appendix 1: Banks by Asset Size, 1990–1998

\YEAR STATE \	1998	1997	1996	1995	1994	1993	1992	1991	1990
Alabama									
< $25 million	14	16	19	21	27	32	36		49
$25 - $50 million	30	40	52	48	55	61	65		73
$50 - $100 million	48	55	51	62	57	59	57		52
$100 - $300 million	53	49	49	44	52	47	44		32
$300 - $500 million	5	7	5	5	9	9	9		9
.5 - $1 billion	5	3	2	1	2	1	1		1
$1 - $3 billion	0	0	0	0	1	1	1		1
$3 - $10 billion	0	2	2	3	4	4	4		4
$10 billion or more	5	3	3	2	0	0	0		0
Alaska									
< $25 million	0	0	0	0	0	0	0		1
$25 - $50 million	0	0	0	0	1	1	1		1
$50 - $100 million	1	1	1	1	1	1	2		1
$100 - $300 million	2	3	4	4	3	3	2		2
$300 - $500 million	1	0	0	0	0	0	0		0
.5 - $1 billion	0	0	1	1	1	1	1		1
$1 - $3 billion	2	2	2	2	2	2	2		2
$3 - $10 billion	0	0	0	0	0	0	0		0
$10 billion or more	0	0	0	0	0	0	0		0
Arizona									
< $25 million	10	9	4	3	3	4	8		8
$25 - $50 million	5	6	3	7	9	10	7		5
$50 - $100 million	10	7	7	7	6	7	8		11
$100 - $300 million	7	9	11	6	6	6	5		6
$300 - $500 million	2	1	1	2	2	2	2		1
.5 - $1 billion	4	3	2	2	1	1	2		2
$1 - $3 billion	1	2	2	1	3	4	3		1
$3 - $10 billion	3	3	4	5	3	2	2		4
$10 billion or more	1	1	1	1	1	1	1		0
Arkansas									
< $25 million	14	19	21	28	33	35	40		49
$25 - $50 million	44	50	50	56	67	68	72		77
$50 - $100 million	66	74	74	74	82	83	81		77
$100 - $300 million	65	65	69	67	63	59	53		45
$300 - $500 million	7	12	11	13	6	7	8		3
.5 - $1 billion	5	4	5	2	3	3	3		5
$1 - $3 billion	1	2	3	3	3	2	2		0
$3 - $10 billion	0	0	0	0	0	0	0		0
$10 billion or more	0	0	0	0	0	0	0		0

California								
< $25 million	21	19	19	24	29	29	46	58
$25 - $50 million	31	40	50	60	68	77	84	92
$50 - $100 million	81	79	94	105	120	122	130	130
$100 - $300 million	115	116	119	126	119	126	119	130
$300 - $500 million	25	28	34	25	26	29	34	27
.5 - $1 billion	28	28	18	17	20	22	22	25
$1 - $3 billion	24	16	17	17	14	11	10	10
$3 - $10 billion	8	7	6	5	4	5	6	5
$10 billion or more	3	3	3	4	4	4	4	5
Colorado								
< $25 million	34	38	44	52	67	89	117	213
$25 - $50 million	48	60	61	65	87	99	113	111
$50 - $100 million	45	50	52	52	59	63	61	72
$100 - $300 million	51	56	53	50	51	59	48	42
$300 - $500 million	9	5	3	5	7	6	3	4
.5 - $1 billion	5	4	5	2	4	2	3	0
$1 - $3 billion	1	1	2	2	2	3	5	3
$3 - $10 billion	2	2	3	3	2	1	0	1
$10 billion or more	0	0	0	0	0	0	0	0
Connecticut								
< $25 million	4	0	0	0	2	2	2	8
$25 - $50 million	1	1	1	5	5	5	4	11
$50 - $100 million	5	9	9	11	13	16	17	20
$100 - $300 million	14	13	13	17	17	17	17	19
$300 - $500 million	2	2	3	1	0	0	2	3
.5 - $1 billion	1	0	0	2	2	2	1	1
$1 - $3 billion	1	1	1	1	1	2	3	3
$3 - $10 billion	0	0	1	1	2	1	1	2
$10 billion or more	0	0	0	1	1	1	1	1
Delaware								
< $25 million	2	2	2	2	3	2	2	6
$25 - $50 million	2	2	2	3	4	3	4	2
$50 - $100 million	5	3	3	3	3	2	5	5
$100 - $300 million	5	5	6	5	4	5	4	6
$300 - $500 million	2	5	6	5	3	3	4	5
.5 - $1 billion	1	1	4	3	5	4	3	5
$1 - $3 billion	8	6	7	8	5	6	7	9
$3 - $10 billion	5	6	6	7	9	10	9	8
$10 billion or more	4	4	3	4	2	1	1	1

Florida								
< $25 million	16	17	17	15	22	24	43	84
$25 - $50 million	42	44	53	74	91	110	118	117
$50 - $100 million	74	84	90	96	96	98	100	83
$100 - $300 million	74	81	82	79	77	75	76	84
$300 - $500 million	16	8	12	16	19	19	23	20
.5 - $1 billion	5	13	16	28	26	25	27	23
$1 - $3 billion	18	15	13	15	15	15	15	12
$3 - $10 billion	5	3	4	9	8	7	3	4
$10 billion or more	0	1	2	1	2	2	2	3
Georgia								
< $25 million	31	30	28	33	40	53	70	87
$25 - $50 million	62	73	86	99	120	125	134	141
$50 - $100 million	115	121	118	132	122	127	116	102
$100 - $300 million	110	100	92	95	80	72	61	58
$300 - $500 million	14	12	15	8	12	11	10	8
.5 - $1 billion	12	11	6	7	3	2	3	5
$1 - $3 billion	2	3	2	2	3	4	4	3
$3 - $10 billion	2	2	3	3	3	2	3	4
$10 billion or more	1	1	4	4	3	3	2	1
Hawaii								
< $25 million	4	3	3	4	4	4	4	7
$25 - $50 million	1	2	2	2	2	2	2	2
$50 - $100 million	1	2	2	1	1	2	1	1
$100 - $300 million	0	1	1	2	2	0	1	3
$300 - $500 million	2	2	2	2	2	4	4	2
.5 - $1 billion	1	1	1	1	1	1	2	3
$1 - $3 billion	1	1	1	1	2	2	1	1
$3 - $10 billion	1	1	1	1	1	1	1	2
$10 billion or more	1	1	1	1	1	1	1	0
Idaho								
< $25 million	1	4	2	1	2	4	3	4
$25 - $50 million	5	2	1	2	4	3	4	5
$50 - $100 million	3	5	5	4	4	6	5	6
$100 - $300 million	7	4	5	6	4	3	3	3
$300 - $500 million	1	1	0	1	1	1	1	0
.5 - $1 billion	0	0	0	0	1	1	1	2
$1 - $3 billion	0	0	1	2	1	1	2	1
$3 - $10 billion	0	0	1	2	2	2	1	1
$10 billion or more	0	0	0	0	0	0	0	0

Illinois								
< $25 million	122	141	146	164	183	207	240	286
$25 - $50 million	155	178	193	207	217	234	233	255
$50 - $100 million	183	183	196	202	215	222	230	237
$100 - $300 million	200	196	213	207	216	217	224	234
$300 - $500 million	35	33	32	33	36	33	39	43
.5 - $1 billion	26	32	33	30	20	27	26	24
$1 - $3 billion	14	10	12	13	10	11	7	2
$3 - $10 billion	4	6	3	3	4	3	4	3
$10 billion or more	6	5	5	5	5	4	3	3
Indiana								
< $25 million	7	12	12	12	17	21	21	34
$25 - $50 million	27	28	37	42	48	47	53	55
$50 - $100 million	42	45	47	53	61	72	79	90
$100 - $300 million	58	63	67	60	55	59	80	86
$300 - $500 million	13	14	15	18	20	17	16	15
.5 - $1 billion	12	13	14	14	10	11	10	10
$1 - $3 billion	7	7	9	8	7	7	8	8
$3 - $10 billion	2	3	3	3	4	3	3	3
$10 billion or more	1	0	0	1	0	0	0	0
Iowa								
< $25 million	77	100	117	128	146	154	173	207
$25 - $50 million	157	159	156	172	173	178	179	186
$50 - $100 million	129	117	120	120	117	123	117	109
$100 - $300 million	65	60	56	54	65	60	57	49
$300 - $500 million	6	6	9	11	12	13	11	6
.5 - $1 billion	5	6	5	3	3	1	3	3
$1 - $3 billion	1	4	3	2	0	0	1	1
$3 - $10 billion	3	1	1	1	1	1	1	1
$10 billion or more	0	0	0	0	0	0	0	0
Kansas								
< $25 million	131	146	157	176	197	211	226	266
$25 - $50 million	107	104	108	112	119	129	135	137
$50 - $100 million	88	94	94	86	89	99	95	97
$100 - $300 million	50	42	44	47	42	41	41	44
$300 - $500 million	10	11	7	7	6	6	8	4
.5 - $1 billion	4	4	4	3	3	2	2	6
$1 - $3 billion	2	1	2	1	1	1	0	1
$3 - $10 billion	1	1	0	1	1	1	1	0
$10 billion or more	0	0	0	0	0	0	0	0

Kentucky								
< $25 million	11	17	19	26	30	41	44	53
$25 - $50 million	58	66	66	61	68	72	78	89
$50 - $100 million	93	95	103	100	106	114	108	106
$100 - $300 million	82	77	71	71	63	64	63	68
$300 - $500 million	5	4	3	3	6	8	9	11
.5 - $1 billion	4	3	4	7	8	5	4	1
$1 - $3 billion	6	7	6	5	3	2	2	2
$3 - $10 billion	1	2	3	3	3	3	3	2
$10 billion or more	1	0	0	0	0	0	0	0
Louisiana								
< $25 million	13	9	10	14	19	20	22	28
$25 - $50 million	33	40	46	51	58	59	59	71
$50 - $100 million	53	50	56	56	58	69	73	74
$100 - $300 million	42	44	44	49	50	52	50	42
$300 - $500 million	4	2	2	0	2	6	7	7
.5 - $1 billion	0	8	7	8	7	6	5	4
$1 - $3 billion	2	1	3	3	3	2	2	3
$3 - $10 billion	1	3	4	4	3	3	3	2
$10 billion or more	2	1	0	0	0	0	0	0
Maine								
< $25 million	0	0	1	1	1	1	1	2
$25 - $50 million	1	1	3	3	2	2	4	5
$50 - $100 million	4	5	4	4	5	7	7	4
$100 - $300 million	9	8	7	7	8	6	5	5
$300 - $500 million	1	2	3	3	1	1	1	1
.5 - $1 billion	1	0	0	0	0	0	0	0
$1 - $3 billion	1	1	1	1	2	3	2	4
$3 - $10 billion	0	0	1	1	1	0	1	0
$10 billion or more	0	0	0	0	0	0	0	0
Maryland								
< $25 million	0	0	1	0	3	4	5	11
$25 - $50 million	4	5	9	10	10	10	12	15
$50 - $100 million	16	22	22	24	26	26	24	22
$100 - $300 million	40	40	40	38	32	33	32	33
$300 - $500 million	8	4	4	5	8	7	7	9
.5 - $1 billion	6	8	9	7	5	5	5	2
$1 - $3 billion	4	2	2	4	4	5	7	5
$3 - $10 billion	1	1	3	2	3	3	3	5
$10 billion or more	1	1	0	1	2	1	1	1

Massachusetts								
< $25 million	2	3	2	2	4	4	2	4
$25 - $50 million	5	4	5	5	6	9	9	10
$50 - $100 million	6	7	6	9	10	11	13	18
$100 - $300 million	11	13	22	22	20	21	21	27
$300 - $500 million	10	9	3	2	2	3	3	7
.5 - $1 billion	1	3	4	3	3	5	5	7
$1 - $3 billion	5	3	3	2	2	2	2	6
$3 - $10 billion	2	2	1	1	3	3	3	2
$10 billion or more	2	2	4	5	3	3	3	4
Michigan								
< $25 million	5	6	5	5	8	8	12	15
$25 - $50 million	28	32	31	34	35	45	46	50
$50 - $100 million	43	51	55	59	66	58	63	68
$100 - $300 million	68	54	62	59	60	62	65	66
$300 - $500 million	8	7	9	9	14	14	13	17
.5 - $1 billion	4	4	5	5	6	7	7	8
$1 - $3 billion	3	3	3	4	6	9	8	6
$3 - $10 billion	2	2	2	2	2	3	3	3
$10 billion or more	4	4	4	3	3	2	2	2
Minnesota								
< $25 million	135	144	165	174	215	222	242	286
$25 - $50 million	158	170	162	175	169	172	167	169
$50 - $100 million	114	112	105	100	106	104	110	110
$100 - $300 million	87	77	72	62	58	61	57	45
$300 - $500 million	9	7	8	6	9	9	10	10
.5 - $1 billion	4	5	3	4	3	2	3	3
$1 - $3 billion	4	2	1	2	1	1	2	1
$3 - $10 billion	1	1	1	0	0	0	0	0
$10 billion or more	2	2	2	2	2	2	2	2
Mississippi								
< $25 million	10	10	11	10	12	13	13	19
$25 - $50 million	14	12	16	17	20	25	28	25
$50 - $100 million	21	31	32	32	36	39	38	44
$100 - $300 million	39	40	38	37	31	30	31	27
$300 - $500 million	5	2	4	6	6	5	5	2
.5 - $1 billion	3	7	6	4	1	1	1	1
$1 - $3 billion	2	2	2	2	3	3	3	3
$3 - $10 billion	2	3	2	2	2	2	2	2
$10 billion or more	0	0	0	0	0	0	0	0

Missouri

< $25 million	59	79	88	98	108	119	140	176
$25 - $50 million	107	116	127	130	144	147	149	159
$50 - $100 million	111	110	111	125	122	130	125	120
$100 - $300 million	78	72	70	73	66	62	67	59
$300 - $500 million	12	12	14	14	14	15	12	15
.5 - $1 billion	8	6	9	8	10	8	8	7
$1 - $3 billion	3	6	4	6	5	5	5	6
$3 - $10 billion	3	3	6	4	3	3	4	1
$10 billion or more	1	0	1	1	1	1	0	1

Montana

< $25 million	22	30	31	35	36	43	50	81
$25 - $50 million	33	34	35	37	40	37	36	39
$50 - $100 million	18	18	19	20	21	24	21	25
$100 - $300 million	11	10	12	9	12	9	9	10
$300 - $500 million	2	1	0	0	1	2	2	0
.5 - $1 billion	0	0	0	1	1	1	1	0
$1 - $3 billion	3	3	3	2	1	1	1	1
$3 - $10 billion	0	0	0	0	0	0	0	0
$10 billion or more	0	0	0	0	0	0	0	0

Nebraska

< $25 million	114	131	144	152	164	172	188	210
$25 - $50 million	90	87	83	84	86	96	93	101
$50 - $100 million	60	61	61	56	62	61	62	53
$100 - $300 million	39	37	31	32	32	23	23	21
$300 - $500 million	6	6	5	5	3	4	3	2
.5 - $1 billion	3	1	1	2	1	1	1	1
$1 - $3 billion	2	2	2	4	4	4	4	4
$3 - $10 billion	1	1	2	1	0	0	0	0
$10 billion or more	0	0	0	0	0	0	0	0

Nevada

< $25 million	2	1	3	2	2	2	1	5
$25 - $50 million	6	4	6	7	6	5	7	5
$50 - $100 million	2	6	4	4	3	4	2	0
$100 - $300 million	6	5	3	3	3	3	3	3
$300 - $500 million	1	0	2	3	3	2	1	1
.5 - $1 billion	0	3	2	1	1	1	1	2
$1 - $3 billion	7	3	3	1	1	1	0	1
$3 - $10 billion	2	3	2	4	3	3	3	2
$10 billion or more	0	0	1	0	0	0	0	0

New Hampshire								
< $25 million	0	1	0	1	1	1	1	2
$25 - $50 million	3	3	6	4	5	5	6	9
$50 - $100 million	5	4	2	5	5	5	5	11
$100 - $300 million	6	7	6	7	7	9	11	16
$300 - $500 million	1	0	1	1	2	3	2	2
.5 - $1 billion	1	3	1	2	2	1	1	3
$1 - $3 billion	1	2	4	2	2	2	2	2
$3 - $10 billion	2	1	0	1	0	0	0	0
$10 billion or more	0	0	0	0	0	0	0	0
New Jersey								
< $25 million	5	5	0	1	3	3	2	10
$25 - $50 million	5	1	1	2	2	5	11	22
$50 - $100 million	3	10	11	17	23	27	24	26
$100 - $300 million	28	30	30	30	33	32	35	37
$300 - $500 million	14	10	12	14	9	10	8	5
.5 - $1 billion	5	4	3	2	3	2	5	8
$1 - $3 billion	6	8	6	9	8	10	11	16
$3 - $10 billion	4	1	1	4	5	8	7	6
$10 billion or more	2	2	2	3	3	2	2	1
New Mexico								
< $25 million	5	5	3	4	5	6	9	11
$25 - $50 million	10	11	14	14	14	17	19	20
$50 - $100 million	15	15	19	18	22	27	24	31
$100 - $300 million	19	20	23	24	21	24	26	23
$300 - $500 million	4	4	4	2	2	3	2	4
.5 - $1 billion	2	1	3	3	2	1	2	0
$1 - $3 billion	2	2	3	3	4	3	2	2
$3 - $10 billion	1	0	0	0	0	0	0	0
$10 billion or more	0	0	0	0	0	0	0	0
New York								
< $25 million	7	7	6	8	9	13	12	20
$25 - $50 million	9	10	14	14	17	18	22	23
$50 - $100 million	26	28	29	30	33	35	31	39
$100 - $300 million	54	47	49	49	42	42	48	41
$300 - $500 million	11	13	14	16	18	21	18	21
.5 - $1 billion	17	18	17	16	17	14	14	15
$1 - $3 billion	12	14	12	14	12	13	13	10
$3 - $10 billion	7	7	8	8	8	9	9	14
$10 billion or more	10	9	10	11	11	10	10	10

North Carolina								
< $25 million	10	8	4	3	3	3	7	11
$25 - $50 million	4	3	5	4	11	13	19	14
$50 - $100 million	11	10	7	13	15	18	20	21
$100 - $300 million	19	16	19	23	20	20	19	18
$300 - $500 million	9	9	8	7	8	8	4	5
.5 - $1 billion	5	6	4	3	2	0	0	0
$1 - $3 billion	2	1	1	0	0	2	3	4
$3 - $10 billion	3	3	4	4	6	4	3	2
$10 billion or more	4	4	4	4	3	3	3	3
North Dakota								
< $25 million	34	38	41	48	53	53	56	64
$25 - $50 million	39	41	45	49	50	53	54	58
$50 - $100 million	22	20	20	17	24	22	21	16
$100 - $300 million	10	11	12	8	8	9	9	10
$300 - $500 million	5	4	3	4	2	2	1	0
.5 - $1 billion	2	2	1	0	1	1	1	1
$1 - $3 billion	2	1	1	1	1	1	1	1
$3 - $10 billion	0	0	0	0	0	0	0	0
$10 billion or more	0	0	0	0	0	0	0	0
Ohio								
< $25 million	24	28	29	31	33	35	39	52
$25 - $50 million	34	41	53	55	54	56	55	56
$50 - $100 million	60	59	51	54	55	62	61	61
$100 - $300 million	52	54	62	60	62	58	64	66
$300 - $500 million	15	17	18	22	19	19	19	22
.5 - $1 billion	14	15	20	12	15	12	11	8
$1 - $3 billion	9	10	13	15	9	12	12	13
$3 - $10 billion	6	6	7	8	9	7	7	10
$10 billion or more	6	5	4	3	2	2	2	0
Oklahoma								
< $25 million	70	83	94	100	111	122	129	155
$25 - $50 million	90	86	90	93	97	110	115	122
$50 - $100 million	80	89	88	93	87	89	93	94
$100 - $300 million	54	48	44	42	42	38	45	38
$300 - $500 million	8	9	8	5	4	5	4	4
.5 - $1 billion	3	2	3	3	5	3	3	4
$1 - $3 billion	2	1	3	5	3	4	4	2
$3 - $10 billion	2	2	2	1	1	0	0	0
$10 billion or more	0	0	0	0	0	0	0	0

Oregon								
< $25 million	5	4	7	6	6	9	12	16
$25 - $50 million	7	8	9	8	9	6	8	10
$50 - $100 million	10	9	7	6	8	10	10	9
$100 - $300 million	16	16	15	15	14	13	11	9
$300 - $500 million	2	3	2	2	1	1	1	2
.5 - $1 billion	1	1	1	2	2	2	2	0
$1 - $3 billion	1	0	0	1	1	2	1	2
$3 - $10 billion	0	0	1	2	2	1	2	1
$10 billion or more	0	0	1	1	1	1	1	1
Pennsylvania								
< $25 million	5	6	6	6	6	6	12	25
$25 - $50 million	16	18	18	23	29	35	37	36
$50 - $100 million	23	29	37	48	53	53	59	65
$100 - $300 million	89	94	97	95	107	110	111	107
$300 - $500 million	31	29	27	20	18	22	20	21
.5 - $1 billion	15	15	12	13	14	16	17	20
$1 - $3 billion	13	15	14	12	10	9	15	18
$3 - $10 billion	2	1	1	2	4	6	6	4
$10 billion or more	3	5	5	5	4	4	4	4
Rhode Island								
< $25 million	0	1	0	0	2	2	3	1
$25 - $50 million	0	1	2	2	0	0	1	1
$50 - $100 million	1	0	0	0	2	2	2	2
$100 - $300 million	1	1	2	2	1	2	2	2
$300 - $500 million	0	0	1	0	0	1	1	2
.5 - $1 billion	2	2	1	1	1	0	1	1
$1 - $3 billion	0	1	1	1	1	1	0	1
$3 - $10 billion	2	2	1	1	1	2	2	1
$10 billion or more	1	1	0	1	1	0	0	0
South Carolina								
< $25 million	10	10	12	11	10	10	11	17
$25 - $50 million	17	18	17	14	17	18	22	27
$50 - $100 million	21	17	21	22	25	28	27	24
$100 - $300 million	21	27	17	12	10	12	11	7
$300 - $500 million	1	1	6	6	4	2	3	4
.5 - $1 billion	2	3	0	0	3	3	3	1
$1 - $3 billion	4	3	3	3	4	3	2	2
$3 - $10 billion	1	1	3	3	2	2	2	3
$10 billion or more	0	0	0	0	0	0	0	0

South Dakota								
< $25 million	26	35	44	44	46	49	48	57
$25 - $50 million	29	27	23	27	28	29	33	33
$50 - $100 million	22	20	23	18	21	20	18	15
$100 - $300 million	15	13	19	20	16	18	18	16
$300 - $500 million	5	5	4	3	6	2	1	1
.5 - $1 billion	5	2	0	0	0	0	1	1
$1 - $3 billion	0	2	2	2	1	2	1	1
$3 - $10 billion	1	1	1	1	1	1	1	0
$10 billion or more	1	1	1	1	1	0	0	1
Tennessee								
< $25 million	10	15	14	21	29	27	31	43
$25 - $50 million	41	49	56	52	57	68	72	80
$50 - $100 million	58	67	63	69	74	73	76	68
$100 - $300 million	72	75	76	75	72	65	59	49
$300 - $500 million	11	13	12	9	6	6	3	2
.5 - $1 billion	5	4	5	4	3	2	2	3
$1 - $3 billion	2	3	6	6	6	4	3	5
$3 - $10 billion	2	4	5	3	3	5	5	3
$10 billion or more	3	2	1	1	1	0	0	0
Texas								
< $25 million	109	129	147	171	197	219	254	332
$25 - $50 million	208	221	232	258	290	299	329	359
$50 - $100 million	231	239	262	270	258	263	265	267
$100 - $300 million	189	186	175	187	190	188	189	176
$300 - $500 million	26	25	31	21	20	19	23	22
.5 - $1 billion	19	21	13	13	10	11	15	13
$1 - $3 billion	9	8	9	8	8	5	7	9
$3 - $10 billion	6	7	5	4	4	4	4	4
$10 billion or more	2	3	3	3	3	3	3	2
Utah								
< $25 million	7	9	9	8	9	11	15	17
$25 - $50 million	11	9	9	8	10	11	11	8
$50 - $100 million	9	10	11	11	7	8	11	15
$100 - $300 million	12	14	10	10	10	11	10	7
$300 - $500 million	4	1	1	1	1	1	1	1
.5 - $1 billion	2	1	2	3	4	3	3	4
$1 - $3 billion	2	2	3	2	1	1	1	1
$3 - $10 billion	1	1	1	2	2	2	2	2
$10 billion or more	2	2	2	0	0	0	0	0

Vermont								
< $25 million	1	1	1	1	2	2	2	3
$25 - $50 million	1	1	2	1	0	0	0	1
$50 - $100 million	4	5	5	5	6	5	6	6
$100 - $300 million	9	8	9	8	7	8	8	12
$300 - $500 million	1	1	0	0	0	0	0	0
.5 - $1 billion	3	3	3	3	4	4	4	4
$1 - $3 billion	2	2	2	2	1	1	1	1
$3 - $10 billion	0	0	0	0	0	0	0	0
$10 billion or more	0	0	0	0	0	0	0	0
Virginia								
< $25 million	7	4	5	7	8	8	16	27
$25 - $50 million	12	17	19	20	24	22	31	35
$50 - $100 million	31	35	36	45	55	62	57	62
$100 - $300 million	76	69	70	60	56	54	49	36
$300 - $500 million	11	11	10	12	9	8	7	8
.5 - $1 billion	8	8	6	6	4	4	2	2
$1 - $3 billion	2	2	1	1	2	1	2	2
$3 - $10 billion	4	3	3	2	4	4	4	4
$10 billion or more	1	2	4	4	2	2	2	2
Washington								
< $25 million	14	17	16	16	14	15	23	31
$25 - $50 million	14	14	15	17	19	22	21	22
$50 - $100 million	17	16	22	25	26	24	25	16
$100 - $300 million	22	25	20	16	16	17	15	16
$300 - $500 million	7	5	5	6	4	2	3	2
.5 - $1 billion	1	2	2	1	1	2	1	1
$1 - $3 billion	3	1	1	2	2	1	2	2
$3 - $10 billion	0	0	2	3	3	3	3	3
$10 billion or more	0	0	1	1	1	1	1	1
West Virginia								
< $25 million	5	7	12	11	8	11	18	29
$25 - $50 million	12	20	20	21	24	31	37	51
$50 - $100 million	26	25	33	40	45	54	56	55
$100 - $300 million	26	31	30	30	34	39	40	35
$300 - $500 million	11	9	11	10	7	8	9	7
.5 - $1 billion	3	4	3	2	0	2	2	2
$1 - $3 billion	5	4	4	4	4	3	2	1
$3 - $10 billion	1	0	0	0	0	0	0	0
$10 billion or more	0	0	0	0	0	0	0	0

Wisconsin									
< $25 million	33	52	57	63	70	79	85		115
$25 - $50 million	76	84	94	96	109	122	121		125
$50 - $100 million	110	108	103	111	110	121	129		123
$100 - $300 million	85	84	81	83	78	86	83		89
$300 - $500 million	18	15	17	19	18	16	16		12
.5 - $1 billion	11	11	5	7	6	7	6		5
$1 - $3 billion	7	3	4	5	5	3	3		3
$3 - $10 billion	4	4	4	3	3	2	2		1
$10 billion or more	0	0	0	0	0	0	0		0
Wyoming									
< $25 million	9	10	11	12	15	15	18		27
$25 - $50 million	14	12	15	15	15	15	21		17
$50 - $100 million	14	17	13	13	10	12	11		12
$100 - $300 million	11	9	11	9	10	9	10		14
$300 - $500 million	1	1	2	2	1	3	2		1
.5 - $1 billion	1	1	0	0	0	0	0		0
$1 - $3 billion	1	2	2	1	2	1	1		0
$3 - $10 billion	1	0	0	1	0	0	0		0
$10 billion or more	0	0	0	0	0	0	0		0
Total 50 States									
< $25 million	1257	1461	1589	1755	2017	2219	2554	0	3322
$25 - $50 million	1906	2055	2203	2365	2595	2786	2941	0	3137
$50 - $100 million	2236	2329	2404	2528	2631	2769	2781	0	2775
$100 - $300 million	2274	2225	2233	2196	2147	2139	2134	0	2073
$300 - $500 million	417	388	409	390	389	398	395	0	380
.5 - $1 billion	275	300	271	262	250	238	247	0	248
$1 - $3 billion	212	193	205	213	192	194	198	0	198
$3 - $10 billion	102	102	114	124	129	126	123	0	119
$10 billion or more	70	65	72	74	63	54	51	0	49

Source: Statistics on Banking, 1998, pp. B-26–B33; 1997, pp. B–26–B–33; Historical 1934–1996.

Appendix 2: Aggregate Condition and Income Data

		1999	1998	1997	1996	Change	% Change
Alabama						1996-1999	1996-1999
Net Income		1,951	1,508	1,118	772	1,179	152.72
Total Assets		177,790	140,861	101,184	63,221	114,569	181.22
Total Deposits		122,527	101,765	72,695	45,477	77,050	189.43
Equity Capital		13,484	11,200	8,293	4,995	8,489	169.95
Alaska							
Net Income		89	89	84	87	2	2.30
Total Assets		5,431	5,147	4,848	5,816	-385	-6.62
Total Deposits		3,953	3,801	3,521	4,202	-249	-5.93
Equity Capital		741	719	685	754	-13	-1.72
Arizona							
Net Income		1,308	783	581	514	794	154.47
Total Assets		47,701	42,261	39,330	48,052	-351	-0.73
Total Deposits		25,897	25,122	22,837	28,221	-2,324	-8.24
Equity Capital		3,972	4,009	3,801	4,316	-344	-7.97
Arkansas							
Net Income		285	285	352	385	-100	-25.97
Total Assets		26,726	25,128	28,734	30,721	-3,995	-13.00
Total Deposits		22,467	21,503	24,703	26,539	-4,072	-15.34
Equity Capital		2,507	2,422	2,738	2,876	-369	-12.83
California							
Net Income		3,177	3,784	5,696	3,939	-762	-19.35
Total Assets		286,752	515,898	474,812	417,224	-130,472	-31.27
Total Deposits		226,292	398,768	361,470	321,516	-95,224	-29.62
Equity Capital		31,382	46,785	45,924	38,863	-7,481	-19.25
Colorado							
Net Income		625	428	422	553	72	13.02
Total Assets		41,618	36,142	33,875	41,012	606	1.48
Total Deposits		33,813	31,263	29,228	34,319	-506	-1.47
Equity Capital		3,082	2,794	2,626	3,211	-129	-4.02
Connecticut							
Net Income		39	60	57	97	-58	-59.79
Total Assets		3,156	6,494	4,772	10,881	-7,725	-71.00
Total Deposits		2,539	5,053	4,020	8,639	-6,100	-70.61
Equity Capital		312	572	442	1,010	-698	-69.11
Delaware							
Net Income		3,682	3,936	2,562	2,207	1,475	66.83
Total Assets		133,239	131,312	127,880	115,166	18,073	15.69
Total Deposits		64,302	54,162	50,819	40,148	24,154	60.16
Equity Capital		15,948	17,083	14,464	12,360	3,588	29.03

Florida						
Net Income	1,070	868	1,334	2,003	-933	-46.58
Total Assets	86,271	81,210	116,932	160,708	-74,437	-46.32
Total Deposits	64,931	62,468	92,117	130,468	-65,537	-50.23
Equity Capital	7,740	6,987	10,300	13,604	-5,864	-43.10
Georgia						
Net Income	1,419	1,122	898	1,552	-133	-8.57
Total Assets	86,238	76,668	69,244	147,075	-60,837	-41.36
Total Deposits	50,830	47,333	46,937	101,591	-50,761	-49.97
Equity Capital	12,464	11,750	8,866	14,987	-2,523	-16.83
Hawaii						
Net Income	234	196	230	217	17	7.83
Total Assets	23,568	24,154	22,891	22,066	1,502	6.81
Total Deposits	16,803	16,603	15,682	15,159	1,644	10.85
Equity Capital	2,081	2,023	1,983	1,823	258	14.15
Idaho						
Net Income	23	21	15	87	-64	-73.56
Total Assets	2,114	1,810	1,427	6,657	-4,543	-68.24
Total Deposits	1,781	1,564	1,230	5,372	-3,591	-66.85
Equity Capital	215	191	150	474	-259	-54.64
Illinois						
Net Income	3,000	2,886	2,678	2,311	689	29.81
Total Assets	328,732	297,301	265,400	247,069	81,663	33.05
Total Deposits	228,409	207,588	194,798	181,330	47,079	25.96
Equity Capital	24,504	23,409	22,071	21,649	2,855	13.19
Indiana						
Net Income	1,006	923	845	902	104	11.53
Total Assets	65,038	73,367	66,523	66,537	-1,499	-2.25
Total Deposits	45,342	54,531	50,893	52,056	-6,714	-12.90
Equity Capital	5,999	6,478	5,509	5,871	128	2.18
Iowa						
Net Income	484	504	580	527	-43	-8.16
Total Assets	44,897	46,594	43,307	42,514	2,383	5.61
Total Deposits	35,820	37,961	35,951	35,033	787	2.25
Equity Capital	3,877	4,135	4,082	3,928	-51	-1.30
Kansas						
Net Income	414	394	357	298	116	38.93
Total Assets	34,761	34,013	31,317	28,607	6,154	21.51
Total Deposits	29,025	28,871	26,704	24,514	4,511	18.40
Equity Capital	3,335	3,277	3,005	2,831	504	17.80

Kentucky							
Net Income		645	639	616	636	9	1.42
Total Assets		51,439	52,310	50,998	52,685	-1,246	-2.36
Total Deposits		37,174	39,922	38,247	39,768	-2,594	-6.52
Equity Capital		4,155	4,458	4,246	4,455	-300	-6.73
Louisiana							
Net Income		548	554	527	568	-20	-3.52
Total Assets		50,781	48,963	46,726	46,966	3,815	8.12
Total Deposits		40,536	39,539	37,592	38,249	2,287	5.98
Equity Capital		4,539	4,384	4,427	4,476	63	1.41
Maine							
Net Income		57	86	63	111	-54	-48.65
Total Assets		5,118	5,001	4,921	9,024	-3,906	-43.28
Total Deposits		3,838	4,035	3,720	6,458	-2,620	-40.57
Equity Capital		398	410	417	812	-414	-50.99
Maryland							
Net Income		581	494	417	403	178	44.17
Total Assets		45,387	44,591	35,220	38,913	6,474	16.64
Total Deposits		34,433	33,538	26,927	30,229	4,204	13.91
Equity Capital		3,893	3,930	3,131	3,619	274	7.57
Massachusetts							
Net Income		1,586	1,566	1,477	1,843	-257	-13.94
Total Assets		169,672	137,540	123,437	153,975	15,697	10.19
Total Deposits		115,603	94,513	84,177	106,623	8,980	8.42
Equity Capital		11,371	9,587	8,374	11,965	-594	-4.96
Michigan							
Net Income		1,908	1,667	1,642	1,542	366	23.74
Total Assets		123,307	117,213	118,829	112,182	11,125	9.92
Total Deposits		88,053	87,006	85,307	84,170	3,883	4.61
Equity Capital		10,966	10,402	10,861	10,255	711	6.93
Minnesota							
Net Income		2,404	2,185	1,925	989	1,415	143.07
Total Assets		157,439	147,791	131,877	72,124	85,315	118.29
Total Deposits		105,583	103,667	97,921	53,852	51,731	96.06
Equity Capital		13,692	12,166	11,644	6,002	7,690	128.12
Mississippi							
Net Income		363	326	440	391	-28	-7.16
Total Assets		29,515	26,897	34,363	28,522	993	3.48
Total Deposits		22,801	21,580	27,849	23,391	-590	-2.52
Equity Capital		2,810	2,632	3,409	2,761	49	1.77

Missouri						
Net Income		968	1,030	760	1,190	-222	-18.66
Total Assets		80,378	79,579	63,418	88,301	-7,923	-8.97
Total Deposits		61,749	61,963	53,518	70,564	-8,815	-12.49
Equity Capital		6,770	6,761	5,575	7,122	-352	-4.94
Montana						
Net Income		145	138	134	114	31	27.19
Total Assets		10,138	9,882	9,029	8,670	1,468	16.93
Total Deposits		8,176	8,176	7,481	7,293	883	12.11
Equity Capital		932	910	814	760	172	22.63
Nebraska						
Net Income		355	329	308	308	47	15.26
Total Assets		28,525	27,968	25,855	27,764	761	2.74
Total Deposits		23,002	23,041	21,606	23,259	-257	-1.10
Equity Capital		2,370	2,355	2,227	2,660	-290	-10.90
Nevada						
Net Income		1,020	753	601	775	245	31.61
Total Assets		32,218	27,647	25,889	32,406	-188	-0.58
Total Deposits		11,445	8,911	8,141	9,725	1,720	17.69
Equity Capital		4,313	3,650	4,038	3,709	604	16.28
New Hampshire						
Net Income		733	443	284	223	510	228.70
Total Assets		22,046	16,073	11,687	10,724	11,322	105.58
Total Deposits		15,462	11,137	8,534	8,997	6,465	71.86
Equity Capital		1,849	1,406	1,324	994	855	86.02
New Jersey						
Net Income		1,290	1,126	916	655	635	96.95
Total Assets		107,882	96,871	79,904	70,031	37,851	54.05
Total Deposits		82,346	74,218	62,418	59,273	23,073	38.93
Equity Capital		8,145	7,850	6,517	5,946	2,199	36.98
New Mexico						
Net Income		176	153	139	199	-23	-11.56
Total Assets		15,955	15,272	11,307	15416	539	3.50
Total Deposits		11,131	11,540	9,003	11,928	-797	-6.68
Equity Capital		1,411	1,367	895	1,222	189	15.47
New York						
Net Income		11,056	7,757	9,455	9,114	1,942	21.31
Total Assets		1,170,273	1,143,650	1,119,205	1,032,230	138,043	13.37
Total Deposits		729,819	677,482	630,699	602,522	127,297	21.13
Equity Capital		83,503	78,651	70,912	66,652	16,851	25.28

North Carolina						
Net Income		11,382	8,271	4,660	1,943	9,439	485.80
Total Assets		936,936	665,882	433,297	191,522	745,414	389.21
Total Deposits		603,990	414,596	271,030	121,450	482,540	397.32
Equity Capital		76,828	58,108	36,162	13,674	63,154	461.85
North Dakota						
Net Income		178	151	102	100	78	78.00
Total Assets		11,578	10,834	8,938	8,544	3,034	35.51
Total Deposits		8,401	8,122	7,559	7,280	1,121	15.40
Equity Capital		1,077	1,021	786	742	335	45.15
Ohio						
Net Income		4,286	3,475	3,358	2,307	1,979	85.78
Total Assets		309,282	267,385	230,595	172,673	136,609	79.11
Total Deposits		187,008	170,449	154,420	117,027	69,981	59.80
Equity Capital		24,742	22,059	18,324	12,782	11,960	93.57
Oklahoma						
Net Income		418	381	368	370	48	12.97
Total Assets		39,628	35,637	34,071	36,134	3,494	9.67
Total Deposits		31,038	28,706	27,993	30,058	980	3.26
Equity Capital		3,602	3,478	3,317	3,380	222	6.57
Oregon						
Net Income		102	126	98	360	-258	-71.67
Total Assets		7,156	6,294	5,778	22,244	-15,088	-67.83
Total Deposits		5,742	5,329	4,749	16,125	-10,383	-64.39
Equity Capital		729	682	650	1,852	-1,123	-60.64
Pennsylvania						
Net Income		2,567	2,758	3,689	3,101	-534	-17.22
Total Assets		195,331	198,352	267,581	143,683	51,648	35.95
Total Deposits		135,345	137,003	194,850	184,271	-48,926	-26.55
Equity Capital		16,550	17,743	23,039	20,322	-3,772	-18.56
Rhode Island						
Net Income		1,276	1,255	1,115	83	1,193	1437.35
Total Assets		102,991	90,523	77,287	6,451	96,540	1496.51
Total Deposits		50,596	56,593	54,764	4,959	45,637	920.29
Equity Capital		9,456	8,951	6,765	551	8,905	1616.15
South Carolina						
Net Income		266	246	209	330	-64	-19.39
Total Assets		20,761	18,974	17,476	26,353	-5,592	-21.22
Total Deposits		16,312	15,606	14,505	21,277	-4,965	-23.34
Equity Capital		1,854	1,826	1,589	2,204	-350	-15.88

South Dakota							
Net Income		792	722	610	682	110	16.13
Total Assets		31,992	29,754	30,333	29,333	2,659	9.06
Total Deposits		11,996	11,660	11,787	13,207	-1,211	-9.17
Equity Capital		3,379	3,119	3,051	2,685	694	25.85
Tennessee							
Net Income		1,201	1,248	1,064	962	239	24.84
Total Assets		90,424	102,557	75,068	75,930	14,494	19.09
Total Deposits		64,832	76,454	56,297	57,185	7,647	13.37
Equity Capital		7,654	8,919	6,815	6,461	1,193	18.46
Texas							
Net Income		2,059	1,900	2,641	2,447	-388	-15.86
Total Assets		181,163	179,695	235,098	205,184	-24,021	-11.71
Total Deposits		143,248	149,093	191,791	168,218	-24,970	-14.84
Equity Capital		14,753	15,256	19,416	259	14,494	5596.14
Utah							
Net Income		1,150	926	718	422	728	172.51
Total Assets		59,231	45,229	39,601	35,969	23,262	64.67
Total Deposits		29,855	22,923	20,197	18,836	11,019	58.50
Equity Capital		5,666	4,494	3,920	3,432	2,234	65.09
Vermont							
Net Income		63	94	87	104	-41	-39.42
Total Assets		7,600	7,602	7,113	6,221	1,379	22.17
Total Deposits		6,098	6,381	5,909	5,206	892	17.13
Equity Capital		636	648	616	511	125	24.46
Virginia							
Net Income		1,363	1,143	990	1,204	159	13.21
Total Assets		80,684	75,001	77,805	89,893	-9,209	-10.24
Total Deposits		54,530	52,006	55,853	64,890	-10,360	-15.97
Equity Capital		6,869	6,598	6,531	7,391	-522	-7.06
Washington							
Net Income		172	158	157	743	-571	-76.85
Total Assets		13,360	12,742	11,647	44,646	-31,286	-70.08
Total Deposits		10,937	10,625	9,897	35,466	-24,529	-69.16
Equity Capital		1,430	1,416	1,196	4,006	-2,576	-64.30
West Virginia							
Net Income		236	346	277	318	-82	-25.79
Total Assets		23,088	23,540	21,598	22,267	821	3.69
Total Deposits		17,291	18,761	17,451	18,011	-720	-4.00
Equity Capital		2,058	2,257	2,088	2,260	-202	-8.94

Wisconsin						
Net Income		828	871	838	812	16	1.97
Total Assets		74,221	81,706	72,479	65,690	8,531	12.99
Total Deposits		53,534	62,195	55,408	51,096	2,438	4.77
Equity Capital		5,934	6,759	6,210	5,447	487	8.94
Wyoming						
Net Income		185	243	190	189	-4	-2.12
Total Assets		7,491	10,146	8,310	8,184	-693	-8.47
Total Deposits		6,062	9,099	7,215	7,017	-955	-13.61
Equity Capital		712	821	713	703	9	1.28
National						
Net Income		71,703	61,800	59,159	52,350	19,353	36.97
Total Assets		5,734,844	5,441,055	5,014,951	4,578,315	1,156,529	25.26
Total Deposits		3,830,776	3,681,444	3,421,727	3,197,136	633,640	19.82
Equity Capital		479,875	462,169	417,778	388,826	91,049	23.42

Source: FDIC State Banking Performance Summary.

Appendix 3: Performance Ratios

	1999	1998	1997	1996	Percent Change
Alabama					
Net interest margin	4.03	4.11	4.18	4.19	-3.82
Noninterest income to average earning assets	1.51	1.39	1.25	1.60	-5.63
Net charge-offs to loans and leases	0.35	0.29	0.32	0.30	16.67
Credit-loss provision to net charge-offs	140.48	127.40	124.75	136.07	3.24
Return on assets	1.15	1.15	1.23	1.29	-10.85
Return on equity	14.50	14.07	15.08	16.03	-9.54
Percent of unprofitable institutions	5.76	5.00	2.28	2.73	110.99
Percent of institutions with earning gains	71.15	59.37	72.00	69.39	2.54
Alaska					
Net interest margin	5.63	5.80	5.78	5.63	0.00
Noninterest income to average earning assets	1.80	1.80	1.71	1.73	4.05
Net charge-offs to loans and leases	0.11	0.21	0.24	0.42	-73.81
Credit-loss provision to net charge-offs	245.57	129.13	151.71	123.81	98.34
Return on assets	1.68	1.79	1.79	1.55	8.39
Return on equity	12.21	12.64	12.49	11.65	4.81
Percent of unprofitable institutions	NA	NA	NA	25.00	NA
Percent of institutions with earning gains	50.00	66.66	83.33	62.50	-20.00
Arizona					
Net interest margin	5.90	6.91	7.38	6.86	-13.99
Noninterest income to average earning assets	8.22	6.48	4.08	3.22	155.28
Net charge-offs to loans and leases	2.49	3.14	3.50	2.52	-1.19
Credit-loss provision to net charge-offs	67.84	80.27	109.65	107.06	-36.63
Return on assets	2.70	2.02	1.49	1.14	136.84
Return on equity	29.18	20.68	15.38	12.14	140.36
Percent of unprofitable institutions	24.44	25.58	17.07	14.28	71.15
Percent of institutions with earning gains	66.66	74.41	73.17	77.14	-13.59
Arkansas					
Net interest margin	4.06	4.10	4.30	4.35	-6.67
Noninterest income to average earning assets	1.08	1.10	1.20	1.27	-14.96
Net charge-offs to loans and leases	0.29	0.27	0.25	0.24	20.83
Credit-loss provision to net charge-offs	150.57	150.61	177.59	144.80	3.98
Return on assets	1.10	1.22	1.28	1.30	-15.38
Return on equity	11.46	12.26	13.46	13.67	-16.17
Percent of unprofitable institutions	8.71	5.94	3.98	1.70	412.35
Percent of institutions with earning gains	59.48	62.37	70.35	79.91	-25.57
California					
Net interest margin	5.15	4.57	4.66	4.81	7.07
Noninterest income to average earning assets	2.62	2.27	2.32	2.41	8.71
Net charge-offs to loans and leases	0.37	0.46	0.32	0.39	-5.13
Credit-loss provision to net charge-offs	139.01	164.79	69.17	46.78	197.16
Return on assets	1.18	0.78	1.22	1.02	15.69
Return on equity	10.68	8.22	12.63	11.23	-4.90
Percent of unprofitable institutions	13.53	13.43	11.30	13.05	3.68
Percent of institutions with earning gains	74.15	65.97	74.70	66.11	12.16

Colorado					
Net interest margin	5.09	5.18	5.32	5.30	-3.96
Noninterest income to average earning assets	2.04	2.21	1.89	2.21	-7.69
Net charge-offs to loans and leases	0.48	0.52	0.39	0.44	9.09
Credit-loss provision to net charge-offs	102.74	119.58	136.97	107.08	-4.05
Return on assets	1.62	1.27	1.33	1.44	12.50
Return on equity	21.59	16.36	16.60	18.08	19.41
Percent of unprofitable institutions	6.91	6.66	6.97	3.58	93.02
Percent of institutions with earning gains	72.34	70.25	66.97	70.40	2.76
Connecticut					
Net interest margin	4.12	4.37	5.01	4.81	-14.35
Noninterest income to average earning assets	3.48	1.51	1.52	1.25	178.40
Net charge-offs to loans and leases	0.38	0.45	0.33	0.56	-32.14
Credit-loss provision to net charge-offs	144.09	82.28	141.56	1.12	12765.18
Return on assets	1.34	0.96	1.20	1.26	6.35
Return on equity	12.90	10.48	13.46	14.32	-9.92
Percent of unprofitable institutions	29.16	14.28		10.71	172.27
Percent of institutions with earning gains	58.33	64.28	69.23	85.71	-31.94
Delaware					
Net interest margin	5.29	6.09	6.21	6.07	-12.85
Noninterest income to average earning assets	15.55	13.10	11.58	10.28	51.26
Net charge-offs to loans and leases	2.98	3.90	4.31	3.43	-13.12
Credit-loss provision to net charge-offs	108.22	91.63	106.25	125.76	-13.95
Return on assets	2.98	3.15	2.15	2.09	42.58
Return on equity	23.13	25.57	19.00	19.71	17.35
Percent of unprofitable institutions	18.18	11.76	5.88	15.38	18.21
Percent of institutions with earning gains	57.57	64.70	79.41	48.71	18.19
Florida					
Net interest margin	4.12	4.21	4.83	4.93	-16.43
Noninterest income to average earning assets	1.67	1.73	2.23	1.64	1.83
Net charge-offs to loans and leases	0.41	0.34	0.37	0.52	-21.15
Credit-loss provision to net charge-offs	99.76	102.83	129.56	119.52	-16.53
Return on assets	1.30	1.16	1.21	1.29	0.78
Return on equity	14.05	13.22	13.77	15.38	-8.65
Percent of unprofitable institutions	25.00	15.20	10.90	7.26	244.35
Percent of institutions with earning gains	53.67	60.80	65.41	69.55	-22.83
Georgia					
Net interest margin	4.52	4.90	5.38	4.59	-1.53
Noninterest income to average earning assets	4.69	4.30	2.48	2.01	133.33
Net charge-offs to loans and leases	0.88	1.16	0.98	0.74	18.92
Credit-loss provision to net charge-offs	99.55	116.41	168.02	140.90	-29.35
Return on assets	1.78	1.61	1.34	1.10	61.82
Return on equity	11.92	10.76	10.56	10.95	8.86
Percent of unprofitable institutions	8.11	8.88	5.66	3.67	120.98
Percent of institutions with earning gains	70.72	61.89	70.53	79.66	-11.22

Hawaii					
Net interest margin	4.50	4.48	4.46	4.33	3.93
Noninterest income to average earning assets	1.88	1.64	1.59	1.61	16.77
Net charge-offs to loans and leases	0.71	0.61	0.44	0.31	129.03
Credit-loss provision to net charge-offs	87.88	129.17	93.76	109.48	-19.73
Return on assets	0.98	0.82	1.03	1.00	-2.00
Return on equity	11.38	9.35	12.00	12.08	-5.79
Percent of unprofitable institutions	20.00	41.66	28.57	21.42	-6.63
Percent of institutions with earning gains	70.00	25.00	57.14	35.71	96.02
Idaho					
Net interest margin	5.12	5.15	5.18	4.86	5.35
Noninterest income to average earning assets	1.07	1.15	0.91	1.22	-12.30
Net charge-offs to loans and leases	0.18	0.12	0.09	0.40	-55.00
Credit-loss provision to net charge-offs	231.64	325.58	450.96	88.91	160.53
Return on assets	1.15	1.30	1.19	1.26	-8.73
Return on equity	11.11	12.33	10.72	15.60	-28.78
Percent of unprofitable institutions	5.88	17.64	29.41	5.88	0.00
Percent of institutions with earning gains	64.70	82.35	58.82	70.58	-8.33
Illinois					
Net interest margin	3.15	3.33	3.55	3.56	-11.52
Noninterest income to average earning assets	1.54	1.65	1.51	1.44	6.94
Net charge-offs to loans and leases	0.27	0.28	0.34	0.34	-20.59
Credit-loss provision to net charge-offs	134.24	130.11	121.44	115.37	16.36
Return on assets	0.97	1.05	1.06	0.96	1.04
Return on equity	12.55	12.73	12.87	11.14	12.66
Percent of unprofitable institutions	6.48	3.89	3.31	4.68	38.46
Percent of institutions with earning gains	59.58	57.44	67.72	70.82	-15.87
Indiana					
Net interest margin	4.29	4.21	4.49	4.49	-4.45
Noninterest income to average earning assets	3.15	2.12	1.27	1.42	121.83
Net charge-offs to loans and leases	0.31	0.35	0.35	0.38	-18.42
Credit-loss provision to net charge-offs	122.26	120.81	116.90	79.86	53.09
Return on assets	1.57	1.36	1.31	1.39	12.95
Return on equity	16.49	14.85	14.86	15.71	4.96
Percent of unprofitable institutions	3.79	5.32	3.24	2.45	54.69
Percent of institutions with earning gains	67.72	64.49	76.21	76.47	-11.44
Iowa					
Net interest margin	3.82	3.89	4.16	4.20	-9.05
Noninterest income to average earning assets	1.33	1.24	1.54	1.37	-2.92
Net charge-offs to loans and leases	0.18	0.29	0.37	0.45	-60.00
Credit-loss provision to net charge-offs	148.15	93.72	113.73	98.58	50.28
Return on assets	1.10	1.19	1.37	1.26	-12.70
Return on equity	12.41	12.76	14.61	13.64	-9.02
Percent of unprofitable institutions	5.23	3.61	2.86	1.71	205.85
Percent of institutions with earning gains	58.31	60.04	66.66	77.51	-24.77

Kansas					
Net interest margin	4.33	4.42	4.60	4.44	-2.48
Noninterest income to average earning assets	1.20	1.18	1.20	1.25	-4.00
Net charge-offs to loans and leases	0.38	0.45	0.43	0.61	-37.70
Credit-loss provision to net charge-offs	122.75	126.57	112.07	94.85	29.41
Return on assets	1.22	1.22	1.25	1.10	10.91
Return on equity	12.67	12.49	12.72	10.99	15.29
Percent of unprofitable institutions	2.06	1.78	2.23	3.12	-33.97
Percent of institutions with earning gains	54.78	60.55	69.97	70.43	-22.22
Kentucky					
Net interest margin	4.12	4.17	4.40	4.34	-5.07
Noninterest income to average earning assets	1.32	1.27	1.17	1.17	12.82
Net charge-offs to loans and leases	0.40	0.37	0.38	0.37	8.11
Credit-loss provision to net charge-offs	109.53	117.89	133.91	110.64	-1.00
Return on assets	1.28	1.29	1.26	1.26	1.59
Return on equity	15.04	15.07	14.47	14.15	6.29
Percent of unprofitable institutions	3.62	6.13	5.90	3.27	10.70
Percent of institutions with earning gains	66.12	60.53	69.37	68.72	-3.78
Louisiana					
Net interest margin	4.35	4.63	4.70	4.83	-9.94
Noninterest income to average earning assets	1.42	1.77	1.59	1.49	-4.70
Net charge-offs to loans and leases	0.51	0.37	0.43	0.38	34.21
Credit-loss provision to net charge-offs	114.41	85.68	100.16	67.33	69.92
Return on assets	1.10	1.19	1.19	1.27	-13.39
Return on equity	12.06	12.30	12.28	13.05	-7.59
Percent of unprofitable institutions	11.76	8.00	5.69	2.90	305.52
Percent of institutions with earning gains	51.63	54.00	55.69	57.55	-10.29
Maine					
Net interest margin	4.54	4.84	5.09	4.93	-7.91
Noninterest income to average earning assets	1.74	2.42	1.68	1.47	18.37
Net charge-offs to loans and leases	0.11	0.26	0.33	0.27	-59.26
Credit-loss provision to net charge-offs	441.59	87.33	73.95	80.09	451.37
Return on assets	1.15	1.78	1.32	1.24	-7.26
Return on equity	14.21	20.31	15.82	12.88	10.33
Percent of unprofitable institutions	NA	NA	NA	5.00	NA
Percent of institutions with earning gains	62.50	64.70	82.35	70.00	-10.71
Maryland					
Net interest margin	4.14	4.20	4.50	4.40	-5.91
Noninterest income to average earning assets	1.53	1.48	1.33	1.37	11.68
Net charge-offs to loans and leases	0.27	0.26	0.20	0.25	8.00
Credit-loss provision to net charge-offs	441.59	120.55	129.58	81.33	442.96
Return on assets	1.30	1.14	1.25	1.10	18.18
Return on equity	14.96	11.23	14.20	12.08	23.84
Percent of unprofitable institutions	5.19	5.00	1.20	4.44	16.89
Percent of institutions with earning gains	68.83	70.00	86.74	73.33	-6.14

Massachusetts					
Net interest margin	3.58	3.59	3.62	3.75	-4.53
Noninterest income to average earning assets	4.35	4.16	3.88	3.88	12.11
Net charge-offs to loans and leases	0.43	0.55	0.44	0.28	53.57
Credit-loss provision to net charge-offs	135.27	105.83	74.03	32.43	317.11
Return on assets	1.04	1.17	1.24	1.22	-14.75
Return on equity	14.84	16.98	17.76	15.86	-6.43
Percent of unprofitable institutions	4.44	6.81	4.34	4.00	11.00
Percent of institutions with earning gains	71.11	65.90	73.91	72.00	-1.24
Michigan					
Net interest margin	4.46	4.40	4.54	4.38	1.83
Noninterest income to average earning assets	2.34	2.23	2.03	1.77	32.20
Net charge-offs to loans and leases	0.26	0.28	0.36	0.28	-7.14
Credit-loss provision to net charge-offs	110.56	122.29	129.15	145.02	-23.76
Return on assets	1.59	1.48	1.41	1.33	19.55
Return on equity	17.71	16.05	15.32	15.08	17.44
Percent of unprofitable institutions	8.77	8.48	9.81	5.68	54.40
Percent of institutions with earning gains	*68.42*	*75.75*	*69.93*	*76.70*	*-10.80*
Minnesota					
Net interest margin	4.53	4.64	4.79	4.54	-0.22
Noninterest income to average earning assets	2.09	2.34	2.22	2.22	-5.86
Net charge-offs to loans and leases	3.39	0.48	0.57	0.20	1595.00
Credit-loss provision to net charge-offs	0.59	88.33	108.59	144.97	-99.59
Return on assets	1.63	1.59	1.48	1.43	13.99
Return on equity	19.25	18.37	17.04	17.34	11.01
Percent of unprofitable institutions	3.01	1.94	2.88	2.11	42.65
Percent of institutions with earning gains	64.78	57.78	57.50	79.38	-18.39
Mississippi					
Net interest margin	4.33	4.42	4.72	4.70	-7.87
Noninterest income to average earning assets	1.32	1.20	1.43	1.37	-3.65
Net charge-offs to loans and leases	0.30	0.28	0.29	0.26	15.38
Credit-loss provision to net charge-offs	134.11	137.87	116.76	121.82	10.09
Return on assets	1.28	1.27	1.31	1.39	-7.91
Return on equity	13.21	12.80	13.31	14.69	-10.07
Percent of unprofitable institutions	8.08	4.16	3.73	2.70	199.26
Percent of institutions with earning gains	68.68	57.29	64.48	74.77	-8.14
Missouri					
Net interest margin	3.96	4.01	4.26	4.16	-4.81
Noninterest income to average earning assets	1.45	1.43	1.19	1.54	-5.84
Net charge-offs to loans and leases	0.23	0.20	0.29	0.28	-17.86
Credit-loss provision to net charge-offs	131.67	144.55	127.93	110.10	19.59
Return on assets	1.22	1.35	1.27	1.38	-11.59
Return on equity	14.32	15.57	14.43	16.71	-14.30
Percent of unprofitable institutions	2.73	3.40	3.96	3.02	-9.60
Percent of institutions with earning gains	64.10	58.37	72.52	72.32	-11.37

Montana					
Net interest margin	4.98	5.19	5.34	5.24	-4.96
Noninterest income to average earning assets	1.19	1.17	1.29	1.19	0.00
Net charge-offs to loans and leases	0.30	0.29	0.30	0.36	-16.67
Credit-loss provision to net charge-offs	101.16	97.85	119.74	111.10	-8.95
Return on assets	1.47	1.44	1.53	5.24	-71.95
Return on equity	15.83	15.53	17.05	15.66	1.09
Percent of unprofitable institutions	1.17	2.24	4.16	5.00	-76.60
Percent of institutions with earning gains	64.70	49.43	68.75	62.00	4.35
Nebraska					
Net interest margin	4.52	4.67	4.78	4.65	-2.80
Noninterest income to average earning assets	2.48	2.60	2.46	2.41	2.90
Net charge-offs to loans and leases	0.71	0.91	0.96	0.85	-16.47
Credit-loss provision to net charge-offs	96.55	105.16	108.54	113.57	-14.99
Return on assets	1.28	1.24	1.24	1.16	10.34
Return on equity	15.01	14.24	14.22	11.90	26.13
Percent of unprofitable institutions	1.99	1.90	1.84	3.03	-34.32
Percent of institutions with earning gains	56.81	59.36	63.80	67.47	-15.80
Nevada					
Net interest margin	6.75	6.48	6.75	7.52	-10.24
Noninterest income to average earning assets	11.50	10.40	8.47	8.05	42.86
Net charge-offs to loans and leases	2.69	2.61	3.33	2.75	-2.18
Credit-loss provision to net charge-offs	98.84	104.43	104.35	107.97	-8.46
Return on assets	3.67	2.99	2.31	2.85	28.77
Return on equity	26.60	18.62	15.67	23.93	11.16
Percent of unprofitable institutions	22.22	25.92	16.00	19.23	15.55
Percent of institutions with earning gains	59.25	59.25	68.00	69.23	-14.42
New Hampshire					
Net interest margin	11.62	9.12	7.76	7.74	50.13
Noninterest income to average earning assets	10.74	8.26	6.27	4.03	166.50
Net charge-offs to loans and leases	3.75	3.67	1.90	1.59	135.85
Credit-loss provision to net charge-offs	208.99	143.55	113.82	111.25	87.86
Return on assets	3.92	2.99	2.57	2.13	84.04
Return on equity	45.10	28.86	24.60	22.71	98.59
Percent of unprofitable institutions	10.52	10.52	14.28	5.00	110.40
Percent of institutions with earning gains	73.68	68.42	61.90	70.00	5.26
New Jersey					
Net interest margin	3.96	4.10	4.57	3.91	1.28
Noninterest income to average earning assets	1.12	1.18	1.28	1.00	12.00
Net charge-offs to loans and leases	0.46	0.33	0.45	0.40	15.00
Credit-loss provision to net charge-offs	90.71	119.86	105.92	75.88	19.54
Return on assets	1.23	1.24	1.23	0.91	35.16
Return on equity	15.85	15.06	14.51	10.70	48.13
Percent of unprofitable institutions	24.00	18.05	9.85	3.03	692.08
Percent of institutions with earning gains	70.66	68.05	71.83	75.75	-6.72

New Mexico					
Net interest margin	4.62	4.65	5.10	5.20	-11.15
Noninterest income to average earning assets	1.09	1.12	1.17	1.42	-23.24
Net charge-offs to loans and leases	0.46	0.40	0.36	0.50	-8.00
Credit-loss provision to net charge-offs	82.44	138.10	100.90	94.53	-12.79
Return on assets	1.13	1.10	1.29	1.33	-15.04
Return on equity	12.91	12.49	16.29	16.55	-21.99
Percent of unprofitable institutions	7.40	10.34	6.89	4.41	67.80
Percent of institutions with earning gains	59.25	56.89	79.31	66.17	-10.46
New York					
Net interest margin	3.13	2.92	2.90	3.22	-2.80
Noninterest income to average earning assets	3.44	2.64	2.59	2.80	22.86
Net charge-offs to loans and leases	0.58	0.53	0.27	0.36	61.11
Credit-loss provision to net charge-offs	69.51	81.48	111.50	97.80	-28.93
Return on assets	1.00	0.68	0.89	0.93	7.53
Return on equity	14.19	10.40	13.82	14.10	0.64
Percent of unprofitable institutions	6.00	7.18	3.26	6.91	-13.17
Percent of institutions with earning gains	69.33	65.35	70.58	69.18	0.22
North Carolina					
Net interest margin	3.88	3.80	3.90	3.58	8.38
Noninterest income to average earning assets	2.42	2.31	1.91	2.02	19.80
Net charge-offs to loans and leases	0.43	0.36	0.41	0.25	72.00
Credit-loss provision to net charge-offs	107.64	101.76	123.60	81.61	31.90
Return on assets	1.23	1.28	1.13	1.06	16.04
Return on equity	14.89	14.98	13.25	15.19	-1.97
Percent of unprofitable institutions	22.53	26.08	24.19	8.77	156.90
Percent of institutions with earning gains	71.83	71.01	69.35	80.70	-10.99
North Dakota					
Net interest margin	4.32	4.19	4.55	4.55	-5.05
Noninterest income to average earning assets	3.39	3.16	1.09	1.08	213.89
Net charge-offs to loans and leases	0.87	0.88	0.43	0.20	335.00
Credit-loss provision to net charge-offs	121.07	107.51	158.72	166.10	-27.11
Return on assets	1.60	1.43	1.18	1.22	31.15
Return on equity	17.00	15.37	13.40	14.02	21.26
Percent of unprofitable institutions	4.38	2.63	0.85	1.62	170.37
Percent of institutions with earning gains	56.14	50.00	54.70	59.34	-5.39
Ohio					
Net interest margin	4.18	4.51	4.88	4.83	-13.46
Noninterest income to average earning assets	3.17	3.28	2.47	2.31	37.23
Net charge-offs to loans and leases	0.53	0.73	0.86	0.80	-33.75
Credit-loss provision to net charge-offs	112.39	109.00	104.69	114.14	-1.53
Return on assets	1.44	1.38	1.50	1.38	4.35
Return on equity	17.43	16.45	18.52	17.70	-1.53
Percent of unprofitable institutions	4.56	2.72	2.12	2.33	95.71
Percent of institutions with earning gains	61.18	61.81	68.51	73.54	-16.81

Oklahoma					
Net interest margin	4.22	4.39	4.48	4.29	-1.63
Noninterest income to average earning assets	1.40	1.47	1.45	1.47	-4.76
Net charge-offs to loans and leases	0.37	0.53	0.50	0.37	0.00
Credit-loss provision to net charge-offs	109.78	111.87	120.63	131.82	-16.72
Return on assets	1.09	1.11	1.15	1.06	2.83
Return on equity	11.59	11.22	11.97	11.31	2.48
Percent of unprofitable institutions	6.33	6.14	3.12	4.51	40.35
Percent of institutions with earning gains	54.33	64.07	68.12	63.55	-14.51
Oregon					
Net interest margin	5.74	5.98	5.87	5.30	8.30
Noninterest income to average earning assets	2.40	3.43	2.64	2.45	-2.04
Net charge-offs to loans and leases	0.48	0.42	0.27	0.48	0.00
Credit-loss provision to net charge-offs	138.99	193.14	175.14	127.56	8.96
Return on assets	1.53	2.17	1.85	1.71	-10.53
Return on equity	14.41	19.44	16.51	19.65	-26.67
Percent of unprofitable institutions	18.18	14.28	12.19	13.95	30.32
Percent of institutions with earning gains	70.45	59.52	73.17	76.74	-8.20
Pennsylvania					
Net interest margin	3.91	4.04	4.21	4.22	-7.35
Noninterest income to average earning assets	2.78	2.81	2.10	1.85	50.27
Net charge-offs to loans and leases	0.25	0.47	0.34	0.23	8.70
Credit-loss provision to net charge-offs	109.00	68.25	51.69	14.47	653.28
Return on assets	1.33	1.45	1.42	1.27	4.72
Return on equity	15.15	16.17	16.65	14.63	3.55
Percent of unprofitable institutions	8.80	5.07	2.83	2.76	218.84
Percent of institutions with earning gains	67.87	68.52	77.35	84.33	-19.52
Rhode Island					
Net interest margin	4.53	4.85	4.68	4.69	-3.41
Noninterest income to average earning assets	4.80	3.77	3.09	2.37	102.53
Net charge-offs to loans and leases	1.32	1.18	0.58	0.42	214.29
Credit-loss provision to net charge-offs	100.44	91.16	90.11	99.69	0.75
Return on assets	1.35	1.50	1.51	1.39	-2.88
Return on equity	13.42	15.45	16.76	15.48	-13.31
Percent of unprofitable institutions	NA	NA	NA	NA	NA
Percent of institutions with earning gains	83.33	100.00	77.77	62.50	33.33
South Carolina					
Net interest margin	4.69	4.69	4.75	4.31	8.82
Noninterest income to average earning assets	1.31	1.27	1.26	1.45	-9.66
Net charge-offs to loans and leases	0.23	0.28	0.32	0.22	4.55
Credit-loss provision to net charge-offs	194.26	143.56	139.41	58.16	234.01
Return on assets	1.35	1.37	1.28	1.29	4.65
Return on equity	14.35	14.54	14.25	15.23	-5.78
Percent of unprofitable institutions	14.28	14.28	13.75	13.92	2.59
Percent of institutions with earning gains	79.22	75.32	81.25	78.48	0.94

South Dakota					
Net interest margin	7.84	7.57	7.32	6.20	26.45
Noninterest income to average earning assets	13.24	11.55	9.86	10.27	28.92
Net charge-offs to loans and leases	3.56	3.57	3.46	2.98	19.46
Credit-loss provision to net charge-offs	120.49	111.09	110.57	116.40	3.51
Return on assets	2.62	2.53	2.09	2.42	8.26
Return on equity	24.81	23.83	20.78	26.13	-5.05
Percent of unprofitable institutions	2.94	2.88	1.88	5.12	-42.58
Percent of institutions with earning gains	60.78	56.73	66.98	58.97	3.07
Tennessee					
Net interest margin	4.22	4.21	4.40	4.27	-1.17
Noninterest income to average earning assets	3.16	3.09	2.73	2.31	36.80
Net charge-offs to loans and leases	0.36	0.47	0.39	0.31	16.13
Credit-loss provision to net charge-offs	110.18	109.08	118.58	115.87	-4.91
Return on assets	1.36	1.28	1.47	1.32	3.03
Return on equity	15.73	14.51	16.45	15.54	1.22
Percent of unprofitable institutions	5.97	4.90	5.17	4.62	29.22
Percent of institutions with earning gains	65.67	58.82	67.24	77.73	-15.52
Texas					
Net interest margin	4.42	4.45	4.31	4.31	2.55
Noninterest income to average earning assets	1.84	1.70	2.44	2.23	-17.49
Net charge-offs to loans and leases	0.50	0.45	0.36	0.34	47.06
Credit-loss provision to net charge-offs	113.33	120.58	107.27	112.67	0.59
Return on assets	1.18	1.11	1.23	1.21	-2.48
Return on equity	14.24	12.65	14.30	14.63	-2.67
Percent of unprofitable institutions	4.90	5.38	4.29	3.07	59.61
Percent of institutions with earning gains	60.87	57.01	61.09	57.58	5.71
Utah					
Net interest margin	6.57	6.78	6.82	6.23	5.46
Noninterest income to average earning assets	4.86	4.97	4.81	3.55	36.90
Net charge-offs to loans and leases	2.23	2.86	2.85	2.76	-19.20
Credit-loss provision to net charge-offs	119.63	106.32	117.43	112.54	6.30
Return on assets	2.32	2.27	1.96	1.25	85.60
Return on equity	22.21	22.29	19.81	12.83	73.11
Percent of unprofitable institutions	11.76	12.00	14.28	12.50	-5.92
Percent of institutions with earning gains	70.58	72.00	75.51	66.66	5.88
Vermont					
Net interest margin	4.68	4.76	4.90	4.99	-6.21
Noninterest income to average earning assets	2.04	1.56	1.49	2.06	-0.97
Net charge-offs to loans and leases	0.27	0.37	0.32	0.42	-35.71
Credit-loss provision to net charge-offs	105.64	71.52	80.81	78.01	35.42
Return on assets	0.83	1.28	1.33	1.70	-51.18
Return on equity	9.88	14.60	16.15	20.39	-51.54
Percent of unprofitable institutions	10.00	4.76	NA	NA	NA
Percent of institutions with earning gains	65.00	66.66	66.66	77.27	-15.88

Virginia					
Net interest margin	5.02	4.73	4.42	4.55	10.33
Noninterest income to average earning assets	4.60	3.59	2.75	2.28	101.75
Net charge-offs to loans and leases	0.62	0.68	0.76	0.62	0.00
Credit-loss provision to net charge-offs	122.43	122.53	111.62	101.67	20.42
Return on assets	1.76	1.60	1.34	1.35	30.37
Return on equity	19.80	17.87	15.52	16.41	20.66
Percent of unprofitable institutions	15.64	6.57	2.64	1.94	706.19
Percent of institutions with earning gains	62.58	61.18	80.13	79.87	-21.65
Washington					
Net interest margin	5.29	5.09	5.39	5.54	-4.51
Noninterest income to average earning assets	1.13	1.22	1.17	2.09	-45.93
Net charge-offs to loans and leases	0.22	0.15	0.21	0.28	-21.43
Credit-loss provision to net charge-offs	181.68	246.12	197.65	114.68	58.42
Return on assets	1.36	1.33	1.44	1.69	-19.53
Return on equity	12.62	12.42	13.95	18.54	-31.93
Percent of unprofitable institutions	20.98	16.66	12.65	7.31	187.00
Percent of institutions with earning gains	61.72	61.53	81.01	68.29	-9.62
West Virginia					
Net interest margin	4.09	4.52	4.61	4.68	-12.61
Noninterest income to average earning assets	1.25	1.80	1.24	1.00	25.00
Net charge-offs to loans and leases	0.45	0.48	0.47	0.32	40.63
Credit-loss provision to net charge-offs	101.70	125.70	119.10	111.56	-8.84
Return on assets	1.06	1.51	1.32	1.44	-26.39
Return on equity	11.65	15.61	13.00	14.51	-19.71
Percent of unprofitable institutions	6.09	6.74	4.00	5.30	14.91
Percent of institutions with earning gains	65.85	51.68	64.00	64.60	1.93
Wisconsin					
Net interest margin	3.72	3.84	4.12	4.18	-11.00
Noninterest income to average earning assets	1.37	1.66	1.47	1.46	-6.16
Net charge-offs to loans and leases	0.19	0.28	0.22	0.19	0.00
Credit-loss provision to net charge-offs	111.78	128.00	168.93	89.69	24.63
Return on assets	1.17	1.14	1.24	1.28	-8.59
Return on equity	14.08	13.38	14.83	15.20	-7.37
Percent of unprofitable institutions	2.67	0.87	3.61	3.02	-11.59
Percent of institutions with earning gains	66.17	71.80	76.66	74.45	-11.12
Wyoming					
Net interest margin	4.69	5.72	5.42	5.52	-15.04
Noninterest income to average earning assets	0.98	0.62	0.57	0.65	50.77
Net charge-offs to loans and leases	0.16	0.15	0.17	0.20	-20.00
Credit-loss provision to net charge-offs	115.61	110.12	92.27	163.02	-29.08
Return on assets	2.14	2.66	2.37	2.34	-8.55
Return on equity	22.95	31.32	27.30	27.81	-17.48
Percent of unprofitable institutions	4.00	3.84	3.77	1.85	116.22
Percent of institutions with earning gains	56.00	71.15	64.15	72.22	-22.46

National					
Net interest margin	4.07	4.07	4.21	4.27	-4.68
Noninterest income to average earning assets	3.06	2.76	2.52	2.45	24.90
Net charge-offs to loans and leases	0.61	0.67	0.64	0.58	5.17
Credit-loss provision to net change-offs	106.75	104.87	108.37	105.07	1.60
Return on assets	1.31	1.19	1.23	1.19	10.08
Return on equity	15.34	13.93	14.69	14.45	6.16
Percent of unprofitable institutions	7.23	6.12	4.84	4.28	68.93
Percent of institutions with earning gains	63.11	61.24	68.37	70.77	-10.82

Source: FDIC State Banking Performance Summary.

130

Appendix 4: Condition Ratios

	1999	1998	1997	1996	Percent Change
Alabama					
Net loans and leases to assets	65.98	66.3	69	66.48	-0.75
Loss allowance to loans and leases	1.3	1.29	1.31	1.34	-2.99
Nonperforming assets to assets	0.57	0.58	0.61	0.49	16.33
Core deposits to total liabilities	59.42	67.07	66.59	65.89	-9.82
Equity capital to total assets	7.58	7.95	8.2	7.9	-4.05
Total capital to risk-weighted assets	11.18	11.34	11.7	12.21	-8.44
Gross 1-4 family mortgages to gross assets	17.73	20.39	23.15	20.24	-12.40
Alaska					
Net loans and leases to assets	55.31	52.74	51.57	55.21	0.18
Loss allowance to loans and leases	1.46	1.42	1.48	1.51	-3.31
Nonperforming assets to assets	0.4	0.41	0.56	0.64	-37.50
Core deposits to total liabilities	72.01	72.36	72.56	72.43	-0.58
Equity capital to total assets	13.65	13.97	13.13	12.97	5.24
Total capital to risk-weighted assets	19.77	20.88	21.98	20.47	-3.42
Gross 1-4 family mortgages to gross assets	9.56	11.12	10.24	10.81	-11.56
Arizona					
Net loans and leases to assets	67.66	70.27	74.61	75.99	-10.96
Loss allowance to loans and leases	1.93	3.11	3.72	2.78	-30.58
Nonperforming assets to assets	0.96	1.85	0.99	0.77	24.68
Core deposits to total liabilities	46.24	56.77	56.98	58.23	-20.59
Equity capital to total assets	8.33	9.49	9.66	8.98	-7.24
Total capital to risk-weighted assets	11.32	13.28	12.83	11.58	-2.25
Gross 1-4 family mortgages to gross assets	7.4	7.9	9.13	11.34	-34.74
Arkansas					
Net loans and leases to assets	60.7	58.05	58.9	56.44	7.55
Loss allowance to loans and leases	1.28	1.26	1.37	1.37	-6.57
Nonperforming assets to assets	0.72	0.74	0.66	0.57	26.32
Core deposits to total liabilities	74.71	77.68	79.03	81.34	-8.15
Equity capital to total assets	9.38	9.64	9.53	9.36	0.21
Total capital to risk-weighted assets	15.41	15.83	15.6	15.67	-1.66
Gross 1-4 family mortgages to gross assets	17.75	17.42	17.96	16.5	7.58
California					
Net loans and leases to assets	65.21	63.62	65.32	64.58	0.98
Loss allowance to loans and leases	1.99	2.08	1.89	2.08	-4.33
Nonperforming assets to assets	0.54	0.52	0.65	0.95	-43.16
Core deposits to total liabilities	70.46	63.17	63.56	63.34	11.24
Equity capital to total assets	10.94	9.07	9.67	9.31	17.51
Total capital to risk-weighted assets	11.91	11.42	11.73	11.69	1.88
Gross 1-4 family mortgages to gross assets	11.69	11.22	14.69	16.84	-30.58

Colorado					
Net loans and leases to assets	52.08	51.36	52.51	57.97	-10.16
Loss allowance to loans and leases	1.28	1.52	1.5	1.49	-14.09
Nonperforming assets to assets	0.4	0.47	0.44	0.41	-2.44
Core deposits to total liabilities	79.27	85.3	85.43	84.98	-6.72
Equity capital to total assets	7.41	7.73	7.75	7.83	-5.36
Total capital to risk-weighted assets	12.07	12.5	12.67	12.48	-3.29
Gross 1-4 family mortgages to gross assets	15.48	14.01	15.12	14.57	6.25
Connecticut					
Net loans and leases to assets	54.32	50.14	63.65	72.8	-25.38
Loss allowance to loans and leases	1.7	2.03	1.9	1.75	-2.86
Nonperforming assets to assets	0.69	0.98	1.48	1.65	-58.18
Core deposits to total liabilities	73.43	79.03	86.41	82.88	-11.40
Equity capital to total assets	9.88	8.8	9.27	9.28	6.47
Total capital to risk-weighted assets	15.67	15.03	14.44	12.59	24.46
Gross 1-4 family mortgages to gross assets	25.58	24.53	29.66	42.24	-39.44
Delaware					
Net loans and leases to assets	61.2	71.02	73.35	75.61	-19.06
Loss allowance to loans and leases	2.82	2.73	2.94	3.04	-7.24
Nonperforming assets to assets	1.36	1.54	1.59	1.62	-16.05
Core deposits to total liabilities	23.34	23.64	20.92	19.87	17.46
Equity capital to total assets	11.97	13.01	11.31	10.73	11.56
Total capital to risk-weighted assets	14.04	14.78	12.73	14.46	-2.90
Gross 1-4 family mortgages to gross assets	8.76	9.25	7.95	7.1	23.38
Florida					
Net loans and leases to assets	65.59	64.94	67.52	67.72	-3.15
Loss allowance to loans and leases	1.31	1.43	1.62	1.63	-19.63
Nonperforming assets to assets	0.56	0.59	0.6	0.78	-28.21
Core deposits to total liabilities	69.93	71.54	75.73	78.99	-11.47
Equity capital to total assets	8.97	8.6	8.81	8.46	6.03
Total capital to risk-weighted assets	13.43	13.08	12.43	13.07	2.75
Gross 1-4 family mortgages to gross assets	22.24	22.28	24.19	26.7	-16.70
Georgia					
Net loans and leases to assets	66.49	64.11	65.62	67.81	-1.95
Loss allowance to loans and leases	1.92	2.35	2.03	1.89	1.59
Nonperforming assets to assets	0.51	0.61	0.78	0.8	-36.25
Core deposits to total liabilities	52.57	57.73	62.43	64.22	-18.14
Equity capital to total assets	14.45	15.33	12.8	10.19	41.81
Total capital to risk-weighted assets	16	17.06	15.26	13.5	18.52
Gross 1-4 family mortgages to gross assets	12.33	12.53	14.96	15.4	-19.94

Hawaii					
Net loans and leases to assets	67.55	67.25	65.8	63.48	6.41
Loss allowance to loans and leases	1.82	1.89	1.7	1.83	-0.55
Nonperforming assets to assets	1.39	1.5	1.39	1.36	2.21
Core deposits to total liabilities	50.61	49.35	48.61	48.76	3.79
Equity capital to total assets	8.83	8.37	8.66	8.26	6.90
Total capital to risk-weighted assets	12.6	11.27	11.52	11.44	10.14
Gross 1-4 family mortgages to gross assets	19.45	20.21	19.04	16.9	15.09
Idaho					
Net loans and leases to assets	63.7	59.27	61.65	67.9	-6.19
Loss allowance to loans and leases	1.34	1.42	1.44	1.72	-22.09
Nonperforming assets to assets	0.39	0.53	0.44	0.47	-17.02
Core deposits to total liabilities	79.16	82.47	83.05	78.7	0.58
Equity capital to total assets	10.16	10.53	10.52	7.12	42.70
Total capital to risk-weighted assets	15.26	16.23	15.88	11.81	29.21
Gross 1-4 family mortgages to gross assets	10.14	9.03	9.05	13.37	-24.16
Illinois					
Net loans and leases to assets	59.86	54.34	55.22	56.23	6.46
Loss allowance to loans and leases	1.23	1.4	1.48	1.67	-26.35
Nonperforming assets to assets	0.48	0.46	0.5	0.52	-7.69
Core deposits to total liabilities	49.67	54.25	57.97	60.25	-17.56
Equity capital to total assets	7.45	7.87	8.32	8.76	-14.95
Total capital to risk-weighted assets	12.28	11.93	12.4	12.49	-1.68
Gross 1-4 family mortgages to gross assets	12.12	12.38	15.13	12.58	-3.66
Indiana					
Net loans and leases to assets	64.27	67.87	67.07	67.42	-4.67
Loss allowance to loans and leases	1.54	1.39	1.49	1.49	3.36
Nonperforming assets to assets	0.62	0.76	0.52	0.53	16.98
Core deposits to total liabilities	66.51	69.97	74.09	77.3	-13.96
Equity capital to total assets	9.22	8.83	8.28	8.82	4.54
Total capital to risk-weighted assets	12.74	12.36	12.81	12.9	-1.24
Gross 1-4 family mortgages to gross assets	21.93	23.44	20.08	20.17	8.73
Iowa					
Net loans and leases to assets	60.83	57.85	59.17	57.81	5.22
Loss allowance to loans and leases	1.37	1.4	1.48	1.53	-10.46
Nonperforming assets to assets	0.41	0.45	0.44	0.48	-14.58
Core deposits to total liabilities	79.25	81.92	83.99	84.24	-5.92
Equity capital to total assets	8.63	8.87	9.43	9.24	-6.60
Total capital to risk-weighted assets	14.04	14.06	15.11	15.26	-7.99
Gross 1-4 family mortgages to gross assets	16.16	15.18	16.22	14.76	9.49

Kansas					
Net loans and leases to assets	60.76	57.72	58.53	54.55	11.38
Loss allowance to loans and leases	1.59	1.67	1.64	1.79	-11.17
Nonperforming assets to assets	0.55	0.56	0.62	0.79	-30.38
Core deposits to total liabilities	81.05	82.89	83.64	85.33	-5.02
Equity capital to total assets	9.59	9.63	9.6	9.9	-3.13
Total capital to risk-weighted assets	14.54	15.02	15.18	16.33	-10.96
Gross 1-4 family mortgages to gross assets	11.84	12.15	12.96	10.67	10.97
Kentucky					
Net loans and leases to assets	67.17	64.38	66.2	66.59	0.87
Loss allowance to loans and leases	1.3	1.39	1.43	1.48	-12.16
Nonperforming assets to assets	0.59	0.51	0.54	0.58	1.72
Core deposits to total liabilities	67.49	69.19	69.2	71.87	-6.09
Equity capital to total assets	8.27	8.52	8.33	8.46	-2.25
Total capital to risk-weighted assets	13.15	13.11	13.28	13.46	-2.30
Gross 1-4 family mortgages to gross assets	22.1	21.56	22.31	21.78	1.47
Louisiana					
Net loans and leases to assets	62.94	59.46	59.51	58	8.52
Loss allowance to loans and leases	1.28	1.3	1.53	1.75	-26.86
Nonperforming assets to assets	0.65	0.64	0.6	0.68	-4.41
Core deposits to total liabilities	73.11	74.91	75.03	77.4	-5.54
Equity capital to total assets	8.94	8.95	9.47	9.53	-6.19
Total capital to risk-weighted assets	13.03	13.05	13.93	14.45	-9.83
Gross 1-4 family mortgages to gross assets	16.68	16.01	15.33	14.27	16.89
Maine					
Net loans and leases to assets	67.55	70.3	64.52	65.96	2.41
Loss allowance to loans and leases	1.87	1.49	1.68	1.89	-1.06
Nonperforming assets to assets	0.58	0.67	0.67	1	-42.00
Core deposits to total liabilities	73.8	76.81	76.85	73.38	0.57
Equity capital to total assets	7.78	8.19	8.48	9	-13.56
Total capital to risk-weighted assets	13.53	13.88	13.87	12.77	5.95
Gross 1-4 family mortgages to gross assets	26.23	26.15	26.6	18.93	38.56
Maryland					
Net loans and leases to assets	64.38	61.92	63.31	61.37	4.90
Loss allowance to loans and leases	1.47	1.51	1.62	1.67	-11.98
Nonperforming assets to assets	0.6	0.63	0.7	0.75	-20.00
Core deposits to total liabilities	69.96	73.26	74.96	77.92	-10.22
Equity capital to total assets	8.58	8.81	8.89	9.3	-7.74
Total capital to risk-weighted assets	13.03	12.99	13.1	13.35	-2.40
Gross 1-4 family mortgages to gross assets	20.12	20.19	22.05	20.93	-3.87

Massachusetts					
Net loans and leases to assets	41.2	46.3	49.15	54.67	-24.64
Loss allowance to loans and leases	1.65	1.57	1.51	2.02	-18.32
Nonperforming assets to assets	0.43	0.43	0.38	0.67	-35.82
Core deposits to total liabilities	36.51	39.92	43.85	52.01	-29.80
Equity capital to total assets	6.7	6.97	6.78	7.77	-13.77
Total capital to risk-weighted assets	11.6	11.35	11.21	11.78	-1.53
Gross 1-4 family mortgages to gross assets	7.14	8.63	9.43	11.3	-36.81
Michigan					
Net loans and leases to assets	75.03	72.95	72.12	71.65	4.72
Loss allowance to loans and leases	1.48	1.58	1.65	1.62	-8.64
Nonperforming assets to assets	0.57	0.51	0.54	0.56	1.79
Core deposits to total liabilities	65.58	69.25	69.74	72.74	-9.84
Equity capital to total assets	8.89	8.87	9.14	9.14	-2.74
Total capital to risk-weighted assets	11.53	1.59	12.03	12.39	-6.94
Gross 1-4 family mortgages to gross assets	18.22	18.72	18.18	15.7	16.05
Minnesota					
Net loans and leases to assets	71.1	73.07	69.75	62.29	14.14
Loss allowance to loans and leases	1.32	1.42	1.67	1.68	-21.43
Nonperforming assets to assets	0.48	0.48	0.69	0.46	4.35
Core deposits to total liabilities	62.56	67.36	71.81	73.55	-14.94
Equity capital to total assets	8.7	8.23	8.83	8.32	4.57
Total capital to risk-weighted assets	11.48	11.64	12.16	12.65	-9.25
Gross 1-4 family mortgages to gross assets	18.87	22.21	17.93	16.4	15.06
Mississippi					
Net loans and leases to assets	61.86	59.42	59.95	58.76	5.28
Loss allowance to loans and leases	1.48	1.56	1.6	1.64	-9.76
Nonperforming assets to assets	0.49	0.45	0.59	0.48	2.08
Core deposits to total liabilities	70.57	75.7	78.01	79.06	-10.74
Equity capital to total assets	9.52	9.79	9.92	9.68	-1.65
Total capital to risk-weighted assets	15.66	16.03	15.78	16.19	-3.27
Gross 1-4 family mortgages to gross assets	18.16	17.23	17.73	15.73	15.45
Missouri					
Net loans and leases to assets	63.45	58.55	61.25	59.35	6.91
Loss allowance to loans and leases	1.38	1.44	1.48	1.58	-12.66
Nonperforming assets to assets	0.52	0.55	0.59	0.6	-13.33
Core deposits to total liabilities	75.21	76.07	84.84	79.16	-4.99
Equity capital to total assets	8.42	8.5	8.79	8.07	4.34
Total capital to risk-weighted assets	12.86	13.3	13.91	12.94	-0.62
Gross 1-4 family mortgages to gross assets	19.56	19.59	18.5	16.52	18.40

Montana					
Net loans and leases to assets	62.23	61.3	63.85	63.08	-1.35
Loss allowance to loans and leases	1.47	1.51	1.57	1.62	-9.26
Nonperforming assets to assets	0.78	0.7	0.7	0.61	27.87
Core deposits to total liabilities	81.19	83.72	83.95	85.49	-5.03
Equity capital to total assets	9.2	9.21	9.02	8.77	4.90
Total capital to risk-weighted assets	13.89	13.88	13.39	13.45	3.27
Gross 1-4 family mortgages to gross assets	13.81	14.85	15.89	15.37	-10.15
Nebraska					
Net loans and leases to assets	65.65	61.78	62.66	60.9	7.80
Loss allowance to loans and leases	1.54	1.69	1.73	1.77	-12.99
Nonperforming assets to assets	0.64	0.69	0.63	0.65	-1.54
Core deposits to total liabilities	78.68	81.33	83.05	84.69	-7.10
Equity capital to total assets	8.31	8.42	8.61	9.58	-13.26
Total capital to risk-weighted assets	13.14	13.2	13.49	13.66	-3.81
Gross 1-4 family mortgages to gross assets	8.47	8.14	8.05	7.64	10.86
Nevada					
Net loans and leases to assets	72.9	69.68	74.22	75.57	-3.53
Loss allowance to loans and leases	5.38	5.1	4.82	3.04	76.97
Nonperforming assets to assets	1.08	1.1	1.25	1.3	-16.92
Core deposits to total liabilities	36.79	32.85	32.65	29.94	22.88
Equity capital to total assets	13.39	13.2	15.6	11.45	16.94
Total capital to risk-weighted assets	15.88	15.19	18.06	12.31	29.00
Gross 1-4 family mortgages to gross assets	9.18	8.43	10.63	7.82	17.39
New Hampshire					
Net loans and leases to assets	69.33	68.48	67.78	72.47	-4.33
Loss allowance to loans and leases	6.57	4.57	2.77	2.4	173.75
Nonperforming assets to assets	1.9	1.26	1.13	1.35	40.74
Core deposits to total liabilities	46.97	59.59	65.95	68.01	-30.94
Equity capital to total assets	8.39	8.75	11.33	9.27	-9.49
Total capital to risk-weighted assets	11.41	11.39	13.35	12.95	-11.89
Gross 1-4 family mortgages to gross assets	9.12	15.97	19.22	21.63	-57.84
New Jersey					
Net loans and leases to assets	56.6	56.62	54.72	61.25	-7.59
Loss allowance to loans and leases	1.4	1.55	1.79	1.61	-13.04
Nonperforming assets to assets	0.38	0.5	0.68	1.09	-65.14
Core deposits to total liabilities	72.43	72.8	75.15	81.14	-10.73
Equity capital to total assets	7.55	8.1	8.16	8.49	-11.07
Total capital to risk-weighted assets	12.02	12.55	12.89	12.81	-6.17
Gross 1-4 family mortgages to gross assets	20.48	20.3	19.02	20.96	-2.29

New Mexico					
Net loans and leases to assets	50.52	48.3	52.87	53.48	-5.53
Loss allowance to loans and leases	1.57	1.81	1.8	1.96	-19.90
Nonperforming assets to assets	0.64	0.71	0.68	0.72	-11.11
Core deposits to total liabilities	66.49	72.14	74.49	74.55	-10.81
Equity capital to total assets	8.84	8.95	7.92	7.93	11.48
Total capital to risk-weighted assets	12.86	14.27	13.64	13.94	-7.75
Gross 1-4 family mortgages to gross assets	11.67	11.54	12.31	14.27	-18.22
New York					
Net loans and leases to assets	45.63	43.65	40.69	48.15	-5.23
Loss allowance to loans and leases	1.88	2.17	2.31	2.35	-20.00
Nonperforming assets to assets	0.69	0.77	0.65	0.75	-8.00
Core deposits to total liabilities	23.24	22.97	22.7	24.98	-6.97
Equity capital to total assets	7.14	6.88	6.34	6.46	10.53
Total capital to risk-weighted assets	12.55	12.44	11.87	12.23	2.62
Gross 1-4 family mortgages to gross assets	6.81	6.45	5.8	5.81	17.21
North Carolina					
Net loans and leases to assets	63.04	58.78	59	64.5	-2.26
Loss allowance to loans and leases	1.57	1.36	1.45	1.4	12.14
Nonperforming assets to assets	0.57	0.5	0.5	0.41	39.02
Core deposits to total liabilities	53.24	56.9	54.29	50.22	6.01
Equity capital to total assets	8.2	8.73	8.35	7.14	14.85
Total capital to risk-weighted assets	10.86	10.65	10.87	10.83	0.28
Gross 1-4 family mortgages to gross assets	20.84	16.93	18.79	23.16	-10.02
North Dakota					
Net loans and leases to assets	65.78	63.27	59.31	58.45	12.54
Loss allowance to loans and leases	2.12	2.14	1.78	1.65	28.48
Nonperforming assets to assets	0.75	0.73	0.72	0.64	17.19
Core deposits to total liabilities	68.87	72.88	84.9	85.67	-19.61
Equity capital to total assets	9.3	9.42	8.8	8.68	7.14
Total capital to risk-weighted assets	13.58	14.23	13.9	14.02	-3.14
Gross 1-4 family mortgages to gross assets	10.83	9.01	7	6.93	56.28
Ohio					
Net loans and leases to assets	70.08	69.75	70.07	70.36	-0.40
Loss allowance to loans and leases	1.45	1.56	1.69	1.84	-21.20
Nonperforming assets to assets	0.62	0.66	0.71	0.65	-4.62
Core deposits to total liabilities	56.37	60.75	62.8	63.91	-11.80
Equity capital to total assets	8	8.25	7.95	7.4	8.11
Total capital to risk-weighted assets	11.07	11.35	11.42	11.69	-5.30
Gross 1-4 family mortgages to gross assets	17.15	16.8	16.32	15.66	9.51

Oklahoma					
Net loans and leases to assets	57.76	54.27	55.22	54.38	6.22
Loss allowance to loans and leases	1.4	1.47	1.51	1.51	-7.28
Nonperforming assets to assets	0.68	0.75	0.78	0.92	-26.09
Core deposits to total liabilities	72.11	76.76	77.99	79.64	-9.46
Equity capital to total assets	9.09	9.76	9.74	9.35	-2.78
Total capital to risk-weighted assets	14.11	15.04	15.19	14.95	-5.62
Gross 1-4 family mortgages to gross assets	11.3	11.01	11.89	11.71	-3.50
Oregon					
Net loans and leases to assets	68.13	63.68	65.7	73.12	-6.82
Loss allowance to loans and leases	1.44	1.51	1.29	1.63	-11.66
Nonperforming assets to assets	0.55	0.57	0.48	0.44	25.00
Core deposits to total liabilities	80.66	86.08	84.25	71.64	12.59
Equity capital to total assets	10.19	10.84	11.24	8.32	22.48
Total capital to risk-weighted assets	12.39	13.65	14.26	11.79	5.09
Gross 1-4 family mortgages to gross assets	8.28	9.44	11.83	9.41	-12.01
Pennsylvania					
Net loans and leases to assets	68.54	68.99	67.03	66.27	3.43
Loss allowance to loans and leases	1.3	1.34	1.54	1.64	-20.73
Nonperforming assets to assets	0.66	0.65	0.71	0.81	-18.52
Core deposits to total liabilities	64.94	66.28	68.95	72.33	-10.22
Equity capital to total assets	8.47	8.95	8.61	8.34	1.56
Total capital to risk-weighted assets	11.84	11.69	11.72	11.79	0.42
Gross 1-4 family mortgages to gross assets	24.29	23.21	21.26	21.49	13.03
Rhode Island					
Net loans and leases to assets	64.75	68.58	66.99	59.55	8.73
Loss allowance to loans and leases	2.5	2.44	2.66	1.59	57.23
Nonperforming assets to assets	0.69	0.61	0.76	0.64	7.81
Core deposits to total liabilities	45.32	54.06	62.36	79.63	-43.09
Equity capital to total assets	9.18	9.89	8.75	8.54	7.49
Total capital to risk-weighted assets	11	10.94	10.74	13.41	-17.97
Gross 1-4 family mortgages to gross assets	11.37	16.57	18.23	19.57	-41.90
South Carolina					
Net loans and leases to assets	68.87	65.49	66.35	60.92	13.05
Loss allowance to loans and leases	1.31	1.33	1.32	1.32	-0.76
Nonperforming assets to assets	0.32	0.32	0.4	0.56	-42.86
Core deposits to total liabilities	74.69	79.66	79.68	77.98	-4.22
Equity capital to total assets	8.93	9.63	9.09	8.36	6.82
Total capital to risk-weighted assets	12.77	13.82	13.56	13.1	-2.52
Gross 1-4 family mortgages to gross assets	19.83	19.92	21.32	20.17	-1.69

South Dakota					
Net loans and leases to assets	75.55	73.6	77.34	75.25	0.40
Loss allowance to loans and leases	4.18	3.6	3.39	2.64	58.33
Nonperforming assets to assets	1.53	1.17	1.41	1.35	13.33
Core deposits to total liabilities	34.51	37.07	34.28	42	-17.83
Equity capital to total assets	10.56	10.48	10.06	9.15	15.41
Total capital to risk-weighted assets	14.84	14.96	13.91	13.42	10.58
Gross 1-4 family mortgages to gross assets	2.9	3.05	3.24	3.32	-12.65
Tennessee					
Net loans and leases to assets	64.5	62.23	65.79	64.22	0.44
Loss allowance to loans and leases	1.4	1.41	1.52	1.56	-10.26
Nonperforming assets to assets	0.71	0.67	0.73	0.97	-26.80
Core deposits to total liabilities	65.11	69.02	71.52	72.57	-10.28
Equity capital to total assets	8.46	8.7	9.08	8.51	-0.59
Total capital to risk-weighted assets	12.52	13.47	13.03	12.89	-2.87
Gross 1-4 family mortgages to gross assets	22.19	21.74	23.76	23.1	-3.94
Texas					
Net loans and leases to assets	54.97	52.39	50.9	51.15	7.47
Loss allowance to loans and leases	1.3	1.36	1.35	1.49	-12.75
Nonperforming assets to assets	0.56	0.51	0.44	0.53	5.66
Core deposits to total liabilities	73.74	77.88	70.57	78.44	-5.99
Equity capital to total assets	8.14	8.49	8.26	8.41	-3.21
Total capital to risk-weighted assets	13.43	13.61	12.99	13.25	1.36
Gross 1-4 family mortgages to gross assets	8.37	8.29	8.5	9.14	-8.42
Utah					
Net loans and leases to assets	69.47	71.61	70.64	73.55	-5.55
Loss allowance to loans and leases	2.29	2.34	2.72	2.57	-10.89
Nonperforming assets to assets	0.78	0.82	0.9	0.75	4.00
Core deposits to total liabilities	36.16	41.27	43.37	45.87	-21.17
Equity capital to total assets	9.57	9.94	9.9	9.54	0.31
Total capital to risk-weighted assets	12.87	13.18	13.75	13.46	-4.38
Gross 1-4 family mortgages to gross assets	7.1	11.58	9.88	9.6	-26.04
Vermont					
Net loans and leases to assets	68.97	65.48	67.33	68.05	1.35
Loss allowance to loans and leases	1.5	1.56	1.73	1.84	-18.48
Nonperforming assets to assets	0.49	0.62	0.98	1.01	-51.49
Core deposits to total liabilities	82.27	87.02	85.86	86.37	-4.75
Equity capital to total assets	8.37	8.53	8.66	8.21	1.95
Total capital to risk-weighted assets	12.97	12.4	12.36	13.02	-0.38
Gross 1-4 family mortgages to gross assets	24.63	24.87	27.03	25.08	-1.79

Virginia					
Net loans and leases to assets	67.67	66.18	63.56	62.09	8.99
Loss allowance to loans and leases	1.6	1.64	1.62	1.69	-5.33
Nonperforming assets to assets	0.76	0.64	0.67	0.84	-9.52
Core deposits to total liabilities	64.82	67.98	69.91	70.59	-8.17
Equity capital to total assets	8.51	8.8	8.39	8.22	3.53
Total capital to risk-weighted assets	12.59	13.17	12.47	13.36	-5.76
Gross 1-4 family mortgages to gross assets	20.84	24.04	22.09	20.12	3.58
Washington					
Net loans and leases to assets	72.07	65.34	66.68	75.78	-4.90
Loss allowance to loans and leases	1.37	1.47	1.42	1.59	-13.84
Nonperforming assets to assets	0.68	0.6	0.61	0.72	-5.56
Core deposits to total liabilities	77.51	81.67	83.22	78.34	-1.06
Equity capital to total assets	10.7	11.11	10.27	8.97	19.29
Total capital to risk-weighted assets	14.21	14.67	14.63	12.08	17.63
Gross 1-4 family mortgages to gross assets	13.07	13.67	15.11	15.2	-14.01
West Virginia					
Net loans and leases to assets	64.07	65.01	64.71	65.34	-1.94
Loss allowance to loans and leases	1.27	1.3	1.34	1.3	-2.31
Nonperforming assets to assets	0.74	0.78	0.8	0.71	4.23
Core deposits to total liabilities	74.41	77.88	80.72	82.59	-9.90
Equity capital to total assets	8.91	9.59	9.67	10.15	-12.22
Total capital to risk-weighted assets	13.71	13.26	14.43	16.32	-15.99
Gross 1-4 family mortgages to gross assets	29.03	31.29	29.25	28.42	2.15
Wisconsin					
Net loans and leases to assets	66.16	64.06	65.63	64.37	2.78
Loss allowance to loans and leases	1.3	1.44	1.43	1.4	-7.14
Nonperforming assets to assets	0.52	0.55	0.57	0.59	-11.86
Core deposits to total liabilities	67.91	73.44	73.21	74.92	-9.36
Equity capital to total assets	7.99	8.27	8.57	8.29	-3.62
Total capital to risk-weighted assets	12.37	12.25	12.55	12.83	-3.59
Gross 1-4 family mortgages to gross assets	21.14	18.94	19.29	18.16	16.41
Wyoming					
Net loans and leases to assets	50.94	54.85	66.15	70.1	-27.33
Loss allowance to loans and leases	1.33	0.9	0.92	1.02	30.39
Nonperforming assets to assets	0.44	0.34	0.38	0.54	-18.52
Core deposits to total liabilities	77.59	88.48	85.32	84.53	-8.21
Equity capital to total assets	8.37	8.09	8.58	8.6	-2.67
Total capital to risk-weighted assets	12.16	14.53	14.05	14.39	-15.50
Gross 1-4 family mortgages to gross assets	14.47	27.46	34.22	35.97	-59.77

National					
Net loans and leases to assets	59.86	58.46	58.15	60.24	-0.63
Loss allowance to loans and leases	1.68	1.77	1.84	1.9	-11.58
Nonperforming assets to assets	0.63	0.65	0.66	0.75	-16.00
Core deposits to total liabilities	51.24	53.98	54.6	57.13	-10.31
Equity capital to total assets	8.37	8.49	8.33	8.2	2.07
Total capital to risk-weighted assets	12.16	12.23	12.23	12.53	-2.95
Gross 1-4 family mortgages to gross assets	14.47	13.9	14.16	14.13	2.41

Source: FDIC State Banking Performance Summary.

Appendix 5: McFadden-Pepper Act of 1927

(February 25, 1927)
44 Stat. 1224
US Code: Title 12
(Revised Excerpts)

Sec. 36. Branch banks

The conditions upon which a national banking association may retain or establish and operate a branch or branches are the following:

(a) Lawful and continuous operation

A national banking association may retain and operate such branch or branches as it may have had in lawful operation on February 25, 1927, and any national banking association which continuously maintained and operated not more than one branch for a period of more than twenty-five years immediately preceding February 25, 1927, may continue to maintain and operate such branch.

(b) Converted State banks

(1) A national bank resulting from the conversion of a State bank may retain and operate as a branch any office which was a branch of the State bank immediately prior to conversion if such office—

(A) might be established under subsection (c) of this section as a new branch of the resulting national bank, and is approved by the

Comptroller of the Currency for continued operation as a branch of the resulting national bank;

(B) was a branch of any bank on February 25, 1927; or

(C) is approved by the Comptroller of the Currency for continued operation as a branch of the resulting national bank. The Comptroller of the Currency may not grant approval under clause (C) of this paragraph if a State bank (in a situation identical to that of the national bank) resulting from the conversion of a national bank would be prohibited by the law of such State from retaining and operating as a branch an identically situated office which was a branch of the national bank immediately prior to conversion.

(2) A national bank (referred to in this paragraph as the "resulting bank"), resulting from the consolidation of a national bank (referred to in this paragraph as the "national bank") under whose charter the consolidation is effected with another bank or banks, may retain and operate as a branch any office which, immediately prior to such consolidation, was in operation as—

(A) a main office or branch office of any bank (other than the national bank) participating in the consolidation if, under subsection (c) of this section, it might be established as a new branch of the resulting bank, and if the Comptroller of the Currency approves of its continued operation after the consolidation;

(B) a branch of any bank participating in the consolidation, and which, on February 25, 1927, was in operation as a branch of any bank; or

(C) a branch of the national bank and which, on February 25, 1927, was not in operation as a branch of any bank, if the Comptroller of the Currency approves of its continued operation after the consolidation. The Comptroller of the Currency may not grant approval under clause (C) of this paragraph if a State bank (in a situation identical to that of the resulting national bank) resulting from the consolidation into a State bank of another bank or banks would be prohibited by the law of such State from retaining and operating as a branch an identically situated office which was a branch of the State bank immediately prior to consolidation.

(3) As used in this subsection, the term "consolidation" includes a merger.

(c) New branches

A national banking association may, with the approval of the Comptroller of the Currency, establish and operate new branches:

(1) Within the limits of the city, town or village in which said association is situated, if such establishment and operation are at the time ex-

pressly authorized to State banks by the law of the State in question; and

(2) at any point within the State in which said association is situated, if such establishment and operation are at the time authorized to State banks by the statute law of the State in question by language specifically granting such authority affirmatively and not merely by implication or recognition, and subject to the restrictions as to location imposed by the law of the State on State banks. In any State in which State banks are permitted by statute law to maintain branches within county or greater limits, if no bank is located and doing business in the place where the proposed agency is to be located, any national banking association situated in such State may, with the approval of the Comptroller of the Currency, establish and operate, without regard to the capital requirements of this section, a seasonal agency in any resort community within the limits of the county in which the main office of such association is located, for the purpose of receiving and paying out deposits, issuing and cashing checks and drafts, and doing business incident thereto: Provided, That any permit issued under this sentence shall be revoked upon the opening of a State or national bank in such community. Except as provided in the immediately preceding sentence, no such association shall establish a branch outside of the city, town, or village in which it is situated unless it has a combined capital stock and surplus equal to the combined amount of capital stock and surplus, if any, required by the law of the State in which such association is situated for the establishment of such branches by State banks, or, if the law of such State requires only a minimum capital stock for the establishment of such branches by State banks, unless such association has not less than an equal amount of capital stock.

(d) Branches resulting from interstate merger transactions
A national bank resulting from an interstate merger transaction (as defined in section 1831u(f)(6) [1] of this title) may maintain and operate a branch in a State other than the home State (as defined in subsection (g)(3)(B) of this section) of such bank in accordance with section 1831u of this title.

(e) Exclusive authority for additional branches

(1) In general
Effective June 1, 1997, a national bank may not acquire, establish, or operate a branch in any State other than the bank's home State (as defined in subsection (g)(3)(B) of this section) or a State in which the bank already has a branch unless the acquisition, establishment, or operation of such branch in such State by such national bank is authorized under this section or section 1823(f), 1823(k), or 1831u of this title.

(2) Retention of branches

In the case of a national bank which relocates the main office of such bank from 1 State to another State after May 31, 1997, the bank may retain and operate branches within the State which was the bank's home State (as defined in subsection (g)(3)(B) of this section) before the relocation of such office only to the extent the bank would be authorized, under this section or any other provision of law referred to in paragraph (1), to acquire, establish, or commence to operate a branch in such State if

(A) the bank had no branches in such State; or

(B) the branch resulted from—

(i) an interstate merger transaction approved pursuant to section 1831u of this title; or

(ii) a transaction after May 31, 1997, pursuant to which the bank received assistance from the Federal Deposit Insurance Corporation under section 1823(c) of this title.

(f) Law applicable to interstate branching operations

(1) Law applicable to national bank branches

(A) In general

The laws of the host State regarding community reinvestment, consumer protection, fair lending, and establishment of intrastate branches shall apply to any branch in the host State of an out-of-State national bank to the same extent as such State laws apply to a branch of a bank chartered by that State,except-

(i) when Federal law preempts the application of such State laws to a national bank; or

(ii) when the Comptroller of the Currency determines that the application of such State laws would have a discriminatory effect on the branch in comparison with the effect the application of such State laws would have with respect to branches of a bank chartered by the host State.

(B) Enforcement of applicable State laws

The provisions of any State law to which a branch of a national bank is subject under this paragraph shall be enforced, with respect to such branch, by the Comptroller of the Currency.

(C) Review and report on actions by Comptroller

The Comptroller of the Currency shall conduct an annual review of the actions it has taken with regard to the applicability of State law to national banks (or their branches) during the preceding year, and shall include in its annual report required under section 14 of this title the results of the review and the reasons for each such ac-

tion. The first such review and report after July 3, 1997, shall encompass all such actions taken on or after January 1, 1992.

(2) Treatment of branch as bank

All laws of a host State, other than the laws regarding community reinvestment, consumer protection, fair lending, establishment of intrastate branches, and the application or administration of any tax or
method of taxation, shall apply to a branch (in such State) of an out-of-
State national bank to the same extent as such laws would apply if the
branch were a national bank the main office of which is in such State.

(3) Rule of construction

No provision of this subsection may be construed as affecting the legal standards for preemption of the application of State law to national banks.

(g) State "opt-in" election to permit interstate branching through de
novo branches

(1) In general

Subject to paragraph (2), the Comptroller of the Currency may approve an application by a national bank to establish and operate a de
novo branch in a State (other than the bank's home State) in which the
bank does not maintain a branch if

  (A) there is in effect in the host State a law that—

    (i) applies equally to all banks; and

    (ii) expressly permits all out-of-State banks to establish de novo
    branches in such State; and

  (B) the conditions established in, or made applicable to this paragraph by, paragraph (2) are met.

(2) Conditions on establishment and operation of interstate branch

  (A) Establishment

  An application by a national bank to establish and operate a de
  novo branch in a host State shall be subject to the same requirements and conditions to which an application for an interstate
  merger transaction is subject under paragraphs (1), Establishment

  (B) Operation

  Subsections (c) and (d)(2) of section *1831u* of this title shall apply
  with respect to each branch of a national bank which is established
  and operated pursuant to an application approved under this subsection in the same manner and to the same extent such provisions
  of such section *1831u* of this title apply to a branch of a national
  bank which resulted from an interstate merger transaction approved pursuant to such section *1831u* of this title.

(3) Definitions

The following definitions shall apply for purposes of this section:

(A) De novo branch

The term "de novo branch" means a branch of a national bank which -

　　(i) is originally established by the national bank as a branch; and

　　(ii) does not become a branch of such bank as a result of -

　　　　(I) the acquisition by the bank of an insured depository institution or a branch of an insured depository institution; or

　　　　(II) the conversion, merger, or consolidation of any such institution or branch.

(B) Home State

The term "home State" means the State in which the main office of a national bank is located.

(C) Host State

The term "host State" means, with respect to a bank, a State, other than the home State of the bank, in which the bank maintains, or seeks to establish and maintain, a branch.

(h) Repealed. Pub. L. 104–208, div. A, title II, Sec. 2204, Sept. 30, 1996, 110 Stat. 3009–405

(i) Prior approval of branch locations

No branch of any national banking association shall be established or moved from one location to another without first obtaining the consent and approval of the Comptroller of the Currency.

(j) "Branch" defined

The term "branch" as used in this section shall be held to include any branch bank, branch office, branch agency, additional office, or any branch place of business located in any State or Territory of the United States or in the District of Columbia at which deposits are received, or checks paid, or money lent. The term "branch," as used in this section, does not include an automated teller machine or a remote service unit.

(k) Branches in foreign countries, dependencies, or insular possessions

This section shall not be construed to amend or repeal section 25 of the Federal Reserve Act, as amended (12 U.S.C. 601 et seq.), authorizing the establishment by national banking associations of branches in foreign countries, or dependencies, or insular possessions of the United States.

(l) "State bank" and "bank" defined

The words "State bank," "State banks," "bank," or "banks," as used in this section, shall be held to include trust companies, savings banks, or other such corporations or institutions carrying on the banking business under the authority of State laws.

Sec. 51. Requisite of capital and surplus

After this section as amended takes effect no national banking association shall be organized with a less capital than $100,000, except that such associations with a capital of not less than $50,000 may be organized in any place the population of which does not exceed six thousand inhabitants. No such association shall be organized in a city the population of which exceeds fifty thousand persons with a capital of less than $200,000, except that in the outlying districts of such a city where the State laws permit the organization of State banks with a capital of $100,000 or less, national banking associations now organized or hereafter organized may, with the approval of the Comptroller of the Currency, have a capital of not less than $100,000. No such association shall hereafter be authorized to commence the business of banking until it shall have a paid-in surplus equal to 20 per centum of its capital: Provided, That the Comptroller of the Currency may waive this requirement as to a State bank converting into a national banking association, but each such State bank which is converted into a national banking association shall, before the declaration of a dividend on its shares of common stock, carry not less than one-half part of its net profits of the preceding half year to its surplus fund until it shall have a surplus equal to 20 per centum of its capital: Provided, That for the purposes of this section any amounts paid into a fund for the retirement of any preferred stock of any such converted State bank out of its net earnings for such half-year period shall be deemed to be an addition to its surplus fund if, upon the retirement of such preferred stock, the amount so paid into such retirement fund for such period may then properly be carried to surplus. In any such case the converted State bank shall be obligated to transfer to surplus the amount so paid into such retirement fund for such period on account of the preferred stock as such stock is retired.

Sec. 72. Qualifications

Every director must, during his whole term of service, be a citizen of the United States, and at least a majority of the directors must have resided in the State, Territory, or District in which the association is located, or within one hundred miles of the location of the office of the association, for at least one year immediately preceding their election, and must be residents of such State or within one-hundred-mile territory of the location of the association during their continuance in office, except that the Comptroller may, in the discretion of the Comptroller, waive the requirement of residency. Every director must own in his or her own right either shares of the capital stock of the association of which he or she is a director the aggregate par value of which is not less than $1,000, or an equivalent interest, as determined by the Comptroller of the Currency, in any company which has control over such association within the meaning of section 1841 of this title. If the capital of the bank does not exceed $25,000, every director must own in his or her own right either shares of such capital stock the aggregate par value of which is not less than $500, or an equivalent interest, as determined by the Comptroller of the Currency, in any company which has control over such association within the meaning of section 1841 of this title. Any director who ceases to be the owner of the required number of shares of the stock, or who becomes in any other manner disqualified, shall thereby vacate his place.

Sec. 321. Application for membership

Any bank incorporated by special law of any State, or organized under the general laws of any State or of the United States, including Morris Plan banks and other incorporated banking institutions engaged in similar business, desiring to become a member of the Federal Reserve System, may make application to the Board of Governors of the Federal Reserve System, under such rules and regulations as it may prescribe, for the right to subscribe to the stock of the Federal Reserve bank organized within the district in which the applying bank is located. Such application shall be for the same amount of stock that the applying bank would be required to subscribe to as a national bank. For the purposes of membership of any such bank the terms "capital" and "capital stock" shall include the amount of outstanding capital notes and debentures legally issued by the applying bank and purchased by the Reconstruction Finance Corporation. The Board of Governors of the Federal Reserve System, subject to the provisions of this chapter and to such conditions as it may prescribe pursuant thereto may permit the applying bank to become a stockholder of such Federal Reserve bank.

Upon the conversion of a national bank into a State bank, or the merger or consolidation of a national bank with a State bank which is not a member of the Federal Reserve System, the resulting or continuing State bank may be admitted to membership in the Federal Reserve System by the Board of Governors of the Federal Reserve System in accordance with the provisions of this section, but, otherwise, the Federal Reserve bank stock owned by the national bank shall be canceled and paid for as provided in section 287 of this title. Upon the merger or consolidation of a national bank with a State member bank under a State charter, the membership of the State bank in the Federal Reserve System shall continue.

Any such State bank which on February 25, 1927, has established and is operating a branch or branches in conformity with the State law, may retain and operate the same while remaining or upon becoming a stockholder of such Federal Reserve bank; but no such State bank may retain or acquire stock in a Federal Reserve bank except upon relinquishment of any branch or branches established after February 25, 1927, beyond the limits of the city, town, or village in which the parent bank is situated: Provided, however, That nothing herein contained shall prevent any State member bank from establishing and operating branches in the United States or any dependency or insular possession thereof or in any foreign country, on the same terms and conditions and subject to the same limitations and restrictions as are applicable to the establishment of branches by national banks except that the approval of the Board of Governors of the Federal Reserve System, instead of the Comptroller of the Currency, shall be obtained before any State member bank may hereafter establish any branch and before any State bank hereafter admitted to membership may retain any branch established after February 25, 1927, beyond the limits of the city, town, or village in which the parent bank is situated. The approval of the Board shall likewise be obtained before any State member bank may establish any new branch within the limits of any such city, town, or village (except within the District of Columbia).

Source: http://www4.law.cornell.edu/uscode/12.

Appendix 6: Riegle-Neal Interstate Banking and Branching Efficiency Act of 1994

TITLE 1—INTERSTATE BANKING AND BRANCH

SEC. 101. INTERSTATE BANKING.

(a) IN GENERAL—Section 3(d) of the Bank Holding Company Act of 1956 (12 U.S.C. 1842 (d)) is amended to read as follows:

'(d) INTERSTATE BANKING—

'(1) APPROVALS AUTHORIZED—

'(A) ACQUISITION OF BANKS—The Board may approve an application under this section by a bank holding company that is adequately capitalized and adequately managed to acquire control of, or acquire all or substantially all of the assets of, a bank located in a State other than the home State of such bank holding company, without regard to whether such transaction is prohibited under the law of any State.

'(B) PRESERVATION OF STATE AGE LAWS—

'(i) IN GENERAL—Notwithstanding subparagraph (A), the Board may not approve an application pursuant to such subparagraph that would have the effect of permitting an out-of-State bank holding company to acquire a bank in a host State that has not been in existence for the minimum period of time, if any, specified in the statutory law of the host State.

'(ii) SPECIAL RULE FOR STATE AGE LAWS SPECIFYING A PERIOD OF MORE THAN 5 YEARS- Notwithstanding clause (i), the Board may approve, pursuant to subparagraph (A), the acquisition of a bank that has been in existence for at least 5 years without regard to any longer minimum period of time specified in a statutory law of the host State.

'(C) SHELL BANKS—For purposes of this subsection, a bank that has been chartered solely for the purpose of, and does not open for business prior to, acquiring control of, or acquiring all or substantially all of the assets of, an existing bank shall be deemed to have been in existence for the same period of time as the bank to be acquired.

'(D) EFFECT ON STATE CONTINGENCY LAWS—No provision of this subsection shall be construed as affecting the applicability of a State law that makes an acquisition of a bank contingent upon a requirement to hold a portion of such bank's assets available for call by a State-sponsored housing entity established pursuant to State law, if—

'(i) the State law does not have the effect of discriminating against out-of-State banks, out-of-State bank holding companies, or subsidiaries of such banks or bank holding companies;

'(ii) that State law was in effect as of the date of enactment of the Riegle Neal Interstate Banking and Branching Efficiency Act of 1994;

'(iii) the Federal Deposit Insurance Corporation has not determined that compliance with such State law would result in an unacceptable risk to the appropriate deposit insurance fund; and

'(iv) the appropriate Federal banking agency for such bank has not found that compliance with such State law would place the bank in an unsafe or unsound condition.

'(2) CONCENTRATION LIMITS—

'(A) NATIONWIDE CONCENTRATION LIMITS—The Board may not approve an application pursuant to paragraph (1)(A) if the applicant (including all insured depository institutions which are affiliates of the applicant) controls, or upon consummation of the acquisition for which such application is filed would control, more than 10 percent of the total amount of deposits of insured depository institutions in the United States.

'(B) STATEWIDE CONCENTRATION LIMITS OTHER THAN WITH RESPECT TO INITIAL ENTRIES— The Board may not approve an application pursuant to paragraph (1)(A) if—

'(i) immediately before the consummation of the acquisition for which such application is filed, the applicant (including any insured depository institution affiliate of the applicant) controls any insured depository institution or any branch of an insured depository institution in the home State of any bank to be acquired or in any host State in which any such bank maintains a branch; and

'(ii) the applicant (including all insured depository institutions which are affiliates of the applicant), upon consummation of the acquisition, would control 30 percent or more of the total amount of deposits of insured depository institutions in any such State.

'(C) EFFECTIVENESS OF STATE DEPOSIT CAPS—No provision of this subsection shall be construed as affecting the authority of any State to limit, by statute, regulation, or order, the percentage of the total amount of deposits of insured depository institutions in the State which may be held or controlled by any bank or bank holding company (including all insured depository institutions which are affiliates of the bank or bank holding company) to the extent the application of such limitation does not discriminate against out-of-State banks, out-of-State bank holding companies, or subsidiaries of such banks or holding companies.

'(D) EXCEPTIONS TO SUBPARAGRAPH (B)—The Board may approve an application pursuant to paragraph (1)(A) without regard to the applicability of subparagraph (B) with respect to any State if—

'(i) there is a limitation described in subparagraph (C) in a State statute, regulation, or order which has the effect of permitting a bank or bank holding company (including all insured depository institutions which are affiliates of the bank or bank holding company) to control a greater percentage of total deposits of all insured depository institutions in the State than the percentage permitted under subparagraph (B); or

'(ii) the acquisition is approved by the appropriate State bank supervisor of such State and the standard on which such approval is based does not have the effect of discriminating against out-of-State banks, out-of-State bank holding companies, or subsidiaries of such banks or holding companies.

'(E) DEPOSIT DEFINED—For purposes of this paragraph, the term 'deposit' has the same meaning as in section 3(1) of the Federal Deposit Insurance Act.

'(3) COMMUNITY REINVESTMENT COMPLIANCE—In determining whether to approve an application under paragraph (1)(A), the Board shall—

'(A) comply with the responsibilities of the Board regarding such application under section 804 of the Community Reinvestment Act of 1977; and

'(B) take into account the applicant's record of compliance with applicable State community reinvestment laws.

'(4) APPLICABILITY OF ANTITRUST LAWS—No provision of this subsection shall be construed as affecting—

'(A) the applicability of the antitrust laws; or

'(B) the applicability, if any, of any State law which is similar to the antitrust laws.

'(5) EXCEPTION FOR BANKS IN DEFAULT OR IN DANGER OF DEFAULT—The Board may approve an application pursuant to paragraph (1)(A) which involves—

'(A) an acquisition of 1 or more banks in default or in danger of default; or

(B) an acquisition with respect to which assistance is provided under section 13(c) of the Federal Deposit Insurance Act; without regard to subparagraph (B) or (D) of paragraph (1) or paragraph (2) or (3).'

(b) STATE TAXATION AUTHORITY NOT AFFECTED—Section 7 of the Bank Holding Company Act of 1956 (12 U. S.C. 1846) is amended—

(1) by striking 'No provision' and inserting '(a) IN GENERAL- No provision'; and

(2) by adding at the end the following new subsection:

'(b) STATE TAXATION AUTHORITY NOT AFFECTED—No provision of this Act shall be construed as affecting the authority of any State or political subdivision of any State to adopt, apply, or administer any tax or method of taxation to any bank, bank holding company, or foreign bank, or any affiliate of any bank, bank holding company, or foreign bank, to the extent that such tax or tax method is otherwise permissible by or under the Constitution of the United States or other Federal law.'

(c) DEFINITIONS—Section 2 of the Bank Holding Company Act of 1956 (12 U. S.C. 1841) is amended by adding at the end the following new subsections:

'(n) INCORPORATED DEFINITIONS—For purposes of this Act, the terms 'insured depository institution,' 'appropriate Federal banking agency,' 'default,' 'in danger of default,' and 'state bank supervisor' have the same meanings as in section 3 of the Federal Deposit Insurance Act.

'(o) OTHER DEFINITIONS—For purposes of this Act, the following definitions shall apply:

'(1) ADEQUATELY CAPITALIZED—The term 'adequately capitalized' means a level of capitalization which meets or exceeds all applicable Federal regulatory capital standards.

'(2) ANTITRUST LAWS—Except as provided in section I 1, the term 'antitrust laws'—

'(A) has the same meaning as in subsection (a) of the first section of the Clayton Act; and

'(B) includes section 5 of the Federal Trade Commission Act to the extent that such section 5 relates to unfair methods of competition.

'(3) BRANCH—The term 'branch' means a domestic branch (as defined in section 3 of the Federal Deposit Insurance Act).

'(4) HOME STATE—The term 'home State' means—

'(A) with respect to a national bank, the State in which the main office of the bank is located;

'(B) with respect to a State bank, the State by which the bank is chartered; and

'(C) with respect to a bank holding company, the State in which the total deposits of all banking subsidiaries of such company are the largest on the later of—

'(i) July 1, 1966; or

'(ii) the date on which the company becomes a bank holding company under, this Act.

'(5) HOST STATE—The term 'host State' means—

'(A) with respect to a bank, a State, other than the home State of the bank, in which the bank maintains, or seeks to establish and maintain, a branch; and

'(B) with respect to a bank holding company, a State, other than the home State of the company, in which the company controls, or seeks to control, a bank subsidiary.

'(6) OUT-OF-STATE BANK—The term 'out-of-State bank' means, with respect to any State, a bank whose home State is another State.

'(7) OUT-OF-STATE BANK HOLDING COMPANY—The term 'out-of-State bank holding company' means, with respect to any State, a bank holding company whose home State is another State.'

(d) SUBSIDIARY DEPOSITORY INSTITUTIONS AS AGENTS—Section 18 of the Federal Deposit Insurance Act (12 U.S.C. 1828) is amended by adding at the end the following new subsection:

'(r) SUBSIDIARY DEPOSITORY INSTITUTIONS AS AGENTS FOR CERTAIN AFFILIATES-

'(1) IN GENERAL—Any bank subsidiary of a bank holding company may receive deposits, renew time deposits, close loans, service loans, and receive payments on loans and other obligations as an agent for a depository institution affiliate.

'(2) BANK ACTING AS AGENT IS NOT A BRANCH—Notwithstanding any other provision of law, a bank acting as an agent in accordance with paragraph (1) for a depository institution affiliate shall not be considered to be a branch of the affiliate.

'(3) PROHIBITIONS ON ACTIVITIES—A depository institution may not—

'(A) conduct any activity as an agent under paragraph (1) or (6) which such institution is prohibited from conducting as a principal under any applicable Federal or State law; or

'(B) as a principal, have an agent conduct any activity under paragraph (1) or (6) which the institution is prohibited from conducting under any applicable Federal or State law.

'(4) EXISTING AUTHORITY NOT AFFECTED—No provision of this subsection shall be construed as affecting—

'(A) the authority of any depository institution to act as an agent on behalf of any other depository institution under any other provision of law; or

'(B) whether a depository institution which conducts any activity as an agent on behalf of any other depository institution under any other provision of law shall be considered to be a branch of such other institution.

'(5) AGENCY RELATIONSHIP REQUIRED TO BE CONSISTENT WITH SAFE AND SOUND BANKING PRACTICES—An agency relationship between depository institutions under paragraph (1) or (6) shall be on terms that are consistent with safe and sound banking practices and all applicable regulations of any appropriate Federal banking agency.

'(6) AFFILIATED INSURED SAVINGS ASSOCIATIONS—An insured savings association which was an affiliate of a bank on July 1, 1994, may conduct activities as an agent on behalf of such bank in the same manner as an insured bank affiliate of such bank may act as agent for such bank under this subsection to the extent such activities are conducted only in—

'(A) any State in which—

'(i) the bank is not prohibited from operating a branch under any provision of Federal or State law; and

'(ii) the savings association maintained an office or branch and conducted business as of July 1, 1994; or

'(B) any State in which—

'(i) the bank is not expressly prohibited from operating a branch under a State law described in section 44(a)(2); and

'(ii) the savings association maintained a main office and conducted business as of July 1, 1994.'

(e) EFFECTIVE DATE—The amendments made by this section shall take effect at the end of the 1-year period beginning on the date of the enactment of this Act.

SEC. 102. INTERSTATE BANK MERGERS.

(a) IN GENERAL—The Federal Deposit Insurance Act (12 U.S.C. 1811 et seq.) is amended by adding at the end the following new section:

SEC. 44. INTERSTATE BANK MERGERS.

'(a) APPROVAL OF INTERSTATE MERGER TRANSACTIONS AUTHORIZED—

'(1) IN GENERAL—Beginning on June 1, 1997, the responsible agency may approve a merger transaction under section 18(c) between insured banks with different home States, without regard to whether such transaction is prohibited under the law of any State.

'(2) STATE ELECTION TO PROHIBIT INTERSTATE MERGER TRANSACTIONS-

'(A) IN GENERAL—Notwithstanding paragraph (1), a merger transaction may not be approved pursuant to paragraph (1) if the transaction involves a bank the home State of which has enacted a law after the date of enactment of the Riegle-Neal Interstate Banking and Branching Efficiency Act of 1994 and before June 1, 1997, that—

(i) applies equally to all out-of-State banks; and

(ii) expressly prohibits merger transactions involving out-of-State banks.

'(B) NO EFFECT ON PRIOR APPROVALS OF MERGER TRANSACTIONS—A law enacted by a State pursuant to subparagraph (A) shall have no effect on merger transactions that were approved before the effective date of such law.

'(3) STATE ELECTION TO PERMIT EARLY INTERSTATE MERGER TRANSACTIONS—

'(A) IN GENERAL—A merger transaction may be approved pursuant to paragraph (1) before June 1, 1997, if the home State of each bank involved in the transaction has in effect, as of the date of the approval of such transaction, a law that—

'(i) applies equally to all out-of-State banks; and

'(ii) expressly permits interstate merger transactions with all out-of-State banks.

'(B) CERTAIN CONDITIONS ALLOWED- A host State may impose conditions on a branch within such State of a bank resulting from an interstate merger transaction if—

'(i) the conditions do not have the effect of discriminating against out-of-State banks, out-of-State bank holding companies, or any subsidiary of such bank or company (other than on the basis of a nationwide reciprocal treatment requirement);

'(ii) the imposition of the conditions is not preempted by Federal law; and

'(iii) the conditions do not apply or require performance after May 31, 1997.

'(4) INTERSTATE MERGER TRANSACTIONS INVOLVING ACQUISITIONS OF BRANCHES—

'(A) IN GENERAL—An interstate merger transaction may involve the acquisition of a branch of an insured bank without the acquisition of the bank only if the law of the State in which the branch is located permits out-of-State banks to acquire a branch of a bank in such State without acquiring the bank.

'(B) TREATMENT OF BRANCH FOR PURPOSES OF THIS SECTION—In the case of an interstate merger transaction which involves the acquisition of a branch of an insured bank without the acquisition of the bank, the branch shall be treated, for purposes of this section, as an insured bank the home State of which is the State in which the branch is located.

'(5) PRESERVATION OF STATE AGE LAWS—

'(A) IN GENERAL—The responsible agency may not approve an application pursuant to paragraph (1) that would have the effect of permitting an out-of-State bank or out-of-State bank holding company to acquire a bank in a host State that has not been in existence for the minimum period of time, if any, specified in the statutory law of the host State.

'(B) SPECIAL RULE FOR STATE AGE LAWS SPECIFYING A PERIOD OF MORE THAN 5 YEARS—Notwithstanding subparagraph (A), the responsible agency may approve a merger transaction pursuant to paragraph (1) involving the acquisition of a bank that has been in existence at least 5 years without regard to any longer minimum period of time specified in a statutory law of the host State.

'(6) SHELL BANKS—For purposes of this subsection, a bank that has been chartered solely for the purpose of, and does not open for business prior to, acquiring control of, or acquiring all or substantially all of the assets of, an existing bank or branch shall be deemed to have been in existence for the same period of time as the bank or branch to be acquired.

'(b) PROVISIONS RELATING TO APPLICATION AND APPROVAL PROCESS—

'(1) COMPLIANCE WITH STATE FILING REQUIREMENTS—

'(A) IN GENERAL—Any bank which files an application for an interstate merger transaction shall—

'(i) comply with the filing requirements of any host State of the bank which will result from such transaction to the extent that the requirement—

'(I) does not have the effect of discriminating against out-of-State banks or out-of-State bank holding companies or subsidiaries of such banks or bank holding companies; and

'(II) is similar in effect to any requirement imposed by the host State on a nonbanking corporation incorporated in another State that engages in business in the host State; and

'(ii) submit a copy of the application to the State bank supervisor of the host State.

'(B) PENALTY FOR FAILURE TO COMPLY—The responsible agency may not approve an application for an interstate merger transaction if the applicant materially fails to comply with subparagraph (A).

'(2) CONCENTRATION LIMITS—

'(A) NATIONWIDE CONCENTRATION LIMITS—The responsible agency may not approve an application for an interstate merger transaction if the resulting bank (including all insured depository institutions which are affiliates of the resulting bank), upon consummation of the transaction, would control more than 10 percent of the total amount of deposits of insured depository institutions in the United States.

'(B) STATEWIDE CONCENTRATION LIMITS OTHER THAN WITH RESPECT TO INITIAL ENTRIES— The responsible agency may not approve an application for an interstate merger transaction if—

'(i) any bank involved in the transaction (including all insured depository institutions which are affiliates of any such bank) has a branch in any State in which any other bank involved in the transaction has a branch; and '(ii) the resulting bank (including all insured depository institutions which would be affiliates of the resulting bank), upon consummation of the transaction, would control 30 percent or more of the total amount of deposits of insured depository institutions in any such State.

'(C) EFFECTIVENESS OF STATE DEPOSIT CAPS—No provision of this subsection shall be construed as affecting the authority of any State to limit, by statute, regulation, or order, the percentage of the total amount of deposits of insured depository institutions in the State which may be held or controlled by any bank or bank holding company (including all insured depository institutions which are affiliates of the bank or bank holding company) to the extent the application of such limitation does not discriminate against out-of-State banks, out-of-State bank holding companies, or subsidiaries of such banks or holding companies.

'(D) EXCEPTIONS TO SUBPARAGRAPH (B)—The responsible agency may approve an application for an interstate merger transaction pursuant to subsection (a) without regard to the applicability of subparagraph (B) with respect to any State if—

' (i) there is a limitation described in subparagraph (C) in a State statute, regulation, or order which has the effect of permitting a bank or bank holding company (including all insured depository institutions which are affiliates of the bank or bank holding company) to control a greater percentage of total deposits of all insured depository institutions in the State than the percentage permitted under subparagraph (B); or

'(ii) the transaction is approved by the appropriate State bank supervisor of such State and the standard on which such approval is based does not have the effect of discriminating against out-of-State banks, out-of-State bank holding companies, or subsidiaries of such banks or holding companies.

'(E) EXCEPTION FOR CERTAIN BANKS—This paragraph shall not apply with respect to any interstate merger transaction involving only affiliated banks.

'(3) COMMUNITY REINVESTMENT COMPLIANCE—In determining whether to approve an application for an interstate merger transaction in which the resulting bank would have a branch or bank affiliate immediately following the transaction in any State in which the bank submitting the application (as the acquiring bank) had no branch or bank affiliate immediately before the transaction, the responsible agency shall—

'(A) comply with the responsibilities of the agency regarding such application under section 804 of the Community Reinvestment Act of 1977;

'(B) take into account the most recent written evaluation under section 804 of the Community Reinvestment Act of 1977 of any bank which would be an affiliate of the resulting bank; and

'(C) take into account the record of compliance of any applicant bank with applicable State community reinvestment laws.

'(4) ADEQUACY OF CAPITAL AND MANAGEMENT SKILLS— The responsible agency may approve an application for an interstate merger transaction pursuant to subsection (a) only if—

'(A) each bank involved in the transaction is adequately capitalized as of the date the application is filed; and

'(B) the responsible agency determines that the resulting bank will continue to be adequately capitalized and adequately managed upon the consummation of the transaction.

'(5) SURRENDER OF CHARTER AFTER MERGER TRANSAC-TION—The charters of all banks involved in an interstate merger transaction, other than the charter of the resulting bank, shall be surrendered, upon request, to the Federal banking agency or State bank supervisor which issued the charter.

'(c) APPLICABILITY OF CERTAIN LAWS TO INTERSTATE BANKING OPERATIONS—

'(1) STATE TAXATION AUTHORITY NOT AFFECTED—

'(A) IN GENERAL—No provision of this section shall be construed as affecting the authority of any State or political subdivision of any State to adopt, apply, or administer any tax or method of taxation to any bank, bank holding company, or foreign bank, or any affiliate of any bank, bank holding company, or foreign bank, to the extent such tax or tax method is otherwise permissible by or under the Constitution of the United States or other Federal law.

'(B) IMPOSITION OF SHARES TAX BY HOST STATES—In the case of a branch of an out-of-State bank which results from an interstate merger transaction, a proportionate amount of the value of the shares of the out-of-State bank may be subject to any bank shares tax levied or imposed by the host State, or any political subdivision of such host State that imposes such tax based upon a method adopted by the host State, which may include allocation and apportionment.

'(2) APPLICABILITY OF ANTITRUST LAWS—No provision of this section shall be construed as affecting—

'(A) the applicability of the antitrust laws; or

'(B) the applicability, if any, of any State law which is similar to the antitrust laws.

'(3) RESERVATION OF CERTAIN RIGHTS TO STATES- No provision of this section shall be construed as limiting in any way the right of a State to—

'(A) determine the authority of State banks chartered by that State to establish and maintain branches; or

'(B) supervise, regulate, and examine State banks chartered by that State.

'(4) STATE-IMPOSED NOTICE REQUIREMENTS—A host State may impose any notification or reporting requirement on a branch of an out-of-State bank if the requirement—

'(A) does not discriminate against out-of-State banks or bank holding companies; and

'(B) is not preempted by any Federal law regarding the same subject.

'(d) OPERATIONS OF THE RESULTING BANK—

'(1) CONTINUED OPERATIONS—A resulting bank may, subject to the approval of the appropriate Federal banking agency, retain and operate, as a main office or a branch, any office that any bank involved in an interstate merger transaction was operating as a main office or a branch immediately before the merger transaction.

'(2) ADDITIONAL BRANCHES—Following the consummation of any interstate merger transaction, the resulting bank may establish, acquire, or operate additional branches at any location where any bank involved in the transaction could have established, acquired, or operated a branch under applicable Federal or State law if such bank had not been a party to the merger transaction.

'(3) CERTAIN CONDITIONS AND COMMITMENTS CONTINUED—If, as a condition for the acquisition of a bank by an out-of-State bank holding company before the date of the enactment of the Riegle-Neal Interstate Banking and Branching Efficiency Act of 1994—

'(A) the home State of the acquired bank imposed conditions on such acquisition by such out-of-State bank holding company; or

'(B) the bank holding company made commitments to such State in connection with the acquisition, the State may enforce such conditions and commitments with respect to such bank holding company or any affiliated successor company which controls a bank or branch in such State as a result of an interstate merger transaction to the same extent as the State could enforce such conditions or commitments against the bank holding company before the consummation of the merger transaction.

'(e) EXCEPTION FOR BANKS IN DEFAULT OR IN DANGER OF DEFAULT—If an application under subsection (a)(1) for approval of a merger transaction which involves 1 or more banks in default or in danger of default or with respect to which the Corporation provides assistance under section 13(c), the responsible agency may approve such application without regard to subsection (b), or paragraph (2), (4), or (5) of subsection (a),

'(f) DEFINITIONS—For purposes of this section, the following definitions shall apply:

'(1) ADEQUATELY CAPITALIZED—The term 'adequately capitalized' has the same meaning as in section 38.

'(2) ANTITRUST LAWS—The term 'antitrust laws'—

'(A) has the same meaning as in subsection (a) of the first section of the Clayton Act; and

'(B) includes section 5 of the Federal Trade Commission Act to the extent such section 5 relates to unfair methods of competition.

'(3) BRANCH—The term 'branch' means any domestic branch.

'(4) HOME STATE—The term 'home State'—

'(A) means—

'(i) with respect to a national bank, the State in which the main office of the bank is located; and

'(ii) with respect to a State bank, the State by which the bank is chartered; and

'(B) with respect to a bank holding company, has the same meaning as in section 2 (o)(4) of the Bank Holding Company Act of 1956.

'(5) HOST STATE—The term 'host State' means, with respect to a bank, a State, other than the home State of the bank, in which the bank maintains, or seeks to establish and maintain, a branch.

'(6) INTERSTATE MERGER TRANSACTION—The term 'interstate merger transaction' means any merger transaction approved pursuant to subsection (a)(1).

'(7) MERGER TRANSACTION—The term 'merger transaction' has the meaning determined under section 18(c)(3).

'(8) OUT-OF-STATE BANK—The term 'out-of-State bank' means, with respect to any State, a bank whose home State is another State.

'(9) OUT-OF-STATE BANK HOLDING COMPANY—The term 'out-of-State bank holding company' means, with respect to any State, a bank holding company whose home State is another State.

'(10) RESPONSIBLE AGENCY—The term 'responsible agency' means the agency determined in accordance with section 18(c)(2) with respect to a merger transaction.

'(11) RESULTING BANK—The term 'resulting bank' means a bank that has tesulted from an interstate merger transaction under this section.'

(b) TECHNICAL AND CONFORMING AMENDMENTS—

(1) REVISED STATUTES—Section 5155 of the Revised Statutes (12 U.S.C. 36) is amended—

(A) by redesignating subsections (d) through (h) as subsections (h) through (l), respectively; and

(B) by inserting after subsection (c) the following new subsections:

'(d) BRANCHES RESULTING FROM INTERSTATE MERGER TRANS-ACTIONS—A national bank resulting from an interstate merger transaction (as defined in section 44(f)(6) of the Federal Deposit Insurance Act) may maintain and operate a branch in a State other than the home State (as defined in subsection (g)(3)(B)) of such bank in accordance with section 44 of the Federal Deposit Insurance Act.

'(e) EXCLUSIVE AUTHORITY FOR ADDITIONAL BRANCHES—

'(1) IN GENERAL—Effective June 1, 1997, a national bank may not acquire, establish, or operate a branch in any State other than the bank's home State (as defined in subsection (g)(3)(B)) or a State in which the bank already has a branch unless the acquisition, establishment, or operation of such branch in such State by such national bank is authorized under this section or section 13(f), 13(k), or 44 of the Federal Deposit Insurance Act.

'(2) RETENTION OF BRANCHES—In the case of a national bank which relocates the main office of such bank from 1 State to another State after May 31, 1997, the bank may retain and operate branches within the State which was the bank's home State (as defined in subsection (g)(3)(B)) before the relocation of such office only to the extent the bank would be authorized, under this section or any other provision of law referred to in paragraph (1), to acquire, establish, or commence to operate a branch in such State if—

'(A) the bank had no branches in such State; or

'(B) the branch resulted from—

'(i) an interstate merger transaction approved pursuant to section 44 of the Federal Deposit Insurance Act; or

'(ii) a transaction after May 31, 1997, pursuant to which the bank received assistance from the Federal Deposit Insurance Corporation under section 13 (c) of such Act.

'(f) LAW APPLICABLE TO INTERSTATE BRANCHING OPERA-
TIONS—

'(1) LAW APPLICABLE TO NATIONAL BANK BRANCHES—

'(A) IN GENERAL—The laws of the host State regarding community reinvestment, consumer protection, fair lending, and establishment of intrastate branches shall apply to any branch in the
host State of an out-of-State national bank to the same extent as
such State laws apply to a branch of a bank chartered by that State,
except—

'(i) when Federal law preempts the application of such State
laws to a national bank; or

'(ii) when the Comptroller of the Currency determines that the
application of such State laws would have a discriminatory effect on the branch in comparison with the effect the application
of such State laws would have with respect to branches of a bank
chartered by the host State.

'(B) ENFORCEMENT OF APPLICABLE STATE LAWS—The provisions of any State law to which a branch of a national bank is subject under this paragraph shall be enforced, with respect to such
branch, by the Comptroller of the Currency.

'(2) TREATMENT OF BRANCH AS BANK—All laws of a host State,
other than the laws regarding community reinvestment, consumer
protection, fair lending, establishment of intrastate branches, and the
application or administration of any tax or method of taxation, shall
apply to a branch (in such State) of an out-of-State national bank to the
same extent as such laws would apply if the branch were a national
bank the main office of which is in such State.

'(3) RULE OF CONSTRUCTION—No provision of this subsection
may be construed as affecting the legal standards for preemption of
the application of State law to national banks..'

(2) ACT OF MAY 1, 1886—Section 2 of the Act entitled 'An Act to en-
able national banking associations to increase their capital stock and to
change their names and locations' and approved May 1, 1886 (12 U.S.C.
30) is amended by adding at the end the following new subsection:

'(c) COORDINATION WITH REVISED STATUTES—In the case of a national bank which relocates the main office of such bank from 1 State to
another State after May 31, 1997, the bank may retain and operate
branches within the State from which the bank relocated such office only
to the extent authorized in section 5155(e)(2) of the Revised Statutes.'

(3) FEDERAL DEPOSIT INSURANCE ACT—

(A) EXCLUSIVE AUTHORITY FOR ADDITIONAL BRANCHES
OF STATE NONMEMBER BANKS— Section 18(d) of the Federal

Deposit Insurance Act (12 U.S. C. 1828(d)) is amended by adding at the end the following new paragraph:

'(3) EXCLUSIVE AUTHORITY FOR ADDITIONAL BRANCHES-

'(A) IN GENERAL—Effective June 1, 1997, a State nonmember bank may not acquire, establish, or operate a branch in any State other than the bank's home State (as defined in section 44(f)(4)) or a State in which the bank already has a branch unless the acquisition, establishment, or operation of a branch in such State by a State non-member bank is authorized under this subsection or section 13(f), 13(k), or 44.

'(B) RETENTION OF BRANCHES—In the case of a State nonmember bank which relocates the main office of such bank from 1 State to another State after May 31, 1997, the bank may retain and oper-ate branches within the State which was the bank's home State (as defined in section 44(f)(4)) before the relocation of such office only to the extent the bank would be authorized, under this section or any other provision of law referred to in subparagraph (A), to ac-quire, establish, or commence to operate a branch in such State if—

'(i) the bank had no branches in such State; or

'(ii) the branch resulted from—

'(I) an interstate merger transaction approved pursuant to section 44; or

'(II) a transaction after May 31, 1997, pursuant to which the bank received assistance from the Corporation under section 13(c).

(B) ACTIVITIES OF BRANCHES OF STATE BANKS RESULTING FROM INTERSTATE MERGER TRANSACTIONS—Section 24 of the Federal Deposit Insurance Act (12 U.S.C. 1831a) is amended by adding at the end the following new subsection:

ACTIVITIES OF BRANCHES OF OUT-OF-STATE BANKS-

'(1) IN GENERAL—The laws of a host State, including laws regard-ing community reinvestment, consumer protection, fair lending, and establishment of intrastate branches, shall apply to any branch in the host State of an out-of-State State bank to the same extent as such State laws apply to a branch of a bank chartered by that State.

'(2) ACTIVITIES OF BRANCHES—An insured State bank that estab-lishes a branch in a host State may not conduct any activity at such branch that is not permissible for a bank chartered by the host State.

'(3) DEFINITIONS—The terms 'host State,' 'interstate merger trans-action,' and 'out-of-State bank' have the same meanings as in section 44(f).'

(4) ACT OF NOVEMBER 7, 1918– The Act entitled 'An Act to provide for the consolidation of the national banking associations.' and approved November 7, 1918 (12 U.S. C. 215 et seq.) is amended—

(A) by redesignating section 2 as section 3.

(B) by redesignating section 3 as section 5;

(C) in the 1st section, by striking 'That (a) any national banking association' and inserting the following:

'SECTION 1. SHORT TITLE.

'This Act may be cited as the 'National Bank Consolidation and Merger Act.'

'SEC. 2. CONSOLIDATION OF BANKS WITHIN THE SAME STATE.

'(a) IN GENERAL—Any national bank'; and

(D) by inserting after section 3 (as so redesignated under subparagraph (A) of this paragraph) the following new section:

'SEC. 4. INTERSTATE CONSOLIDATIONS AND MERGERS.

'(a) IN GENERAL—A national bank may engage in a consolidation or merger under this Act with an out-of-State bank if the consolidation or merger is approved pursuant to section 44 of the Federal Deposit Insurance Act.

'(b) SCOPE OF APPLICATION—Subsection (a) shall not apply with respect to any consolidation or merger before June 1, 1997, unless the home State of each bank involved in the transaction has in effect a law described in section 44(a)(3) of the Federal Deposit Insurance Act.

'(c) DEFINITIONS—The terms 'home State' and 'out-of-State bank' have the same meaning as in section 44(f) of the Federal Deposit Insurance Act.'

(5) HOME OWNERS' LOAN ACT—Section 3 of the Home Owners' Loan Act (12 U.S. C. 1462a) is amended—

(A) by redesignating subsections (f) through (i) as subsections (g) through [j]respectively; and

(B) by inserting after subsection (e), the following new subsection:

'(f) STATE HOMESTEAD PROVISIONS—No provision of this Act or any other provision of law administered by the Director shall be construed as superseding any homestead provision of any State constitution, including any implementing State statute, in effect on the date of enactment of the Riegle-Neal Interstate Banking and Branching Efficiency Act of 1994, or any subsequent amendment to such a State constitutional or statutory provision in effect on such date, that exempts the homestead of any person from foreclosure, or forced sale, for the payment of all debts, other than a purchase money obligation relating to the homestead, taxes due on the homestead, or an obligation arising from work and material used in constructing improvements on the homestead.'

SEC. 103. STATE 'OPT-IN' ELECTION TO PERMIT INTERSTATE BRANCHING THROUGH DE NOVO BRANCHES.

(a) NATIONAL BANKS—Section 5155 of the Revised Statutes (12 U.S.C. 36) is amended by inserting after subsection (f) (as added by section 102(b)) the following new subsection:

'(g) STATE' OPT-IN' ELECTION TO PERMIT INTERSTATE BRANCHING THROUGH DE NOVO BRANCHES—

'(1) IN GENERAL—Subject to paragraph (2), the Comptroller of the Currency may approve an application by a national bank to establish and operate a de novo branch in a State (other than the bank's home State) in which the bank does not maintain a branch if—

'(A) there is in effect in the host State a law that—

'(i) applies equally to all banks; and

'(ii) expressly permits all out-of-State banks to establish de novo branches in such State; and

'(B) the conditions established in, or made applicable to this paragraph by, paragraph (2) are met.

'(2) CONDITIONS ON ESTABLISHMENT AND OPERATION OF INTERSTATE BRANCH—

'(A) ESTABLISHMENT—An application by a national bank to establish and operate a de novo branch in a host State shall be subject to the same requirements and conditions to which an application for an interstate merger transaction is subject under paragraphs (1), (3), and (4) of section 44(b) of the Federal Deposit Insurance Act.

'(B) OPERATION—Subsections (c) and (d)(2) of section 44 of the Federal Deposit Insurance Act shall apply with respect to each branch of a national bank which is established and operated pursuant to an application approved under this subsection in the same manner and to the same extent such provisions of such section 44 apply to a branch of a national bank which resulted from an interstate merger transaction approved pursuant to such section 44.

'(3) DEFINITIONS—The following definitions shall apply for purposes of this section:

'(A) DE NOVO BRANCH—The term 'de novo branch' means a branch of a national bank which—

'(i) is originally established by the national bank as a branch; and

'(ii) does not become a branch of such bank as a result of—

'(I) the acquisition by the bank of an insured depository institution or a branch of an insured depository institution; or

'(II) the conversion, merger, or consolidation of any such institution or branch.

'(B) HOME STATE—The term 'home State' means the State in which the main office of a national bank is located.

'(C) HOST STATE—The term 'host State' means, with respect to a bank, a State, other than the home State of the bank, in which the bank maintains, or seeks to establish and maintain, a branch..'

(b) STATE BANKS—Section 18(d) of the Federal Deposit Insurance Act (12 U.S.C. 1828(d)) is amended by inserting after paragraph (3) (as added by section 102(b)(3) of this title) the following new paragraph:

'(4) STATE 'OPT-IN' ELECTION TO PERMIT INTERSTATE BRANCHING THROUGH DE NOVO BRANCHES—

'(A) IN GENERAL—Subject to subparagraph (B), the Corporation may approve an application by an insured State nonmember bank to establish and operate a de novo branch in a State (other than the bank's home State) in which the bank does not maintain a branch if—

'(i) there is in effect in the host State a law that—

'(I) applies equally to all banks; and

'(II) expressly permits all out-of-State banks to establish de novo branches in such State; and

'(ii) the conditions established in, or made applicable to this paragraph by, subparagraph (B) are met.

'(B) CONDITIONS ON ESTABLISHMENT AND OPERATION OF INTERSTATE BRANCH—

'(i) ESTABLISHMENT—An application by an insured State nonmember bank to establish and operate a de novo branch in a host State shall be subject to the same requirements and conditions to which an application for a merger transaction is subject under paragraphs (1), (3), and (4) of section 44 (b).

'(ii) OPERATION—Subsections (c) and (d)(2) of section 44 shall apply with respect to each branch of an insured State nonmember bank which is established and operated pursuant to an application approved under this paragraph in the same manner and to the same extent such provisions of such section apply to a branch of a State bank which resulted from a merger transaction under such section 44.

'(C) DE NOVO BRANCH DEFINED—For purposes of this paragraph, the term 'de novo branch' means a branch of a State bank which—

'(i) is originally established by the State bank as a branch; and

'(ii) does not become a branch of such bank as a result of—

'(I) the acquisition by the bank of an insured depository institution or a branch of an insured depository institution; or

'(II) the conversion, merger, or consolidation of any such institution or branch.

'(D) HOME STATE DEFINED—The term 'home State' means the State by which a State bank is chartered.

'(E) HOST STATE DEFINED—The term 'host State' means, with respect to a bank, a State, other than the home State of the bank, in which the bank maintains, or seeks to establish and maintain, a branch.'

SEC. 104. BRANCHING BY FOREIGN BANKS.

(a) IN GENERAL—Section 5(a) of the International Banking Act of 1978 (12 U.S.C. 3103(a)), is amended to read as follows:

'(a) INTERSTATE BRANCHING AND AGENCY OPERATIONS—

'(1) FEDERAL BRANCH OR AGENCY—Subject to the provisions of this Act and with the prior written approval by the Board and the Comptroller of the Currency of an application, a foreign bank may establish and operate a Federal branch or agency in any State outside the home State of such foreign bank to the extent that the establishment and operation of such branch would be permitted under section 5155(g) of the Revised Statutes or section 44 of the Federal Deposit Insurance Act if the foreign bank were a national bank whose home State is the same State as the home State of the foreign bank.

'(2) STATE BRANCH OR AGENCY—Subject to the provisions of this Act and with the prior written approval by the Board and the appropriate State bank supervisor of an application, a foreign bank may establish and operate a State branch or agency in any State outside the home State of such foreign bank to the extent that such establishment and operation would be permitted under section 18(d)(4) or 44 of the Federal Deposit Insurance Act if the foreign bank were a State bank whose home State is the same State as the home State of the foreign bank.

'(3) CRITERIA FOR DETERMINATION—In approving an application under paragraph (1) or (2), the Board and (in the case of an application under paragraph (1)) the Comptroller of the Currency—

'(A) shall apply the standards applicable to the establishment of a foreign bank office in the United States under section 7(d);

'(B) may not approve an application unless the Board and (in the case of an application under paragraph (1)) the Comptroller of the Currency—

'(i) determine that the foreign bank's financial resources, including the capital level of the bank, are equivalent to those required for a domestic bank to be approved for branching under section 5155 of the Revised Statutes and section 44 of the Federal Deposit Insurance Act; and

'(ii) consult with the Secretary of the Treasury regarding capital equivalency, and

'(C) shall apply the same requirements and conditions to which an application for an interstate merger transaction is subject under paragraphs (1), (3), and (4) of section 44(b) of the Federal Deposit Insurance Act.

'(4) OPERATION—Subsections (c) and (d)(2) of section 44 of the Federal Deposit Insurance Act shall apply with respect to each branch and agency of a foreign bank which is established and operated pursuant to an application approved under this subsection in the same manner and to the same extent such provisions of such section apply to a domestic branch of a national or State bank (as such terms are defined in section 3 of such Act) which resulted from a merger transaction under such section 44,

'(5) EXCLUSIVE AUTHORITY FOR ADDITIONAL BRANCHES— Except as provided in this section, a foreign bank may not, directly or indirectly, acquire, establish, or operate a branch or agency in any State other than the home State of such bank.

'(6) REQUIREMENT FOR A SEPARATE SUBSIDIARY—If the Board or the Comptroller of the Currency, taking into account differing regulatory or accounting standards, finds that adherence by a foreign bank to capital requirements equivalent to those imposed under section 5155 of the Revised Statutes and section 44 of the Federal Deposit Insurance Act could be verified only if the banking activities of such bank in the United States are carried out in a domestic banking subsidiary within the United States, the Board and (in the case of an application under paragraph (1)) the Comptroller of the Currency may approve an application under paragraph (1) or (2) subject to a requirement that the foreign bank or company controlling the foreign bank establish a domestic banking subsidiary in the United States.

'(7) ADDITIONAL AUTHORITY FOR INTERSTATE BRANCHES AND AGENCIES OF FOREIGN BANKS— Notwithstanding paragraphs (1) and (2), a foreign bank may, with the approval of the Board and the Comptroller of the Currency, establish and operate a Federal branch or Federal agency or, with the approval of the Board and the appropriate State bank supervisor, a State branch or State agency in any State outside the foreign bank's home State if—

'(A) the establishment and operation of a branch or agency is expressly permitted by the State in which the branch or agency is to be established; and

'(B) in the case of a Federal or State branch, the branch receives only such deposits as would be permissible for a corporation organized under section 25A of the Federal Reserve Act,

'(9) HOME STATE OF DOMESTIC BANK DEFINED—For purposes of this subsection, the term 'home State' means—

'(A) with respect to a national bank, the State in which the main office of the bank is located—and

'(B) with respect to a State bank, the State by which the bank is chartered.'

(b) CONTINUED AUTHORITY FOR LIMITED BRANCHES, AGENCIES, OR COMMERCIAL LENDING COMPANIES—Section 5(b) of the International Banking Act of 1978 (12 U.S.C. 3103(b)) is amended by adding at the end the following new sentence:

'Notwithstanding subsection (a), a foreign bank may continue to operate, after the enactment of the Riegle-Neal Interstate Banking and Branching Efficiency Act of 1994, any Federal branch, State branch, Federal agency, State agency, or commercial lending company subsidiary which such bank was operating on the day before the date of the enactment of such Act to the extent the branch, agency, or subsidiary continues, after the enactment of such Act, to engage in operations which were lawful under the laws in effect on the day before such date.

(c) CLARIFICATION OF BRANCHING RULES IN THE CASE OF A FOREIGN BANK WITH DOMESTIC BANK SUBSIDIARY—Section 5 of the International Banking Act of 1978 (12 U.S.C. 3103) is amended by adding at the end the following new subsection:

'(d) CLARIFICATION OF BRANCHING RULES IN THE CASE OF A FOREIGN BANK WITH A DOMESTIC BANK SUBSIDIARY—In the case of a foreign bank that has a domestic bank subsidiary within the United States—

'(1) the fact that such bank controls a domestic bank shall not affect the authority of the foreign bank to establish Federal and State branches or agencies to the extent permitted under subsection (a); and

'(2) the fact that the domestic bank is controlled by a foreign bank which has Federal or State branches or agencies in States other than the home State of such domestic bank shall not affect the authority of the domestic bank to establish branches outside the home State of the domestic bank to the extent permitted under section 5155(g) of the Revised Statutes or section 18(d)(4) or 44 of the Federal Deposit Insurance Act, as the case may be.

(d) HOME STATE DETERMINATIONS—Section 5(c) of the International Banking Act of 1978 (12 U.S.C. 3103(c)) is amended to read as follows:

'(c) DETERMINATION OF HOME STATE OF FOREIGN BANK—For the purposes of this section—

'(1) in the case of a foreign bank that has any branch, agency, subsidiary commercial lending company, or subsidiary bank in more than 1 State, the home State of the foreign bank is the 1 State of such States which is selected to be the home State by the foreign bank or, in default of any such selection, by the Board; and

'(2) in the case of a foreign bank that does not have a branch, agency, subsidiary commercial lending company, or subsidiary bank in more than 1 State, the home State of the foreign bank is the State in which the foreign bank has a branch, agency, subsidiary commercial lending company, or subsidiary bank.

SEC. 105. COORDINATION OF EXAMINATION AUTHORITY.

Section 10 of the Federal Deposit Insurance Act (12 U.S.C. 1820) is amended by inserting after subsection (g) the following new subsection:

'(h) COORDINATION OF EXAMINATION AUTHORITY—

'(1) IN GENERAL—The appropriate State bank supervisor of a host State may examine a branch operated in such State by an out-of-State insured State bank that resulted from an interstate merger transaction approved under section 44 or a branch established in such State pursuant to section 5155(g) of the Revised Statutes or section 18(d)(4)—

'(A) for the purpose of determining compliance with host State laws, including those that govern banking, community reinvestment, fair lending, consumer protection, and permissible activities; and

'(B) to ensure that the activities of the branch are not conducted in an unsafe or unsound manner.

'(2) ENFORCEMENT—If the State bank supervisor of a host State determines that there is a violation of the law of the host State concerning the activities being conducted by a branch described in paragraph (1) or that the branch is being operated in an unsafe and unsound manner, the State bank supervisor of the host State or, to the extent authorized by the law of the host State, a State law enforcement officer may undertake such enforcement actions and proceedings as would be permitted under the law of the host State as if the branch were a bank chartered by that host State.

'(3) COOPERATIVE AGREEMENT—The State bank supervisors from 2 or more States may enter into cooperative agreements to facilitate State regulatory supervision of State banks, including cooperative agreements relating to the coordination of examinations and joint participation in examinations.

'(4) FEDERAL REGULATORY AUTHORITY—No provision of this subsection shall be construed as limiting in any way the authority of an appropriate Federal banking agency to examine or to take any enforcement actions or proceedings against any bank or branch of a bank for which the agency is the appropriate Federal banking agency.'

SEC. 106. BRANCH CLOSURES.

Section 42 of the Federal Deposit Insurance Act (12 U.S.C. 1831r-1) is amended by adding at the end the following new subsection:

'(d) BRANCH CLOSURES IN INTERSTATE BANKING OR BRANCHING OPERATIONS—

'(1) NOTICE REQUIREMENTS—In the case of an interstate bank which proposes to close any branch in a low- or moderate-income area, the notice required under subsection (b)(2) shall contain the mailing address of the appropriate Federal banking agency and a statement that comments on the proposed closing of such branch may be mailed to such agency.

'(2) ACTION REQUIRED BY APPROPRIATE FEDERAL BANKING AGENCY—If, in the case of a branch referred to in paragraph (1)—

'(A) a person from the area in which such branch is located—

'(i) submits a written request relating to the closing of such branch to the appropriate Federal banking agency; and

'(ii) includes a statement of specific reasons for the request, including a discussion of the adverse effect of such closing on the availability of banking services in the area affected by the closing of the branch—and

'(B) the agency concludes that the request is not frivolous, the agency shall consult with community leaders in the affected area and convene a meeting of representatives of the agency and other interested depository institution regulatory agencies with community leaders in the affected area and such other individuals, organizations, and depository institutions (as defined in section 19(b)(1)(A) of the Federal Reserve Act) as the agency may determine, in the discretion of the agency, to be appropriate, to explore the feasibility of obtaining adequate alternative facilities and services for the affected area, including the establishment of a new branch by another depository institution, the chartering of a new depository institution, or the establishment of a community development credit union, following the closing of the branch.

'(3) NO EFFECT ON CLOSING—No action by the appropriate Federal banking agency' under paragraph (2) shall affect the authority of an interstate bank to close a branch (including the timing of such closing) if the requirements of subsections (a) and (b) have been met by such bank with respect to the branch being closed.

'(4) DEFINITIONS—For purposes of this subsection, the following definitions shall apply:

'(A) INTERSTATE BANK DEFINED—The term 'interstate bank' means a bank which maintains branches in more than 1 State.

'(B) LOW- OR MODERATE-INCOME AREA—The term 'low- or moderate income area' means a census tract for which the median family income is—

'(i) less than 80 percent of the median family income for the metropolitan statistical area (as designated by the Director of the Office of Management and Budget) in which the census tract is located; or

'(ii) in the case of a census tract which is not located in a metropolitan statistical area, less than 80 percent of the median family income for the State in which the census tract is located, as determined without taking into account family income in metropolitan statistical areas in such State.'

SEC. 107. EQUALIZING COMPETITIVE OPPORTUNITIES FOR UNITED STATES AND FOREIGN BANKS.

(a) REGULATORY OBJECTIVES—Section 6 of the International Banking Act of 1978 (12 U.S.C. 3104) is amended—

(1) by redesignating subsections (a) through (c) as subsections (b) through (d), respectively—and

(2) by inserting after 'sec. 6' the following new subsection:

'(a) OBJECTIVE—In implementing this section, the Comptroller and the Federal Deposit Insurance Corporation shall each, by affording equal competitive opportunities to foreign and United States banking organizations in their United States operations, ensure that foreign banking organizations do not receive an unfair competitive advantage over United States banking organizations.'

(b) REVIEW OF REGULATIONS—

(1) IN GENERAL—Each Federal banking agency, after consultation with the other Federal banking agencies to assure uniformity, shall revise the regulations adopted by such agency under section 6 of the International Banking Act of 1978 to ensure that the regulations are consistent with the objective set forth in section 6(a) of the International Banking Act of 1978.

(2) SPECIFIC FACTORS—In carrying out paragraph (1), each Federal banking agency shall consider whether to permit an uninsured branch of a foreign bank to accept initial deposits of less than $100,000 only from—

(A) individuals who are not citizens or residents of the United States at the time of the initial deposit;

(B) individuals who—

(i) are not citizens of the United States;

(ii) are residents of the United States-, and

(iii) are employed by a foreign bank, foreign business, foreign government, or recognized international organization;

(C) persons to whom the branch or foreign bank has extended credit or provided other nondeposit banking services;

(D) foreign businesses and large United States businesses;

(E) foreign governmental units and recognized international organizations; and

(F) persons who are depositing funds in connection with the issuance of a financial instrument by the branch for the transmission of funds.

(3) REDUCTION IN REGULATORY DE MINIMIS EXEMPTION—In carrying out paragraph (1), each Federal banking agency shall limit any exemption which is—

(A) available under any regulation prescribed pursuant to section 6(d) of the International Banking Act of 1978 providing for the acceptance of initial deposits of less than $100,000 by an uninsured branch of a foreign bank; and

(B) based on a percentage of the average deposits at such branch; to not more than 1 percent of the average deposits at such branch.

(4) ADDITIONAL RELEVANT CONSIDERATIONS—In carrying out paragraph (1), each Federal banking agency shall also consider the importance of maintaining and improving the availability of credit to all sectors of the United States economy, including the international trade finance sector of the United State economy.

(5) DEADLINE FOR PRESCRIBING REVISED REGULATIONS—Each Federal banking agency—

(A) shall publish final regulations under paragraph (1) in the Federal Register not later than 12 months after the date of enactment of this Act—and

(B) may establish reasonable transition rules to facilitate any termination of any deposit-taking activities that were permissible under regulations that were in effect' before the date of enactment of this Act.

(6) DEFINITIONS—For purposes of this subsection—

(A) the term 'Federal banking agency' means—

(i)the Comptroller of the Currency with respect to Federal branches of foreign banks; and

(ii) the Federal Deposit Insurance Corporation with respect to State branches of foreign banks; and

(B) the term 'uninsured branch' means a branch of a foreign bank that is not an insured branch, as defined in section 3(s)(3) of the Federal Deposit Insurance Act (12 U.S.C. 1813(s)(3)).

(c) AMENDMENT AFFIRMING THAT CONSUMER PROTECTION LAWS APPLY TO FOREIGN BANKS—Section 9(b) of the International Banking Act of 1978 (12 U. S.C. 3106a) is amended—

(1) in paragraph (1)—

(A) by redesignating subparagraphs (A) and (B) as subparagraphs (B) and (C), respectively; and

(B) by inserting after 'which'—the following new subparagraph: '(A) impose requirements that protect the rights of consumers in financial transactions, to the extent that the branch, agency, or commercial lending company engages in activities that are subject to such laws; and

(2) in paragraph (2)—

(A) by redesignating subparagraphs (A) and (B) as subparagraphs (B) and (C), respectively; and

(B) by inserting after 'which'—the following new subparagraph: '(A) impose requirements that protect the rights of consumers in financial transactions, to the extent that the branch, agency, or commercial lending company engages in activities that are subject to such laws.

(d) INSURED BANKS IN TERRITORIES NOT TREATED AS FOREIGN BANKS FOR PURPOSES OF RETAIL DEPOSIT-TAKING RULE—Section 6(d) of the International Banking Act of 1978 (12 U. S.C. 3104(c)) (as so redesignated by subsection (a)(1) of this section) is amended by adding at the end the following new paragraph:

'(3) INSURED BANKS IN U.S. TERRITORIES—For purposes of this subsection, the term 'foreign bank' does not include any bank organized under the laws of any territory of the United States, Puerto Rico, Guam, American Samoa, or the Virgin Islands the deposits of which are insured by the Federal Deposit Insurance Corporation pursuant to the Federal Deposit Insurance Act..'

(e) AMENDMENT RELATING TO SHELL BRANCHES—

(1) IN GENERAL- Section 7 of the International Banking Act of 1978 (12 U.S.C. 3105) is amended by adding at the end the following new subsection:

'(k) MANAGEMENT OF SHELL BRANCHES—

'(1) TRANSACTIONS PROHIBITED—A branch or agency of a foreign bank shall not manage, through an office of the foreign bank which is located outside the United States and is managed or controlled by such branch or agency, any type of activity that a bank organized under the laws of the United States, any State, or the District of Columbia is not permitted to manage at any branch or subsidiary of such bank which is located outside the United States.

'(2) REGULATIONS—Any regulations promulgated to carry out this section—

'(A) shall be promulgated in accordance with section 13; and

'(B) shall be uniform, to the extent practicable.

(2) EFFECTIVE DATE—The amendment made by paragraph (1) shall become effective at the end of the 180–day period beginning on the date of enactment of this Act.

(f) MEETING COMMUNITY CREDIT NEEDS—Section 5(a) of the International Banking Act of 1978 (12 U. S. C. 3103 (a)) (as amended by section 104 of this Act) is amended by inserting after paragraph (7) the following new paragraph:

'(8) CONTINUING REQUIREMENT FOR MEETING COMMUNITY CREDIT NEEDS AFTER INITIAL INTERSTATE ENTRY BY ACQUISITION—

'(A) IN GENERAL—If a foreign bank acquires a bank or a branch of a bank, in a State in which the foreign bank does not maintain a branch, and such acquired bank is, or is part of, a regulated financial institution (as defined in section 803 of the Community Reinvestment Act of 1977), the Community Reinvestment Act of 1977 shall continue to apply to each branch of the foreign bank which results from the acquisition as if such branch were a regulated financial institution.

'(B) EXCEPTION FOR BRANCH THAT RECEIVES ONLY DEPOSITS PERMISSIBLE FOR AN EDGE ACT CORPORATION— Paragraph (1) shall not apply to any branch that receives only such deposits as are permissible for a corporation organized under section 25A of the Federal Reserve Act to receive.

SEC. 108. FEDERAL RESERVE BOARD STUDY ON BANK FEES.

(a)IN GENERAL—Section 1002 of the Financial Institutions Reform, Recovery, and Enforcement Act of 1989 (12 U.S.C. 1811 note) is amended to read as follows:

'SEC. 1002. SURVEY OF BANK FEES AND SERVICES.

'(a) ANNUAL SURVEY REQUIRED—The Board of Governors of the Federal Reserve System shall obtain a sample, which is representative by geographic location and size of the institution, of—

(1) certain retail banking services provided by insured depository institutions; and

'(2) the fees, if any, which are imposed by such institutions for providing any such service, including fees imposed for not sufficient funds, deposit items returned, and automated teller machine transactions.

'(b) ANNUAL REPORT TO CONGRESS REQUIRED—

'(1) PREPARATION—The Board of Governors of the Federal Reserve System shall prepare a report of the results of each survey conducted pursuant to subsection (a).

'(2) CONTENTS OF THE REPORT—Each report prepared pursuant to paragraph (1) shall include—

'(A) a description of any discernible trend, in the Nation as a whole and in each region, in the cost and availability of retail banking services which delineates differences on the basis of size of the institution and engagement in multistate activity; and

'(B) a description of the correlation, if any, among the following factors:

'(i) An increase or decrease in the amount of any deposit insurance premium assessed by the Federal Deposit Insurance Corporation against insured depository institutions.

'(ii) An increase or decrease in the amount of the fees imposed by such institutions for providing retail banking services.

'(iii) A decrease in the availability of such services.

'(3) SUBMISSION TO CONGRESS—The Board of Governors of the Federal Reserve System shall submit an annual report to the Congress not later than September 1, 1995, and not later than June 1 of each subsequent year.

(b) SUNSET- The requirements of subsection (a) shall not apply after the end of the 7–year period beginning on the date of enactment of this Act.

SEC. 109. PROHIBITION AGAINST DEPOSIT PRODUCTION OFFICES.

(a) REGULATIONS—The appropriate Federal banking agencies shall prescribe uniform regulations effective June 1, 1997, which prohibit any out-of-State bank from using any authority to engage in interstate branching pursuant to this title, or any amendment made by this title to any other provision of law, primarily for the purpose of deposit production.

(b) GUIDELINES FOR MEETING CREDIT NEEDS—Regulations issued under subsection (a) shall include guidelines to ensure that interstate branches operated by an out-of-State bank in a host State are reasonably helping to meet the credit needs of the communities which the branches serve.

(c) LIMITATION ON OUT-OF-STATE LOANS—

(1) LIMITATION—Regulations issued under subsection (a) shall require that, beginning no earlier than 1 year after establishment or acquisition of an interstate branch or branches in a host State by an out-of-State bank, if the appropriate Federal banking agency for the out-of-State bank determines that the bank's level of lending in the host State relative to the deposits from the host State (as reasonably determinable from available information including the agency's sampling of the bank's loan files during an examination or such data as is otherwise available) is less than half the average of total loans in the host State relative to total deposits from the host State (as determinable from relevant sources) for all banks the home State of which is such State—

(A) the appropriate Federal banking agency for the out-of-State bank shall review the loan portfolio of the bank and determine whether the bank is reasonably helping to meet the credit needs of the communities served by the bank in the host State; and

(B) if the agency determines that the out-of-State bank is not reasonably helping to meet those needs—

(i) the agency may order that an interstate branch or branches of such bank in the host State be closed unless the bank provides reasonable assurances to the satisfaction of the appropriate Federal banking agency that the bank has an acceptable plan that will reasonably help to meet the credit needs of the communities served by the bank in the host State, and

(ii) the out-of-State bank may not open a new interstate branch in the host State unless the bank provides reasonable assurances to the satisfaction of the appropriate Federal banking agency that the bank will reasonably help to meet the credit needs of the community that the new branch will serve.

(2) CONSIDERATIONS—In making a determination under paragraph (1)(A), the appropriate Federal banking agency shall consider—

(A) whether the interstate branch or branches of the out-of-State bank were formerly part of a failed or failing depository institution;

(B) whether the interstate branch was acquired under circumstances where there was a low loan-to-deposit ratio because of the nature of the acquired institution's business or loan portfolio;

(C) whether the interstate branch or branches of the out-of-State bank have a higher concentration of commercial or credit card lending, trust services, or other specialized activities;

(D) the ratings received by the out-of-State bank under the Community Reinvestment Act of 1977;

(E) economic conditions, including the level of loan demand, within the communities served by the interstate branch or branches of the out-of-State bank; and

(F) the safe and sound operation and condition of the out-of-State bank.

(3) Branch closing procedure—

(A) NOTICE REQUIRED—Before exercising any authority under paragraph (1)(B) (i), the appropriate Federal banking agency shall issue to the bank a notice of the agency's intention to close an interstate branch or branches and shall schedule a hearing.

(B) HEARING—Section 8(h) of the Federal Deposit Insurance Act shall apply to any proceeding brought under this paragraph.

(d) APPLICATION—This section shall apply with respect to any interstate branch established or acquired in a host State pursuant to this title or any amendment made by this title to any other provision of law.

(e) DEFINITIONS—For the purposes of this section, the following definitions shall apply:

(1) APPROPRIATE FEDERAL BANKING AGENCY, BANK, STATE, AND STATE BANK—The terms 'appropriate Federal banking agency,' 'bank,' 'state,' and 'state bank,' have the same meanings as in section 3 of the Federal Deposit Insurance Act.

(2) HOME STATE—The term 'home State' means—

(A) in the case of a national bank, the State in which the main office of the bank is located; and

(B) in the case of a State bank, the State by which the bank is chartered.

(3) HOST STATE—The term 'host State' means a State in which a bank establishes a branch other than the home State of the bank.

(4) INTERSTATE BRANCH—The term 'interstate branch' means a branch established pursuant to this title or any amendment made by this title to any other provision of law.

(5) OUT-OF-STATE BANK—The term 'out-of-State bank' means, with respect to any State, a bank the home State of which is another State and, for purposes of this section, includes a foreign bank, the home State of which is another State.

SEC. 110. COMMUNITY REINVESTMENT ACT EVALUATION OF BANKS WITH INTERSTATE BRANCHES.

(a) IN GENERAL—Section 807 of the Community Reinvestment Act of 1977 (12 U.S.C. 2906) is amended by adding at the end the following new subsections:

'(d) INSTITUTIONS WITH INTERSTATE BRANCHES—

'(1) STATE-BY-STATE EVALUATION—In the case of a regulated financial institution that maintains domestic branches in 2 or more States, the appropriate Federal financial supervisory agency shall prepare—

'(A) a written evaluation of the entire institution's record of performance under this title, as required by subsections (a), (b), and (c); and

'(B) for each State in which the institution maintains 1 or more domestic branches, a separate written evaluation of the institution's record of performance within such State under this title, as required by subsections (a), (b), and (c).

'(2) MULTISTATE METROPOLITAN AREAS—In the case of a regulated financial institution that maintains domestic branches in 2 or more States within a multistate metropolitan area, the appropriate Federal financial supervisory agency shall prepare a separate written evaluation of the institution's record of performance within such metropolitan area under this title, as required by subsections (a), (b), and (c). If the agency prepares a written evaluation pursuant to this paragraph, the scope of the written evaluation required under paragraph (1)(B) shall be adjusted accordingly.

'(3) CONTENT OF STATE LEVEL EVALUATION—A written evaluation prepared pursuant to paragraph (1)(B) shall—

'(A) present the information required by subparagraphs (A) and (B) of subsection (b)(1) separately for each metropolitan area in which the institution maintains I or more domestic branch offices and separately for the remainder of the nonmetropolitan area of the State if the institution maintains 1 or more domestic branch offices in such nonmetropolitan area; and

'(B) describe how the Federal financial supervisory agency has performed the examination of the institution, including a list of the individual branches examined.

'(e) DEFINITIONS—For purposes of this section the following definitions shall apply:

'(1) DOMESTIC BRANCH—The term 'domestic branch' means any branch office or other facility of a regulated financial institution that accepts deposits, located in any State.

'(2) METROPOLITAN AREA—The term 'metropolitan area' means any primary metropolitan statistical area, metropolitan statistical area, or consolidated metropolitan statistical area, as defined by the Director of the Office of Management and Budget, with a population of 250,000 or more, and any other area designated as such by the appropriate Federal financial supervisory agency.

'(3) STATE—The term 'state' has the same meaning as in section 3 of the Federal Deposit Insurance Act.

(b) SEPARATE PRESENTATION—Section 807(b)(1) of the Community Reinvestment Act of 1977 (12 U. S.C. 2906(b)(1)) is amended—

(1) by redesignating subparagraphs (A) through (C) as clauses (i) through (iii), respectively;

(2) by striking 'The public' and inserting the following:

'(A) CONTENTS OF WRITTEN EVALUATION—The public'; and (3)by adding at the end the following new subparagraph:

'(B) METROPOLITAN AREA DISTINCTIONS—The information required by clauses (i) and (ii) of subparagraph (A) shall be presented separately for each metropolitan area in which a regulated depository institution maintains one or more domestic branch offices.'

SEC. 111. RESTATEMENT OF EXISTING LAW.

No provision of this title and no amendment made by this title to any other provision of law shall be construed as affecting in any way—

(1) the authority of any State or political subdivision of any State to adopt, apply, or administer any tax or method of taxation to any bank, bank holding company, or foreign bank, or any affiliate of any such bank, bank holding company, or foreign bank, to the extent that such tax or tax method is otherwise permissible by or under the Constitution of the United States or other Federal law;

(2) the right of any State, or any political subdivision of any State, to impose or maintain a nondiscriminatory franchise tax or other nonproperty tax instead of a franchise tax in accordance with section 3124 of title 31, United States Code—or

(3) the applicability of section 5197 of the Revised Statutes or section 27 of the Federal Deposit Insurance Act.

SEC. 112. GAO REPORT ON DATA COLLECTION UNDER INTERSTATE BRANCHING.

(a) IN GENERAL—The Comptroller General of the United States shall submit to the Congress, not later than 9 months after the date of enactment of this Act, a report that—

(1) examines statutory and regulatory requirements for insured depository institutions to collect and report deposit and lending data; and (2) determines what modifications to such requirements are needed, so that the implementation of the interstate branching provisions contained in this title will result in no material loss of information important to regulatory or congressional oversight of insured depository institutions.

(b) CONSULTATION—The Comptroller General, in preparing the report required by this section, shall consult with individuals representing the appropriate Federal banking agencies, insured depository institutions, consumers, community groups, and other interested parties.

(c) DEFINITIONS—For purposes of this section, the terms 'appropriate Federal banking agency' and 'insured depository institution' have the same meanings as in section 3 of the Federal Deposit Insurance Act.

SEC. 113. MAXIMUM INTEREST RATE ON CERTAIN FMHA LOANS.

(a) IN GENERAL—Section 307(a) of the Consolidated Farm and Rural Development Act (7 U.S.C. 1927(a)) is amended—

(1) in paragraph (3)(A), by striking 'Except' and inserting 'Notwithstanding the provisions of the constitution or laws of any State limiting the rate or amount of interest that may be charged, taken, received, or reserved, except'; and

(2) in paragraph (5)—

(A) by striking '(5) The' and inserting '(5)(A) Except as provided in subparagraph (B), the'; and

(B) by adding at the end the following new subparagraph:

'(B) In the case of a loan made under section 31 OB as a guaranteed loan, subparagraph (A) shall apply notwithstanding the provisions of the constitution or laws of any State limiting the rate or amount of interest that may be charged, taken, received, or reserved.'

(b)EFFECTIVE DATES—

(1) IN GENERAL—Except as provided in paragraphs (2) and (3), the amendments made by subsection (a) shall apply to a loan made, insured, or guaranteed under the Consolidated Farm and Rural Devel-

opment Act (7 U.S.C. 1921 et seq.) in a State on or after the date of enactment of this Act.

(2) STATE OPTION—Except as provided in paragraph (3), the amendments made by subsection (a) shall not apply to a loan made, insured, or guaranteed under the Consolidated Farm and Rural Development Act in a State after the date (that occurs during the 3 -year period beginning on the date of enactment of this Act) on which the State adopts a law or certifies that the voters of the State have voted in favor of a provision of the constitution or law of the State that states that the State does not want the amendments made by subsection (a) to apply with respect to loans made, insured, or guaranteed under such Act in the State.

(3) TRANSITIONAL PERIOD—In any case in which a State takes an action described in paragraph (2), the amendments made by subsection (a) shall continue to apply to a loan made, insured, or guaranteed under the Consolidated Farm and Rural Development Act in the State after the date the action was taken pursuant to a commitment for the loan that was entered into during the period beginning on the date of enactment of this Act, and ending on the date on which the State takes the action.

SEC. 114. NOTICE REQUIREMENTS FOR BANKING AGENCY DECISIONS PREEMPTING STATE LAW.

Chapter 4 of title LXII of the Revised Statutes (12 U.S.C. 21 et seq.) is amended by adding at the end the following new section:

'SEC. 5244. INTERPRETATIONS CONCERNING PREEMPTION OF CERTAIN STATE LAWS.

'(a) NOTICE AND OPPORTUNITY FOR COMMENT REQUIRED—Before issuing any opinion letter or interpretive rule, in response to a request or upon the agency's own motion, that concludes that Federal law preempts the application to a national bank of any State law regarding community reinvestment, consumer protection, fair lending, or the establishment of intrastate branches, or before making a determination under section 5155(f)(1)(A)(ii) of the Revised Statutes, the appropriate Federal banking agency (as defined in section 3 of the Federal Deposit Insurance Act) shall—

'(1) publish in the Federal Register notice of the preemption or discrimination issue that the agency is considering (including a description of each State law at issue);

'(2) give interested parties not less than 30 days in which to submit written comments; and

'(3) in developing the final opinion letter or interpretive rule issued by the agency, or making any determination under section 5155(f)(1)(A)(ii) of the Revised Statutes, consider any comments received.

'(b) PUBLICATION REQUIRED—The appropriate Federal banking agency shall publish in the Federal Register—

'(1) any final opinion letter or interpretive rule concluding that Federal law preempts the application of any State law regarding community reinvestment, consumer protection, fair lending, or establishment of intrastate branches to a national bank; and

'(2) any determination under section 5155(f)(1)(A)(ii) of the Revised Statutes.

'(c) EXCEPTIONS—

'(1) NO NEW ISSUE OR SIGNIFICANT BASIS—This section shall not apply with respect to any opinion letter or interpretive rule that—

'(A) raises issues of Federal preemption of State law that are essentially identical to those previously resolved by the courts or on which the agency has previously issued an opinion letter or interpretive rule; or

'(B) responds to a request that contains no significant legal basis on which to make a preemption determination.

'(2) JUDICIAL, LEGISLATIVE, OR INTRAGOVERNMENTAL MATERIALS—This section shall not apply with respect to materials prepared for use in judicial proceedings or submission to Congress or a Member of Congress, or for intragovernmental use.

'(3) EMERGENCY—The appropriate Federal banking agency may make exceptions to subsection (a) if—

'(A) the agency determines in writing that the exception is necessary to avoid a serious and imminent threat to the safety and soundness of any national bank; or

'(B) the opinion letter or interpretive rule is issued in connection with—

'(i) an acquisition of 1 or more banks in default or in danger of default (as such terms are defined in section 3 of the Federal Deposit Insurance Act)—or

'(ii) an acquisition with respect to which the Federal Deposit Insurance Corporation provides assistance under section 13(c) of the Federal Deposit Insurance Act.

SEC. 115. MORATORIUM ON EXAMINATION FEES UNDER THE INTERNATIONAL BANKING ACT OF 1978.

(a) BRANCHES, AGENCIES, AND AFFILIATES—Section 7(c)(1)(D) of the International Banking Act of 1978 shall not apply with respect to any examination under section 7(c)(1)(A) of such Act which begins before or during the 3–year period beginning on July 25, 1994.

(b) REPRESENTATIVE OFFICES—The provision of section 10(c) of the International Banking Act of 1978 relating to the cost of examinations under such section shall not apply with respect to any examination under such section which begins before or during the 3-year period beginning on July 25, 1994.

Source: http://thomas.loc.gov/.

Bibliography

Abbate, Anthony S. "Interstate Banking: More Harm than Good," *American Banker* CLXI, no. 3 (January 4, 1996): p. 18.

Annual Report to the Congress on Retail Fees and Services of Depository Institutions. Board of Governors of the Federal Reserve System, June 1999.

Averch, H., and L.L. Johnson. "Behavior of the Firm under Regulatory Constraints," *American Economic Review* 53 (December, 1963): pp. 1052–1069.

Baker, Bruce. "Riegle-Neal Interstate Banking and Branching Efficiency Act of 1994." Unpublished paper from the law firm of Schiff Hardin & Waite, pp. 1–10.

Calem, Paul S. "The Impact of Geographic Deregulation on Small Banks." *Business Review* (Federal Reserve Bank of Philadelphia) (November–December, 1994) pp. 17–31.

Calomiris, Charles W., and Jason Karceski. *Is the Bank Merger Wave of the 1990's Efficient? Lessons from Nine Case Studies.* Washington, DC: The AEI Press, 1998.

Caves, Douglas W., Laurits R. Christensen, and Joseph A. Swanson. "The High Cost of Regulating U.S. Railroads," *Regulation* IV, no. 1 (January/February 1981): pp. 41–46.

Cocheo, Steve. "Banking Reviews the Blueprints." *ABA Banking Journal* LXXXIII, no. 4 (April 1991): pp. 33, 35, 37, 39, and 40.

Demetz, Harold. "Industry Structure, Market Rivalry, and Public Policy." *Journal of Law and Economics* XVI no. 1 (April 1973): pp. 1–10.

Domis, Olaf de Senerpont. "Texas Wins Big in Fight to Ban Cross-Border Branching." *American Banker* CLXI, no. 100 (May 24, 1996): pp. 1 and 2.

Eager, Robert C. "The New Federal Interstate Banking and Branching Legislation." *Bankers Magazine* 178 no. 6 (November/December 1995): pp. 23–28.

Economides, Nicholas, R. Glen Hubbard, and Darius Palia. "The Political Economy of Branching Restrictions and Deposit Insurance: A Model of Monopolistic Competition among Small and Large Banks." *Journal of Law and Economics* XXXIX no. 2 (October 1996): pp. 667–704.

Edelstein, Haskell. "Banks Face Potential for Increased Taxes." *Bank Management* LXXI no. 4 (July/August 1995): pp. 57, 58 and 60.

Finn, Edwin A. Jr., ed. *American Banker's Banking Fact Book.* New York: American Banker, 1991.

Goelzer, Daniel L., Simon Zornoza, and Eli D. Cohen. "New Banking Legislation: The Riegle-Neal Interstate Banking and Branching Efficiency Act of 1994." Unpublished paper from the law firm of Baker and McKenzie. October 1994, pp. 1–7.

Graham, David R., and Daniel P. Kaplan. "Airline Deregulation Is Working." *Regulation* V, no. 3 (May/June 1982): pp. 26–32.

Hilton, George W. "The Consistency of the Interstate Commerce Act." *Journal of Law & Economics* IX (October 1966): pp. 87–114.

Indick, Murray A., and Satish M. Kini. "The Interstate Banking and Branching Efficiency Act: New Options, New Problems." *Banking Law Journal* 112 no. 2 (February 1995): pp. 100–123.

"Interstate Branching: Who's Opting In, Who's Opting Out, Who's Looking at the Options." *ABA Banking Journal*, LXXXVII, no. 10 (October 1995): p. 12.

Jayaratne, Jith, and Philip E. Strahan. "Entry Restrictions, Industry Evolution, and Dynamic Efficiency: Evidence from Commercial Banking." *Journal of Law and Economics*, XLI (April 1998): pp. 239–273.

Jordan, William A. "Producer Protection, Prior Market Structure and the Effects of Government Regulation." *Journal of Law & Economics* XV no. 1 (April 1972): pp. 151–176.

Kane, Edward J. "De Jure Interstate Banking: Why Only Now?" *Journal of Money, Credit and Banking* 28 no. 2 (May 1996): pp. 141–161.

Keeton, William R. "Multi-Office Bank Lending to Small Businesses: Some New Evidence." *Economic Review* (Federal Reserve Bank of Kansas City) 80 no. 2 (Second Quarter 1995): pp. 45–57.

———. "Do Bank Mergers Reduce Lending to Businesses and Farmers? New Evidence from Tenth District States." *Economic Review* (Federal Reserve Bank of Kansas City) 82 no. 3 (Third Quarter 1996): pp. 63–76.

Klebaner, Benjamin J. *American Commercial Banking: A History.* Boston: Twayne Publishers, 1990.

Koch, Timothy W., and S. Scott MacDonald. *Bank Management.* Fort Worth, TX: Dryden Press, 2000.

Mabley, Robert E., and Walter Strack. "Deregulation–A Green Light for Trucking Efficiency." *Regulation* V, no. 4 (July/August 1982): pp. 36–56.

Madura, Jeff. *Financial Markets and Institutions.* 4th ed. Cincinnati, OH: South-Western College Publishing, 1998.

Mastasar, Ann B. and Joseph N. Heiney. "Big Banks/Small Customers: The Impact of Riegle-Neal on the Banking Relationship." Presented at the Tenth Annual Conference of the International Association for Business and Society (IABS) in Paris, France, June 24–27, 1999. Published in the *1999 Proceedings*, pp. 361–366.

———. "The Impact of Geographic Regulations on the Profitability of American Banks." Presented at the Atlantic Economic Society Sessions at the American Economics Association (Allied Social Sciences Association) Conference in New Orleans, January 4, 1997. Unpublished.

Matasar, Ann B., and Mark Holtzblatt. "Banking on Europe: The Implications of European Integration on the Global Planning of US Banks." Presented at the Midwest Business Administration Association Meeting in Chicago and published in the *Midwest Journal of Finance and Insurance* 8, no. 1 (March 1994).

Matasar, Ann B., and Deborah D. Pavelka. "Industry-Specific Corporate Responsibility with an International Dimension: The Case of Foreign Bank Compliance with CRA." *Business and Society* 36, no. 3 (September 1997): pp. 280–295.

McConnell, Bill. "After Long Fight for Branching Power, Banks Seem in No Hurry to Use It." *American Banker* CLXI, no. 64 (April 3, 1996): p. 1.

Peltzman, Sam. "Toward a More General Theory of Regulation," *Journal of Law & Economics* XIX, no. 2 (August 1976): pp. 211–240.

Peoples, James. "Deregulation and the Labor Market," *Journal of Economic Perspectives* 12, no. 3 (summer 1998): pp. 111–130.

Rhoades, Stephen A., and Donald T. Savage. "Interstate Branching: A Cost-Saving Alternative?" *Bankers Magazine* 176 no. 4 (July/August 1993): pp. 34–40.

Rhoads, Christopher. "Branching: A Trickle Instead of a Flood." *American Banker* CLXI, no. 136 (July 18, 1996): p. 9.

Rose, Peter. *Banking across State Lines: Public and Private Consequences.* Westport, CT: Quorum Books, 1997.

Rose, Peter, and James W. Kolari. *Financial Institutions.* 5th ed. Chicago: Irwin, 1995.

Roussakis, Emmanuel. *Commercial Banking in an Era of Deregulation.* 3d ed. Westport, CT: Praeger, 1997.

Schranz, Mary S. "Takeovers Improve Firm Performance: Evidence from the Banking Industry." *Journal of Political Economy* 101, no. 2 (1993): pp. 299–326.

Sloss, James. "Regulation of Motor Freight Transportation: A Quantitative Evaluation of Policy." *Bell Journal of Economics and Management Science* 1 no. 2 (autumn 1970): pp. 327.

Smith, Daniel R. "After interstate: 8 banks or 8,000?" *ABA Banking Journal* LXXXIV, no. 9 (September 1994): p. 17.

Spann, Robert M., and Edward W. Erickson. "The Economics of Railroading: The Beginning of Cartelization and Regulation." *Bell Journal of Economics and Management Science* 1, no. 2 (autumn 1970): p. 227.

Spiegel, John W., and Alan Gart. "What Lies behind the Bank Merger and Acquisition Frenzy?" *Business Economics* XXXI, no. 2 (April 1996): pp. 47–52.

Spong, Kenneth. *Banking Regulation*. Kansas City, MO: Division of Bank Supervision and Structure, Federal Reserve Bank of Kansas City, 1990.

Statistics on Banking: A Statistical History of the United States Banking Industry. Vols. 1–3. Washington, DC: Federal Deposit Insurance Corporation, 1997.

Statistics on Banking: Statistical Profile on the United States Banking Industry–1997. Washington, D.C.: Federal Deposit Insurance Corporation, 1998.

Stigler, George J. "The Theory of Economic Regulation," *Bell Journal of Economics and Management Science* 2, no. 1 (spring 1971): pp. 3–21.

Stigler, George J., and Claire Friedland. "What Can Regulators Regulate? The Case of Electricity." *Journal of Law & Economics* V (October 1962): pp. 1–16.

"Summary of Selected Provisions of the Riegle-Neal Interstate Banking and Branching Efficiency Act of 1994." Unpublished paper from the law firm of Vedder, Price, Kaufman & Kammholz. Presented at the Fifth Annual Banking Law Update. November 16, 1994, pp. 1–10.

U.S. Congress. House. Committee on Banking and Financial Services. *Hearing on Bank Mergers*. 105th Congress, 2nd session, April 29, 1998.

Wahl, Melissa. "As Banks Merge, New Ones Emerge." *Chicago Tribune*, June 30, 1998, pp. Business 1 & 2.

Wheelock, David C. "Nationwide Branching: The Implications." *Bank Management* LXX, no. 5 (September/October 1994): pp. 54, 55, and 57–59.

Winston, Clifford. "U.S. Industry Adjustment to Economic Deregulation." *Journal of Economic Perspectives* 12, no. 3 (summer 1998): pp. 89–110.

Index

About the Authors

ANN B. MATASAR is Amoco Distinguished Professor of International Business at the Walter E. Heller College of Business Administration, Roosevelt University, in Chicago.

JOSEPH N. HEINEY is Professor of Economics in the Center for Business and Economics at Elmhurst College in Elmhurst, Illinois. He previously held the positions of Director of the Center for Business and Economics, and Coleman Foundation Distinguished Chair in Business.